W9-CFQ-639

ALSO BY FRYE GAILLARD

AS

LONG

AS

THE

WATERS

FLOW

As Long
As the Waters Flow

NATIVE AMERICANS

IN THE SOUTH AND THE EAST

Text by
Frye Gaillard
Photographs by
Carolyn DeMeritt

Foreword by
Vine Deloria, Jr.

JOHN F. BLAIR, PUBLISHER
WINSTON-SALEM, NORTH CAROLINA

DESIGN DEBRA LONG HAMPTON

PRINTED AND BOUND BY R. R. DONNELLEY & SONS

The paper in this book meets the guidelines for
permanence and durability of the Committee
on Production Guidelines for Book Longevity
of the Council on Library Resources.

Library of Congress Cataloging-in-Publication Data

Gaillard, Frye, 1946–

    As long as the waters flow : Native Americans in the south and the
east / text by Frye Gaillard ; photographs by Carolyn DeMeritt.

      p.   cm.

    Includes bibliographical references and index.

    ISBN 0-89587-219-6 (alk. paper)

    1. Indians of North America—Southern States—Government
relations.   2. Indians of North America—East (U.S.)—Government
relations.   3. Indians of North America—Southern States—Ethnic
identity.   4. Indians of North America—East (U.S.)—Ethnic identity.
I. DeMeritt, Carolyn.   II. Title.

E78.S65G35   1998   98–29171

975'.00497—dc21

CONTENTS

Foreword

AMERICAN HISTORY BOOKS IMPLY that when the federal government moved the large Indian tribes westward in the 1830s, the eastern United States was virtually cleared of Indian villages and settlements. In this regard, they are badly mistaken. At least half of the native inhabitants of this region remained where they were and continued community life at the margins of white occupation. The people simply adapted to the economies of the area, although with great sacrifices; they did not look to the federal government as much as they sought some kind of accommodation with state and local governments. And while they lived on the edge of white towns and cities, they nevertheless preserved as much of their culture as a racially discriminating society could allow them.

Two distinct practices can be identified east of the Mississippi.

In New England and New York and small parts of Ohio, Indiana, Michigan, and Wisconsin, many Indians were given state reservations or small federal reservations or were simply gathered in traditional areas, where they lived without any recognition at all. These areas were settled systematically following the New England practice in which land-holding companies occupied townships that had been surveyed and opened to settlers under federal supervision. With the exception of the Six Nations of the Iroquois in New York, the federal government did virtually nothing to provide these eastern Indians with services due them under treaties or to protect them from unscrupulous land speculators, who connived to get the Indian reservations and allotments.

In the southern United States, most settlement was by individual entrepreneurs who moved up rivers and streams and established plantations, the streams providing the only viable means of transporting the products of commercial agriculture. The mountains and foothills and the swamps and inlets on the coast and along large rivers were usually the last areas of the South settled by whites. Although the large southeastern tribes—the Cherokees, Creeks, Choctaws, Chickasaws, and Seminoles—ceded their claims to large tracts of land in removal treaties, much of the land they ceded was neither owned nor occupied by them. Rather, beginning in southern New Jersey and extending clear down the eastern seaboard and to eastern Texas, there were small Indian villages beholden to no one but themselves—to people who had occupied these remote areas for many hundreds of years.

With the exception of Virginia, which had reservations dating from the 1600s, and the Catawbas, who had signed treaties with the United States around the time of the American Revolution, most Indian groups had little to do with the federal government. Often, they had to purchase lands that could support settlements and live under state laws, because they had no status with the federal government. Or they lived in well-organized communities in obscure locations in the small towns of the South. They maintained extensive networks of trade, intermarriage, and social relationships. Deprived of ordinary community services, they relied heavily on traditional medicines and foods and used traditional building materials and often traditional ways of building homes. Their desire was simply to be left alone to be themselves. When they were classified as African-Americans for educational purposes, some of them bitterly resisted, others refused to send their children to school, and still others obeyed but with an air of anger.

There is no question that the federal government knew of the small Indian groups.

During the New Deal, Indian commissioner John Collier sent anthropologists to contact some of these groups with the intent of making the Indian Reorganization Act applicable to them. Thus, the Chitimachas of Louisiana and some of the Lumbees of Robeson County, North Carolina, were declared "Indians" under the bureau's protection, and their communities were recognized as being eligible for federal services and status. Had World War II not intervened in this recognition process, there is no question that thirty and perhaps as many as a hundred small, identifiable groups of Indians would have received federal status during the 1940s. Instead, many of them have had to struggle in the years since then to achieve the recognition they deserve. Some of them are involved in that struggle even now.

I first came across these people in 1965, when I was director of the National Congress of American Indians. In the NCAI files, I found correspondence from Chief Swimming Eel of the Schaghticoke Indians of Connecticut. Somehow, this elder had managed to get his tribe's land claim accepted in the Indian Claims Commission. Unfortunately, the lawyer he hired did not believe the Indians had rights to land, so he allowed the claim to expire for want of prosecution, which nearly broke the old man's heart.

Several years later, I received a letter from Chief Joseph Pierite of the Tunicas of Louisiana. Over the next several years, he told me some incredible stories of his people and introduced me to Claude Medford, Jr., who was part Choctaw, a dropout from graduate school, and probably the leading expert on southeastern Indian communities and cultures. Claude had traveled, mostly by thumb, all over the Atlantic seaboard gathering information on basketry and the other crafts that had been preserved by forgotten Indian communities. Later, when I was the chairman of the Institute for the Development of Indian Law, I had a staff member work on the history of the Tunicas, and eventually they achieved federal recognition as a tribe. The most impressive aspect of the Tunicas' claim was that they could trace their chiefs back to the French occupation of Louisiana and so had a pedigree far more comprehensive than even most of the western tribes.

Over the years, then, I have tried to be helpful to these communities. Thus, when my old friend Frye Gaillard told me he was writing a book about the eastern Indian communities, I was very enthusiastic. Their stories are as dramatic as anything in the West. Many of them have retained the old ways, and although they have not had the western reservation experience, they have faced obstacles equally difficult. Living on the edge of a hostile society with no legal status means a kind of discrimination that few people can contemplate. Not only do these people suffer oppression, but they are also viewed as aliens by federal and state agencies and by federally recognized tribes. During the days of the poverty programs, many of them had to fight desperate and lonely fights to avoid a sweeping wave of integration and homogenization.

Gaillard's book both recounts the struggles and highlights the people and their leaders, bringing their stories vividly to life while identifying areas of contemporary concern. Ideally, the Bureau of Indian Affairs should give serious thought to improving the process whereby these people will be recognized as Indians and take their rightful place within the protective powers of the federal government—as well as their rightful place in American history. May this book hasten that day.

Vine Deloria, Jr.

AS

LONG

AS

THE

WATERS

FLOW

Prologue

SHE COULD HAVE LIVED ANYWHERE in the world, and did for a while—New Orleans, Pensacola, a hillside farm in eastern Connecticut—but something always drew her back home. She had left the village when she was a girl, moving to New Orleans to live with an aunt. Her father thought it was better that way. Times were hard in the tiny community of Poarch, Alabama—just a few Creek Indians huddled in the flatlands north of Mobile. Most of them scratched out a living from the soil, working long hours in the sun, bringing in the harvest for their neighbors who were white. As far as Noah McGhee was concerned, it was not the kind of place to raise a little girl, especially not one as bright as LaVerne, so he sent her away. He was proud when she graduated from high school, and prouder still when she got her nursing degree from Tulane. Noah was a medicine man himself. He gathered his herbs from the Alabama forests, and people came to him from all over the county, believing in the healing power of his touch and the Indian words that took away the pain.

LaVerne believed in her father also. Even with her training at the great university and her distant adventures as the wife of a pilot, she never really strayed very far from home—from the Indian community she had known as a child. Later, she began to understand why. She came home to stay in the 1970s, roaming through the territory of the Creeks, searching out the graves and the crumbling chimney of the old family home, now covered with vines. She knew that her spirit was part of this place in a way that was difficult to explain. She was like a lot of Indian people that way—discovering in the closing years of the century that, against all odds, her native identity was still intact. She was proud of that fact, proud that her people had managed to survive—particularly in the East, where, as a matter of United States policy, the Indian nations were supposed to disappear.

Some of them did. In encounters going back to the sixteenth century, Native Americans died by the thousands at the hands of the European invaders. In the country that became the United States, the catastrophe unfolded in the 1540s. The Spanish explorer Hernando

De Soto marched through the Indian lands, stopping in what is now Alabama. There, he encountered the great chief Tazcaluza, a regal man with jet-black hair who was offended by the startling demands of the Spaniards. They asked for warriors to carry their supplies and women to satisfy their desires, and when they threatened to make a prisoner of Tazcaluza himself, the fighting broke out and lasted for the better part of a day. At the end, the Indian forces were defeated, their casualties estimated at more than two thousand.

But that was merely a start. For the next two centuries, European diseases swept through the Indian nations of the East, killing what many scholars believe was 90 percent of the native population. "We had no immunity," says Tom Porter, an Iroquois leader from New York State. "All the Europeans had to do was touch the Indian people and they died."

In addition to the fevers, which ranged from influenza to the measles, there was the simple fact that the whites kept coming—kept filling up the land, which had been promised to the Indians for as long as the waters would continue to flow. The solution devised in 1830, and confirmed by an act of Congress, was to move the Indian people to the West. The forced migrations, known today as the Trail of Tears, continued off and on for twenty years, and although some of the people escaped, hiding most often in the mountains or the swamps, the survivors never found peace. For more than a century, they endured an un-

relenting assault, their land base shrinking, their children sent away to Indian schools where they were beaten if they spoke in their own native tongue. Yet through it all, they managed to survive not only physically but spiritually as well.

In the 1970s, when LaVerne McGhee left her suburban world in Connecticut and moved back home, she discovered that many things were still the same. There had always been a strong sense of community—a people who were deeply attached to each other and who nurtured a feeling of connection to their place. Those qualities were at the heart of their identity and had not dissipated through the years. But now there was more—the scattered signs of economic progress as the Indians paved their roads and built better houses and started enterprises to give people jobs. But in addition to those physical symbols of hope, there was a change that took LaVerne by surprise and quickened her pulse. There was the sound of drumbeats coming from the forest. She soon discovered that at least once a month, Creek traditionalists young and old gathered in a clearing deep in the woods to sing their songs in the ancestors' tongue and dance sometimes until it was almost dawn. William Bailey was a leader in the group, a handsome, dark-eyed man in his thirties who had learned the traditional language and the prayers and who believed, he said, that "the Creator, who gave us all of these things, is still there to teach."

He tried to do a little teaching himself,

bringing back the language and the ancient ceremonies of his tribe, and it gave him a certain reassurance to know that he was not alone. Barry Dana, for example, was a Penobscot man about his age who worked at an Indian school in Maine. He took his students on camping trips to the woods, during which they traveled by canoe and lived off the land, as the native people had always done. He gave lessons in the language, which he had learned himself from a basket maker named Madeline Shay, who had lived for thirty years in Connecticut, where, as far as she knew, there was nobody else who understood Penobscot. But she spoke it every day in her head, committing herself to the words until the day she finally moved back home and found a willing pupil in Barry. He quickly discovered that the language was hard, its syntax bearing no resemblance to English. But he kept working at it, for how could he not? Shay herself had been so tenacious, so committed to preserving the traditions of her people, that Barry decided he could do no less.

For many different reasons in many different places, there are people like Dana and Madeline Shay—Native Americans reasserting their identity, doing what they can to keep the culture alive. Many of them say they were inspired in part by the civil-rights movement of the 1960s, which created a different kind of climate in America, a time in which people felt freer to speak. But even in the dark ages— the first fifty years of the twentieth century,

when almost everything seemed lost—there were Indian leaders who kept stepping forward and proclaiming that the spirit of the people wouldn't die.

It seems clear today that those leaders were right, and this book in part is a celebration of survival—the resilience of a culture that could well have disappeared. It's a story that resonates with the rest of us—or at least it should, for there are lessons in the Indian way of life that transcend the Native American community. Some, of course, are almost a cliché. There is a respect for the earth and a belief in the duty of the people to protect it. But those notions of ecology are connected in the end to something even larger. For many Indian people, there's a gratitude at the heart of their traditional theology—and a different understanding of the nature of things. In a world where many of us live in the present, behaving as if it's the beginning and the end, Native Americans from every tribe in the country—and certainly from those represented here—understand that the present is connected to the past, that their lives are part of a much bigger story. This is true even in the worst of times, and there is a resilience that flows from that understanding, and a duty to those who are not yet born.

It is true, inevitably, that every tribe is different, and each of their stories could be a book of its own. But these are the threads that bind them together. It is not necessary to idealize, to ignore the blemishes that are part of

RAY LITTLETURTLE, LUMBEE TRADITIONALIST,
ROBESON COUNTY, NORTH CAROLINA, 1997

the history of every people on earth, including the Indians. Nor should we forget that the threats to their culture have not been erased. There is a backlash brewing in the non-Indian world, and governmental policies that can do great harm, and divisions among the Indian people themselves, many of which are shortsighted and petty. We deal with those issues in the pages that follow, but the primary message is more optimistic. The people and communities whose lives we describe—the Native Americans of the South and East—have survived nearly five hundred years of contact with a European culture that intended to destroy them.

There's an urgency in their spirit of revival. "As human beings," says Ray Littleturtle, a Lumbee traditionalist from North Carolina, "we are running out of time." But Littleturtle says that, at least for a while, the Indians are living in an era of hope. In the closing years of the twentieth century, their identity is getting stronger, not fading away, as their enemies and many of their friends had predicted.

In the words and photographs of this book, we have set out to record that story of hope and to give it a face. Our interest began with the Catawba Indians of South Carolina, who embarked on a struggle to recover lost land in the 1970s. In the wake of that effort, there was a powerful rebirth of their Indian identity, a pride in a culture that had once seemed doomed. We talked about that with Wenonah Haire, the director of the tribe's new cultural center, and with Gilbert Blue, the chief, and they told us their story was not unique. In one way or another, it was being repeated among tribes throughout the South and the East, and they urged us to write those stories as well.

We set out to do it, traveling—over the course of nearly two years—from Florida to Maine, from the Great Lakes to Louisiana, and to many points in between. Even then, however, we could not do it justice. There are too many tribes, too many communities of Indian people, to tell every story as fully as we'd like. But this book is a start, a suggestion of the richness of the Indian experience. We are grateful to the hundreds of Native Americans who embraced our efforts and offered their wisdom, and who believed, as we do, that the story of the Indian people is worth telling.

We hope the results are worthy of their trust.

Frye Gaillard and Carolyn DeMeritt

KEITH BROWN, CATAWBA NATION, SOUTH CAROLINA, 1996

CHAPTER ONE
The Catawba Renaissance

THERE IS A PATH THROUGH THE WOODS winding by the river where the deep, brown waters are swollen with the rain. Keith Brown is standing alone on the bank, his thoughts drifting back to a desolate time. He spent his childhood just up the stream—his family of twelve in a three-room cabin. His father worked for a while in the mills, then got sick, and his mother had to pick up the load. But hard times were common to the people all around, for Keith and his neighbors were Catawba Indians—the scattered remnants of a once-proud band that had roamed the forests and the broad riverbanks, raising their crops and hunting buffalo and deer.

They were the Iswa Catawba—the People of the River—and there were sixteen towns scattered up and down the banks, sturdy and prosperous when the white man came. But the buffalo vanished, and the wars and the smallpox took their toll, and then in 1763, the Catawbas made a treaty. They gave up all but 144,000 acres just south of Charlotte in ex-

change for guarantees against further encroachment. But the whites kept coming, kept seizing the land, and in 1840, the Catawbas tried again to make a deal. They met at Nations Ford on the banks of their river, sitting down with officials from South Carolina and renouncing their title to the 144,000 acres in exchange for the promise of a new reservation. The agreement was never ratified by Congress, and no reservation was ever established—just a single square mile within the land they had lost.

By the time Keith Brown was coming of age, the Catawbas as a tribe were almost gone. Nobody spoke the language anymore, or performed the dances, or dressed any differently from their white neighbors. There were some potters still working with the clay, digging from the veins that ran near the river, straining and massaging the rust-colored soil, building their elaborate pieces by hand. But even these artists were starting to disappear—and with them a final link to the past.

In the 1960s, Keith Brown, among others, decided to leave. He joined the army and set out to make his way in the world, and for a time, he never expected to return. And yet there was something stirring inside him—"an Indian spirit, or whatever it was"—that seemed to keep pulling in the direction of home. He heard that things were slowly getting better, but when he finally came back, he could hardly believe it. The reservation of the 1990s was different—startling, almost, to those who had left it. There were potters and dancers and Catawba drum groups and people who were trying to relearn the language. There were newly paved roads and eighty new houses and a tribal headquarters that was state of the art. A "Catawba renaissance," some people called it, and Keith, for one, could not disagree.

He applied immediately for a job with the tribe, putting together exhibits and conducting occasional impromptu tours for the visitors who were starting to appear every week. On one of those tours, he led a couple of guests through the woods, where the leaves were slowly turning gold with the season and the ferns were rustling gently on the floor of the forest. He talked about the changes his people had seen, about a struggle for survival that began in the 1970s and—slowly at first, and then more dramatically—gained an inevitable momentum through the years.

This is the story the Catawbas have to tell. It is a story of vision and bitter dissent, of hope and patience and people coming home—of the survival of a culture and the revival of Indian identity and pride. And it's a story, Brown says, that keeps getting better.

It begins, in a way, with Gilbert Blue—the Catawba chief for nearly twenty-five years, a man who also left the reservation for a time. He joined the navy in 1951, adding his name to a long list of Indian veterans. It was a proud tradition among the Catawbas. They have fought in every American war going all the way back to the French and Indian, and their cemetery markers bear witness to the fact.

Blue fought in Korea, serving on a destroyer in the South China Sea, and perhaps more important, he had a chance to see the world. He visited Australia and the Philippines, and having sampled those cultures, he found himself thinking a little more about his own. He remembered his grandfather Samuel Taylor Blue, a slender man about six-foot-one with high cheekbones and jet-black hair. The elder Blue was a chief and a steadfast believer in Indian identity. He still spoke the language—the last man to do it—and he would take his grandson on walks through the woods, talking to him earnestly about the traditions of his people, trying to pass along what it means to be Catawba. He talked about the land and the sense of being part of the history of a people. By the time Gilbert Blue returned from the navy, he found himself stirred by the old man's stories, and he was

GILBERT BLUE, CATAWBA CHIEF,
CATAWBA NATION, SOUTH CAROLINA, 1996

beginning to wear the outward symbols of his pride—a beaded necklace, an Indian-head tattoo on his arm.

He knew that some of the Catawbas were making it. A few, at least, had gone off to college and were building good lives for themselves and their families. But far too many of the others were drifting, caught in the poverty of the rural South without any sense of identity to sustain them. Blue was determined to do something about it, and when he was elected chief in 1973, he found himself thinking about a claim to the land.

"Our people," he declared, "would never have been in poverty if we had had our land."

It was about that time that he met Don Miller, a lawyer for the Native American Rights Fund, a public-interest firm in Boulder, Colorado. Miller was energetic and capable, and he had helped represent the Penobscot and Passamaquoddy Indians in asserting their claim to two-thirds of Maine—a claim that was settled for $80 million. After studying the issue for the better part of a year, Miller told Blue the Catawbas had a case.

In 1976, they made an announcement: The tribe would pursue its claim to the 144,000 acres, much of it prime York County real estate, chunks of subdivisions and farms near the community of Rock Hill, South Carolina. Blue did his best to set a tone of moderation. "We are not being radical," he told one reporter. "We are not going to take developed land, shopping centers. That's not our intention. We

are not going to get condemnation rights. People who own the land now bought it in good faith. We are not trying to push anybody out. But the land is rightfully ours, and we are going to negotiate for the best settlement we can."

Despite Blue's attempts at reassurance, the Catawba land claim cast a pall over York County development. Land titles suddenly had "Catawba exceptions"—stipulations, in effect, that the titles might not apply if the Indians won their case.

It was then that the torrent of opposition began. Whites organized to battle the claim, which was no surprise. What stunned Gilbert Blue was that some of the Catawbas began to fight him, too. They agreed, to be sure, that the tribe had been wronged, but lacking Blue's interest in identity and land, they simply wanted money as a salve for the wounds. There was logic in their preference, of course. Many of these Catawbas were poor, and they had little patience with the dreams of Gilbert Blue—all his talk about a new reservation and restoring the spiritual identity of a people. In the end, the chief was forced to compromise, pledging to seek cash payments to individuals, as well as land for a larger reservation and additional federal money for tribal development.

The Catawbas came together around that position, but almost immediately, their case began to go badly in the courts. It was clear that the federal judge was hostile, and there

MARANDA LEACH, TWELVE-YEAR-OLD CATAWBA DANCER,
CATAWBA NATION, SOUTH CAROLINA, 1997

were times when the tribe seemed likely to lose. Blue grew so discouraged at one point that he told Don Miller he was tempted to quit. The whole ordeal was simply too much. He could see his hair turning gray, and the lines on his face were getting deeper all the time, and his teenage children were growing up without him. Let somebody else take the heat for a while.

But in the end, of course, he did not quit. "I kept thinking about my people," he says, and he was bolstered also by his Mormon faith and his conviction that God was not really indifferent. All of it fit with his Indian's sense of time, a belief in the cyclical nature of history. For more than two hundred years, his people had been caught on the cycle's downside, their homeland vanishing, their identity slowly beginning to fade. But it's all an eye blink in the great sweep of history, and Blue was convinced that their time would come again.

Now, apparently, it has, and the turning point came in a curious way—with what appeared at first to be a piece of bad news. United States district judge Joseph Wilson—who seemed to rule against the tribe every chance he got, rejecting its position at nearly every procedural point in the case—ruled in 1991 that the Catawbas were not eligible to file a class-action lawsuit. The issue had been hanging for more than a decade, and Wilson's ruling left the Catawbas little choice. To prevail in their claim, they would have to sue every white landowner in the area—all 61,767 of them. Most observers assumed that it couldn't be done, or wouldn't be, for the expense alone seemed prohibitive. But the Catawbas and their lawyers decided to try it.

The word spread quickly around York County. The Catawbas were filing more than sixty thousand lawsuits, and as soon as it happened, the effect would be chaos—gridlock in the courts and a terrifying freeze in the real-estate market. Suddenly, state officials who had shown little interest in a political settlement were eager to see if something could be worked out. Led by Representative John Spratt, a team of state and federal negotiators began meeting regularly with the Catawba leadership, and the result was a land settlement in 1994. It was a sweeping agreement in which the tribe received much of what it was seeking: an expanded reservation, modest cash payments for individual Catawbas, $50 million for development and education, and federal recognition of their status as a tribe. In return, the Catawbas renounced any further claim to the land.

Not everybody was happy with the terms. One of the dissenters was the Catawbas' assistant chief, Fred Sanders, who had been perhaps the most strong-willed leader in the tribe—a catalyst at least as important as Blue. Like the chief, he was a man of modest means and education—they worked together for a tire manufacturer in South Carolina. Sanders was tough and smart, and he traveled the country in pursuit of the claim and was deeply disappointed in the final result. It was true the Catawbas got something from the deal, but Sanders hated what they had to give up. Under the final terms of the settlement, their status was not like any other tribe's. They were denied police jurisdiction on their own reservation. Their children were allowed to attend the public schools only if they paid a special tuition as a substitute for taxes on reservation land. (The latter provision was a major step backward, since the land had never been taxed in the past.) And on top of that, even a settlement of $50 million was worth far less than the value of the land they were seeking to recover.

All in all, Sanders was insulted on behalf of his tribe. "In my opinion," he wrote in a letter to President Clinton, "it means the death of the Catawba Nation."

Gilbert Blue disagreed. He understood that the settlement was flawed, but he thought it was probably the best they could do, and he urged the members of the tribe to accept it. His mind raced back over twenty years of struggle—to the day they had decided to file the lawsuit, and the multiple agonies in the years after that. Now, at last, they had an agreement, and for Blue, it was not the end of the story but a place for the Catawba Nation to start.

Fred Sanders could never accept that position, and when the settlement was approved in 1993, he resigned his position as assistant chief and moved to New Mexico. Three years later, at the age of seventy, he was working part-time on his college degree and giving lectures on the perils of being a leader. But many of his allies remained with the tribe, joining forces with Blue to try to make the best of what they had won, and in the next several years, their progress was clear. Federal money poured in by the millions—grants for improving reservation roads, building new houses, and putting in septic tanks and sewers. There were scholarships for college-age Catawbas and new jobs on the reservation itself, and many of the people who had scattered through the years were now coming home.

Keith Brown—the army vet who returned in the nineties and went to work for the tribe, guiding visitors through the new reservation—was one. His friend and neighbor Faye Greiner was another. She had worked for years in Pontiac, Michigan, as a radio dispatcher for a local bus company but found herself still dreaming of home.

"I felt something pulling inside me," she says. "I thought to myself, 'I'm going back and live off the land.'"

For a while, at least, she almost did. At the age of fifty-four, she returned from Michigan to South Carolina and moved in with her mother, Evelyn George, a master potter who worked in the old way, as the Catawbas had done it for a thousand years—digging up clay from the veins near the river, rolling it out by hand, bending it gradually into intricate shapes, scraping, polishing, then burning each pot in a hardwood fire. The techniques came back quickly to Faye, the memories of how she had done it as a child, and she began to make some pots of her own—and baskets, too, a Catawba art that had all but disappeared. She made her money that way for a while, living simply in a rusty old trailer with no electricity and a kerosene heater that doubled as a stove.

It shocked her to discover that in the 1990s, many of the tribal members lived that way— 75 percent in substandard houses and trailers like her own. But the tribe was beginning to do something about it. With federal grants pouring in in the wake of the settlement, the Catawbas were building new houses and renovating others, and before too long, they built one for Faye, tidy and secure, with gray vinyl siding and rust-colored shutters. It is nestled on a bluff on Cemetery Road, and on an autumn morning a few months back, she was working with the flowers still blooming in her yard, listening to the deer hunters' guns in the woods.

"There is something about this place," she said, "a feeling that comes from somewhere inside. It's the Indian part—this sense of attachment to a piece of the earth where your people have lived for so many years. I just have a feeling now that I'm home."

John George has the same kind of feeling,

though in a physical sense, he never really left. Instead, he spent thirty years with the bottle, beginning each day with a fifth of whiskey and a six-pack of beer. Miraculously enough, he survived until New Year's morning in 1995, when he decided to quit. He had met Earl Carter, a medicine man with the Lumbee Tribe who told him it was time to purify his body. Carter had detected some quality in George, some spark inside him that would give him the power to heal himself—and perhaps to heal other people as well. George decided to give it a try. After quitting cold turkey, he headed west to Cherokee country, where he checked himself into a treatment center, and when he emerged, he embarked on the path of becoming a healer—a medicine man for his people.

With the help of two botanists from Winthrop University and historians' records at the Library of Congress, he searched the forests of the Catawba Reservation for medicinal plants used in the old days. He found the ingredients for a traditional cough remedy made by his grandmother, an elixir composed of 8 different plants—barks and roots all boiled into syrup. In all, he discovered 110 different plants used over the course of the centuries for healing. But as a Native American healer, he spends his energies on the patient, not the ailment, trying to use a holistic approach. He works in tandem with the tribal M.D. and has become, since his triumph over the bottle, the first medicine

ANNA BROWN BRANHAM, CATAWBA NATION, SOUTH CAROLINA, 1996

man in ninety-five years to be officially recognized by the tribe.

A man with smooth, copper skin and dark, steady eyes, he is a symbol today that the old ways survive—at least in slightly modified form. But there are others, too, who make that case. Many of them are artists—tribal musicians like Warren Sanders, who composes new songs on his river-cane flute, and his wife, Cheryl Sanders, who makes fine pottery, and their neighbor Anna Branham, who is known for her beadwork.

"A few years ago," says Wenonah Haire, director of the tribe's cultural center, "our heritage was about to disappear. We had only a few people still making pottery, and nobody spoke the language anymore. Now, we have more than sixty potters and language classes that meet at the center. We have drum groups and people tanning hides and reviving the old storytelling traditions. We have seventeen people who work for the center—a well-trained archivist, an architectural department, a tribal historian at the Library of Congress."

Dr. Haire, who oversees all of that, is typical of the new leadership in the tribe. She is competent and smart, a dentist by trade, a woman who grew up close to tribal politics. Her father, Buck George, is a longtime leader, and she remembers the heated discussions in the seventies about how to pursue the Catawbas' land claim and their rightful status as a recognized tribe. She also has two children now, and because of them, the cultural restoration among the Catawbas has become her "obsession."

She is perhaps most proud of the master potters—a group of seven who have kept the sacred tradition alive and are teaching it now to those who are young. For all of the masters—Georgia Harris, Earl Robbins, and the others—the art itself is only part of it. The greater honor, by far, is to teach—to deliver their gift to the next generation—and there are pupils today who are showing great promise.

Probably the most gifted is a young Catawba by the name of Monty Branham. Already, he has lived a colorful life, a paratrooper when he was in his twenties, then a NASCAR mechanic living on the edge. He liked it there. He has experimented with alcohol and drugs and with the adrenalin rush of jumping out of planes and the roar and the speed of the NASCAR circuit. But he's calmer now, a handsome man of thirty-five with large, dark eyes that are steady and soft.

The change began on an ordinary day. He was helping put a roof on a house at Lake Norman, a resort community outside Charlotte, when he stopped for a while to stare at the sunset. It was red and gold, as if the lake itself were on fire, and he says he was caught in the beauty of it all when he saw the buffalo coming through the clouds. One of them turned in his direction and told him it was time to return to his people—and then, just as suddenly, the vision was gone. He thought

EARL ROBBINS, MASTER POTTER,
CATAWBA NATION, SOUTH CAROLINA, 1996

for a moment that he was losing his mind, and later brooded for days about whether it was real. But then he decided to take it as a sign. That was 1992, after all, a turning point in the history of his people. The land-claim struggle was nearing its end, and a spirit of revival seemed to be in the air, and Monty, who had never laid claim to his culture, suddenly felt the need to give it a try.

He knew he probably should have done it before. He was a direct descendant of Samuel Taylor Blue, the last of the Catawba chiefs to speak the language—a man who believed that the land and the river had a spirit of their own, and so did the people, and that one day again, all of these would be strong. That was the old man's article of faith, and he did his best to pass it on to his heirs. Monty thinks that it's starting to happen. The signs of renewal seem to be all around—particularly in the pottery, which has become his primary link to the past. It is, he says, far more than a craft. It is also a gift—a testament to what his people can accomplish.

And so he spends his hours with the clay, re-creating the traditional shapes—the snake pots, pitchers, peace pipes, and canoes—and in all of that, he stands as a symbol of the renaissance around him.

"Our generation is hungry for it," he says. "It's a part of our life we feel like we missed, and a part we need, and we're happy now to be finding it again."

There are still some problems.

There are bickering factions within the tribe, and political infighting that is sometimes nasty, and problems with the state of South Carolina. Tribal administrator Wanda Warren says that in the land-claim struggle, the state was driven all along by the question, How do we protect ourselves from the Indians? Three years after the settlement was signed, that same attitude could still be found. There were controversies looming over the issues of hunting rights and education, and the Catawbas once again were headed to court.

But even in that frustrating arena—the political battleground between the tribe and the state, where hard feelings have simmered for two hundred years—there has been some progress. The most important example came in 1996 in the area of law enforcement, when the Catawba Nation, working with the state, helped train three deputies to patrol the reservation and the area around it. That same year, the tribe started work on a new health clinic and led the push for a regional museum—both of which would serve not only the Catawbas but their neighbors as well.

For Wanda Warren, it's simply a matter of enlightened self-interest—a part of the Catawbas' great quest to survive and to live in peace with the people around them. She is certain now that they will succeed. The political groundwork has mostly been laid, and there have been some sound economic investments, and the culture is stronger than it's been in a century.

"The Catawbas today," says historian Tom Blumer of the Library of Congress, "are back once again to the seventeenth century."

In Indian time, it's a good place to be—a time when the Catawbas were at the peak of their power—and among the ranks of Native Americans, their recent achievements have won them respect. In the fall of 1996, they hosted a gathering of eastern tribes in Myrtle Beach. They entertained a visitor from another part of the world, who came, he said, to pay his respects. He was an Aleut prophet who lived on an island in the Bering Sea, a handsome, dark-eyed man full of poetic words. He said that in the realm of the spirit, a healing wind had arisen in the East and was blowing west through native communities all the way to Alaska. It brought with it life—an invitation to a new vitality—and it was clear that many of the people were listening.

For Gilbert Blue, the spiritual explanation is the best. How else can he understand or explain the changes taking place in his own tribe—the restoration of a culture that was almost dead among a people who had lived on the brink of extinction? As a Mormon minister as well as a chief, he has told his people many times that everything moves in God's own time. It seems to him now, as he looks at the evidence mounting all around, that the time of the Indian once again has arrived.

JIM BOWMAN, CHEROKEE TRIBAL COUNCIL MEMBER,
ROBBINSVILLE, NORTH CAROLINA, 1996

CHAPTER TWO
The Ghost of Junaluska

MAJOR JIM BOWMAN IS BACK HOME NOW, back among the mountains where he roamed as a child. There were times in the highlands of Vietnam when he thought about the Indian blood in his veins, and it gave him an extra measure of pride. It required all the courage and skill he could muster to lead his men on the midnight missions, when the moon was new or hidden by the clouds. They traveled in silence through the bamboo forests, scrambling along ridge tops steeper than the Smokies, and it was a deadly and dangerous game that they played. Bowman was a Special Forces commander, in the company most often of the Montagnards, a tribal people in the central highlands who could live for days on sumac roots and sometimes drank the blood of a tiger. Together, they would search out the Vietcong, slipping into their trenches, and many times after the fighting was over, when he tried to put the ugliness out of his mind— the sound of the screams and the expressions of terror and pain on the faces—he thought about the Cherokee fighters of the past.

On his mother's side, he was descended indirectly from the great Junaluska, who fought at the side of Andrew Jackson in a war against the Creeks. The turning point came at Horseshoe Bend, where the Tallapoosa River doubles back on itself, creating a narrow peninsula of land. The Creeks were holding their own for a while, protected on three sides by the water and massed behind a barricade on the fourth. They taunted General Jackson and dared him to charge, until Junaluska and his warriors swam across the river and attacked the main Creek force from behind. In the panic and pandemonium that followed, the Creeks were slaughtered, and according to Jackson's testimony, the Tallapoosa's waters ran crimson with the blood.

"The carnage was dreadful," he wrote to his wife—but better the Indians' blood than his own.

Jackson had a practical streak that way. He forged his alliance with the Cherokee fighters—and the Choctaws, too—in his war with the Creeks. But a few years later, running for president, he campaigned strongly for Indian removal. In much of the East, the tribes had been decimated by the wars, but in the South, they had not. The Cherokees, the Choctaws, and even a faction of the Creeks still held onto a portion of their lands, and as Jackson understood it, they were simply in the way.

Following his election in 1828, the Indians sent delegations to see him, led most often by men of erudition and courage, people like the Cherokee chief John Ross, who had adopted many of the white man's ways. He owned a plantation in the north Georgia hills and represented a tribe with its own written language and a vast population that was literate and wise. The Cherokees had long ago stopped waging war with the whites, deciding before the turn of the nineteenth century that there was no way to win. Ross, among others, believed that when the nation understood their accomplishments—their literacy rate and their economic progress and their heartfelt alliance in the war against the Creeks—a man as honorable as Andrew Jackson would find support for doing what was right.

But Jackson held firm to his campaign promises, dealing curtly with the Cherokee delegations and once telling Junaluska, his former ally at the Battle of Horseshoe Bend, "Sir, your audience is at an end. I cannot help you."

The Trail of Tears—or, in the Cherokee language, "the Trail Where We Cried"—soon followed. It was a journey in the winter of 1838, a forced removal to the hills of Oklahoma, and although the records are inexact, as many as four thousand Cherokees died along the way. They were the victims of icy winds from the north, and too little food, and a rash of epidemics that swept through the tribe. At least a few of them managed to escape, hiding in the hills, sometimes in caves or steep mountain passes, and a handful of others like Chief Junaluska traveled all the way to Oklahoma before slipping away to make the trip back home.

Jim Bowman had studied that history for years, and the time finally came in Vietnam

when he decided once and for all to embrace it. He had other options. Though his hair was dark and his skin had an unmistakable hue, he was only one-sixteenth Cherokee—enough to be recorded on the tribal rolls but not so much that he couldn't have chosen to live as a white man. But the mountains of North Carolina were calling, and once his military service was over, he came back home and built a house just a few miles from Junaluska's grave.

In the years since then, he has quietly emerged as a leader in the tribe, one of many in the Cherokee Nation who don't want to see their culture slip away. They know it could happen. Their language, for example, is becoming more rare. There are still some elders who speak it every day, especially back in the full-blood communities, in places like Snowbird deep in the hills. But there is a dividing line between the current generations. Many of those in their fifties or younger are the masters of only a phrase here and there, and out of 11,500 people on the rolls, only a few understand their alphabet.

One of the people who wants to change that is the Cherokees' principal chief, Joyce Dugan, who was elected in 1995. She knows that the members of the Eastern Band—the descendants of those who escaped the Trail of Tears—are confronted by terrible problems every day. Reservation unemployment is 45 percent in the winter season, and even when the tourists pour in during the summer, the rate still hovers at around 10 percent. Health problems, especially diabetes, are rampant, and

JOYCE DUGAN, CHEROKEE CHIEF, CHEROKEE, NORTH CAROLINA, 1997

teenage gangs not very different from those in the city—the Cryps and the Bloods, they call themselves—are becoming an issue for the Cherokee police.

"We have all the problems of any rural community—unemployment, health—and we need more things for our children to do," admits Chief Dugan.

She regards those issues as critical, and she and the members of the Cherokee government, including Jim Bowman, one of the stalwarts on the tribal council, work every day to try to find solutions. But intertwining their way through all of that—through every aspect of the life of the tribe—are larger and subtler issues of the spirit.

The chief encountered them first among the children. In 1966, she began a long career in education as a teacher's aide in the Cherokee schools. There were not many Indians working back then—not a single Cherokee teacher in the Bureau of Indian Affairs school system, until Dugan set out to change things. She worked her way through the ranks from teacher's aide to school superintendent, hiring other Indians for the Cherokee classrooms and becoming a role model for the tribe in the process. She was also a wife and a mother, and by the time she decided to run for chief, she was widely admired among the members of the tribe.

She had a gift for articulating their needs, especially the struggles of Cherokee children trying to learn how to live in two worlds. They were surrounded, of course, by the world of the whites. The total isolation of the Great Smoky Mountains, where their ancestors fled from the Trail of Tears, had long since ended with the coming of the roads and the television age. But they still wanted to live as Indians, caught in a resurgence of Cherokee pride that seemed almost to be coming out of nowhere.

Dugan thought it was healthy—a miracle, really—that their native identity was still intact, still existed at all after the battering it had taken down through the years. Almost from the start, as Dugan understood it, the official policy of the United States government was one of destruction. First came the wars of annihilation, the battles over land, and when those were decided, the government declared its war on the culture.

Its passion, quite clearly, was for Indians to be like everybody else. That policy peaked in the twentieth century—in Joyce Dugan's own generation, in fact—when boarding schools run by the BIA punished young Indians for speaking their language. The message was clear. The Cherokee language was a badge of shame, and with the exception of a stubborn few who resisted, a generation of Indians simply ceased to speak it. Dugan's own family was affected by the change. Her parents spoke Cherokee to each other but always addressed their children in English.

The result of it now is that the Cherokee chief, like the vast majority of people in her tribe, knows only bits and pieces of the language. Running for chief in the 1990s, she promised to address that problem head on. Cherokee again would be taught in the schools, would be a symbol of pride, and she would establish a special division of the government to set about preserving the traditions of the people—the pottery, the basket making and the carving, the stickball games played by the men. Burial grounds would be spared desecration, even when they stood in the path of development, and the tribe once again would celebrate its history.

It was a message that clearly struck a chord with the people, and Dugan immediately discovered some allies—leaders like Bowman who served on the council. They were interested in the tangible measures of progress—more jobs, better roads, and effective health care. But they were also committed to the spiritual and cultural health of the tribe, and as the 1990s drew to a close, they were beginning to feel a new sense of hope—an optimism that for two hundred years had not been an easy thing to sustain.

Every weekday morning precisely at nine, Robert Bushyhead disembarks from his car. He spends these mornings at the home of his daughter, a two-story house at the end of a lane that twists its way through a canopy of trees. It's a peaceful setting for the work they have started, a job that now has an urgency about it. Bushyhead, now in his eighties, holds a place of honor among his people. He is a handsome man with olive brown skin and sil-

ver gray hair that he wears swept back and hanging to his shoulders. He is one of those who still speaks the language, and even more significantly, he knows how to read and write it as well, a dying art among the Cherokee people. He doesn't want to take that knowledge to the grave, and so each day, despite the crippling effects of diabetes, he works with his daughter, Jean Bushyhead-Blanton, to record what he knows.

Jean is a teacher on leave from her classroom who has learned to take what her father remembers and turn it into audiotapes for the children. Sometimes, she is startled by the depth of his knowledge—gained, she knows, from a lifetime of study that began in the schools of the BIA. He remembers—with a smile that seems to be forgiving—the punishments inflicted on those like himself who insisted on speaking the Cherokee language. "Sometimes," he says, "they would wash your mouth out with soap. Other times, it was even the strap."

But in Bushyhead's case, the punishments failed. He spoke Cherokee every time he went home, for it was the only language in his parents' household, and even now, nearly eighty years later, it is the language he prefers to speak in his own. But he loves the English language also. Even before his boarding-school days, he picked it up quickly from white missionaries who gave him a lesson one day in his yard. His first English word was *Jesus*, he says, and many years later, he thinks it was probably a good place to start. He never forgot the missionaries' kindness and the love of learning they helped to instill. When boarding school ended after only eight years, he went to work for a while in the forests, cutting lumber in the mountains of North Carolina, but he yearned every day for a college education, and eventually, he says, "the doors of opportunity were opened."

He took his degree from Carson-Newman College and was soon ordained a Baptist minister, becoming known for his eloquence in Cherokee and English. He also worked for a while as an actor, and was the first in the cast of *Unto These Hills*—an outdoor drama about the Trail of Tears—to use his native language in the play. He always loved the sound of the words, the upward lilt at the end of each phrase, and even the complicated structure gave him pleasure.

He admired Sequoyah, the Cherokee scholar who wrote it all down—a silversmith in Georgia who was illiterate when it came to the English language but who was able nevertheless to devise a system for writing in his own. It was not an alphabet per se, but a syllabary with eighty-six characters, each of which stood for a Cherokee sound. It was approved officially in 1821, and seven years later, the Cherokees began a weekly newspaper, as the ability to read spread quickly through the tribe.

Robert Bushyhead is eager to build on Sequoyah's achievement, and part of his work in the final years of his life is to create a new Cherokee dictionary. He and his daughter are building it together, settling in most mornings in front of the computer, where the old man pronounces a Cherokee word, then defines it, after which they work out two different spellings—one a phonetic rendition in English, the other from the syllabary of Sequoyah.

For Bushyhead, the best part is that the work is not taking place in a vacuum. It's gradually finding its way to the schools, where Cherokee speakers conduct special classes and every teacher at the elementary level spends at least twenty minutes a day on the language.

Delores Davis is pleased by that. As a member of the Cherokee Tribal Council, she is fiercely proud of her Indian identity even though she no longer speaks Cherokee. Her grandmother did. In fact, she never spoke any English, and neither did her children until they went to boarding school. There, they were punished for their Cherokee ways, and as a result of that act of governmental coercion, the language died in their household. Delores doesn't speak it and neither do her children. But the good news is that it's now coming back. Her granddaughter, who is three years old, is picking it up at her day-care center, taught most often by the tribal elders.

"She can sing three songs," says Davis with pride, "and they are teaching it now in the Cherokee schools."

Jean Bushyhead-Blanton thinks the work is important. "It's in the pilot stage right now," she says, "but we have to keep going. To speak

Cherokee is to be Cherokee. The way you speak and the way you think is who you are."

Lynne Harlan sees other measures as well. As cultural director for the Eastern Band, she has a deep interest in history and art, the ingredients that give the culture its richness.

Until she began her job in 1996, she had been away from the reservation for a while. In the 1980s, she split her time between the University of Oklahoma and the University of North Carolina at Asheville, where she took her degree in public history before going to work for the Smithsonian Institution. After a decade or so, she decided it was time to come back home, and upon her return, she found a lot of people like herself—Cherokees by choice, people who could have lived anywhere in the world but gave in eventually to the yearning inside.

"I just drifted back," says Major Jim Bowman, who spent thirty years in the military before coming home. "These mountains are a part of who I am."

Lynne Harlan agrees, and it pleases her to know that she's in good company. In addition to Bowman, one of the progressive members of the tribal council, there are also artists like Amanda Crowe, whose fame in the realms of sculpture and carving began taking shape when she was still a child. At the age of four, she found a piece of root and promptly carved the figure of a bear. Later, she did some hum-

mingbirds and squirrels, and by the time she entered her teenage years, her art had emerged as a sturdy consolation against the tragedies that were starting to tear at her life. Her Cherokee father had deserted the family, and a few years later, when her English mother died, Amanda went to live in a foster home. Even as a child, she had cared for her mother with tenderness and strength, lifting her physically when she could no longer walk, carrying her to the door and out into the yard, where she could gaze at the mountains rolling off in the distance. But now it was time to get on with her life, and her guardians decided to send her to Chicago, where she studied at the Chicago Institute of Art and became a sculptor. She worked sometimes in metal and stone, but wood was her favorite. It is an ancient form of Cherokee art—taking a piece of walnut or cherry and carving out the shapes that are hidden inside. Amanda could see them if she stared hard enough—the form and the movement that were eager to escape—and then, she says, "my fingers just seemed to know what to do."

When she graduated, one of Chicago's philanthropists, Mrs. C. D. Kelley, gave her a car, and Amanda immediately headed south to Mexico—"tearing up the roads," she remembers with a smile. She was a young woman by then, and the adventure was grand. She studied for a while with Diego Rivera, the charismatic painter of Mexican murals who had learned the techniques of the European

AMANDA CROWE, CHEROKEE ARTIST, CHEROKEE, NORTH CAROLINA, 1997

masters but whose understanding of his work was fundamentally different. "It surges from the people," he tried to explain, a revolutionary force for dignity and justice. Almost invariably, the subjects of his massive wall paintings were Indians—farmers, miners, teachers, and fighters, all of them struggling against the forces of oppression.

It's difficult to assess his effect on Amanda—"He didn't mean that much to me," she insists—but in her own way, she became like the teachers in some of his murals. She returned to the reservation and for the next forty years shared her talents with the Cherokee children. She taught art in the elementary school and sculpture in the high school a few years later, and she estimates that a third of her woodcarving students are still working at it, selling their wares, keeping the tribal traditions alive. Now past seventy, Crowe continues to do her own carving, slowed sometimes by the pain of arthritis. But there is still a twinkle of mischief in her eyes. She drives a blue Trans Am, and if the mood is right, she'll try to crank up the Model A Ford that occupies a place of honor in her basement. The Smithsonian has a permanent display of her carvings, which makes her proud, but she is frustrated, too, by the concessions to age that forced her recently to give up teaching.

"I wanted to help my people do better," she says, and other Cherokee artists feel the same.

A few miles away, one of Crowe's friends, Emma Taylor, is still making baskets. She, too,

has achieved her share of acclaim. She has her own Smithsonian exhibition and has taught basket making from the reservation to Japan. Now nearly eighty, she lives on a hill in the community of Birdtown, not far from where she learned basket making from her mother. They would gather the materials they needed from the woods—the white oak, river cane, and maple, sometimes honeysuckle when the weather was colder and the wood was dry—and then together they would build their baskets, coloring the strands with a bloodroot dye. Sixty years later, she is still working at it, and has passed the tradition along to her children.

One of her daughters, Katrina Maney, lives down the mountain at the end of a well-worn path through the trees. She remembers some early advice from her mother. Baskets, Emma said, will bring in money when nothing else does—maybe thirty-five dollars for one you can make in a couple of hours. But the purpose, of course, goes deeper than that. The Cherokee crafts are a tie to the past, and as the skills are passed to new generations, they are a tie that helps hold families together.

"The other day," explains Lynne Harlan, the cultural director for the tribe, "I saw a group of women gathering vines for their baskets. They were sitting beside the Tuckasegee River like Cherokee Indians have done for years. There's a continuum of culture that makes us one, that makes us a family. We have always been in this place together. This is where the

Creator put us. The fundamental thing that makes us Indian is that spirit of community that keeps us together."

As the twentieth century draws to a close, Harlan is convinced that the spirit is strong. She finds it in the distant Cherokee communities—places like Snowbird deep in the hills, where Mose Wachacha can see from his driveway the route of the Trail of Tears through the valley. Wachacha is a former tribal council member, a distant descendant of Chief Junaluska who worries sometimes that the old ways are dying. He fought for his country in World War II, keeping the warrior tradition alive, and he still speaks the language, even though he knows that most people don't. But he also sees some reason for hope.

Not far away, there's a day-care center on Jackson Branch Road, an unimposing little building set back on a hill. Every morning at ten, the tribal elders—old women, mostly, who speak Cherokee—pay a visit to the children. Sequoyah's syllabary is posted on the wall, and the little ones seem to pick it up quickly. Lula Rattler is happy about that. She works as a cook's assistant at the center, and she wants her grandson to grow up proud. She understands that life can be hard for young Native Americans, especially those in a place like Snowbird, where there's a price to be paid for the peaceful isolation. There weren't many jobs for her husband, for example, before his diabetes left him disabled, and he had to leave

home to find work as a welder somewhere in Tennessee.

Their neighbor Ed Chekelelee faced the same kind of struggle. He worked for twenty-one years as a logger, a brutal occupation where the work isn't steady, but he says he loved his time in the woods in a way that's difficult to define. He's disabled now, still another victim of diabetes, and has dialysis treatments three times a week. But whatever the difficulties he has faced—hard work, poor health, and extended periods of forced unemployment—he finds Snowbird a source of consolation. It's a community of fewer than eight hundred people spread through the mountains near the Tennessee line. Four of his children are there with their families, and even the son who has moved away—a source of grief sometimes to Chekelelee—lives in Murphy, barely forty miles from the rest of the clan.

"We're pretty close-knit," Ed admits with a smile. "A fellow from Florida came by the other day and wanted to buy a piece of my property. I told him I wasn't tired of it yet. I've only lived here for sixty-eight years."

That sense of community, perhaps the most durable of Cherokee values, is invisible to the tourists who pour into the reservation every summer. They see instead the commercial strip in the town of Cherokee, a gaudy and dismal representation in which the stereotypes are like a pair of facing mirrors—Indians fulfilling what they've come to assume are the lowest expectations of the whites. There are shops full of foreign-made trinkets—Indian statues

AUSTIN RATTLER, AGE 2, STUDENT OF THE CHEROKEE LANGUAGE,
SNOWBIRD, NORTH CAROLINA, 1997

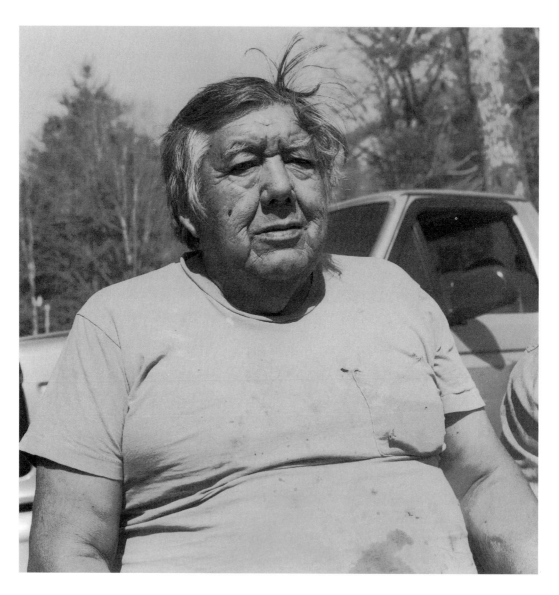

ED CHEKELELEE, CHEROKEE ELDER, SNOWBIRD, NORTH CAROLINA, 1997

made of plaster, complete with inauthentic attire—and there are captive bears that drink Kool-Aid poured from plastic cups by the tourists, and, of course, there's the gambling—bingo and slot machines in smoke-filled rooms that are crammed to capacity beneath the endless flicker of the neon lights.

Gambling was controversial among the Cherokees at first. But it became less so when the payments began to arrive every December, per capita allotments accounting for 50 percent of the take. The payments were substantially less than a fortune—sixteen hundred dollars in 1996—but they came at a time when people could use them, when their children needed coats or shoes for the winter, and when Christmas, for many, was not a season full of promise.

For others, of course, the payments have offered less noble possibilities. The poverty that afflicts the Cherokee people has always had a dark underside. In the 1980s, a social worker told Paul Hemphill, one of the South's most sympathetic journalists, "I see the underbelly. Even when it's the [tourist] season and there are plenty of jobs, the jobs are women's work. That emasculates the men, to their minds, and so they drink. You know, they feel like they're supposed to uphold this image of the macho Indian and all that. And then when it's the off-season, they get their food stamps, or their welfare check, or else the women bring home their paychecks, and they pile into cars and go over to the ABC store in Bryson City for their liquor. And when that money runs out, which doesn't take very long, they 'go Indian' for a while—that means they just start eating beans and don't buy anything or go out—before they start trying to con their social worker. It's a welfare state, no doubt about it."

As harsh as it sounds, there is still some truth behind that assessment. The difference today is the climate that surrounds it, the sense of mission that begins at the highest levels of the tribe. The principal chief, Joyce Dugan, offers a vision that is fundamentally different from the debate that existed a decade ago, when, as one critic put it, one faction wanted to throw off the shackles of language and culture, pull away from the tourists, and bring in heavy industry and jobs. The other group saw that approach as absurd—the tourists were their lifeblood, and the strategy was simply to pander even more to the tasteless inclinations of the visitors, increasing the addiction to the white man's money.

Dugan believes the tribe can do better. With her election as chief, she set out first to reorganize the government, with seven divisions instead of a bewildering maze of twenty-six. There are departments for tourism and economic development, for building infrastructure and providing fire protection and police, and for the first time ever, there is a branch of government commissioned to strengthen the Cherokee culture. The chief is convinced that the heritage can survive in the twenty-first century—indeed, that it must, if the tribe is to confront its range of spiritual and economic problems.

ORIGINAL CHEROKEE CASINO, CHEROKEE, NORTH CAROLINA, 1997

"We have to establish who we are," she says, "and we need a concerted effort at the top."

That effort has taken a variety of forms—support for the language and Cherokee art, the teaching of traditional dances and games, an official reverence for the Cherokee past. Under Dugan's leadership, the tribe has enforced old policies against the excavation of burial sites, even to the point of moving its casino when construction threatened to desecrate a grave. In 1996, it bought a piece of property called Ferguson Field in a lush river valley outside Cherokee, where the "mother town" of Kituwah once stood. It was the place where, on October 17, 1816, a dozen chiefs, including Junaluska, vowed that they would never give up their land.

Knowing that story, Jim Bowman supported the purchase of the land. Of all the heroes of Cherokee history, the one that intrigued him the most was Junaluska. He was a soldier first of all, just as Bowman had been, and there were missions in the mountains of Vietnam that resembled the Battle of Horseshoe Bend, the fighting intense and hand to hand. In addition to that, Junaluska was a sad and ironic symbol, betrayed by his ally, Andrew Jackson. But if he endured the Trail of Tears with his people, he also emerged in the end as a hero, coming home to the mountains of North Carolina and living his life in the place that he loved.

When Bowman returned to the reservation, he paid a visit to Junaluska's grave and was disappointed to find it in a state of disrepair. Years ago, the D.A.R. had put up a marker with a little fence around it, but now the site was trashy and forgotten, hidden away on a brushy hilltop that it took a deliberate effort to find. With others who were interested in Cherokee history, Bowman began to imagine the possibilities—a more elaborate marker and perhaps a museum about the Trail of Tears, something that might appeal to the tourists while at the same time treating Junaluska with respect.

In Bowman's mind, his people's history is a precious resource—a source of pride and a source of jobs, if they think about it right, and he knows that kind of thinking is essential. It is true enough that there is more hope now in Cherokee country than there has been for many years, but from the vantage point of the 1990s, the century just ahead looks rocky and hard. Some people argue that the Cherokees are doomed, if not by the social problems they face then eventually by the pattern of racial intermarriage that leaves the bloodline thinner all the time.

Jim Bowman doesn't know about that. Maybe the Indians will eventually disappear. But for now, he says, the Cherokees are here, just as they have been for ten thousand years. That fact alone is reason to be proud.

EDDIE TULLIS, CREEK TRIBAL CHAIRMAN, POARCH, ALABAMA, 1997

CHAPTER THREE

Legacies of the Choctaws and Creeks

RUTHIE MAE RACKARD REMEMBERS how it was. As an elder in the Poarch Creek Band of Indians, she lived through the days when the greatest Indian confederacy in the South was reduced to a hovel of run-down houses. They were scattered through the woods in southern Alabama—in communities like Hog Fork, Poarch, and Head of Perdido, where families of two and three generations crowded together in rough-hewn cabins and braced themselves against the heat and the cold and the vagaries of poverty and racial segregation. They had no indoor plumbing or heat, except perhaps for a brick fireplace, and no relief at all from the Alabama summers. They worked as farmers, loggers, sharecroppers, and migrants—whatever they could find to do with their hands—and those who dreamed of a better way of life would sometimes stand and stare in dismay as the school buses passed their children on the roads.

"It was rough and hard," says Houston McGhee, a longtime leader in the Poarch Creek Tribe. But things are better today. In fact, the change is stunning. There are paved roads now, replacing the rutted clay paths where mules and wagons once rumbled into town, and there are more than 160 new houses, many of them painted in pastel colors, and there is a sewer system built for the twenty-first century. The tribe raises cattle and catfish and corn, has a buffalo herd, and runs a motel, and unemployment has dropped in the past twenty years from nearly 65 percent to less than 5.

The changes began in the 1940s with a charismatic leader named Calvin McGhee, who dressed himself in Plains Indian regalia and drove off to Washington in a pulpwood truck to meet with presidents and members of Congress and remind them of promises made in the past. When Calvin died in 1970, the mantle was passed to Houston, his son, and then to Eddie Tullis, a tribal chairman who had a different style. Instead of eagle feathers, he was partial to suits and white, starched collars, but his fundamental vision was the same as Calvin's. He believed that his people could compete with anybody.

He understood the strength of the Indian

community, all the old habits of survival and trust—the toughness to endure the brutality of the South and still come out intact. In a way, the Indians were better off than the blacks, less hated certainly, and less often the targets of physical violence. But in the end, it was still a white man's world, and if the Indians were to make it, they would do it on their on. Tullis came to believe that they could, that it was possible to add a new set of skills to the qualities that had served them well in the past, and his faith was sustained—in part, at least—by the experience of the Choctaw people up the road.

The Choctaws lived in eastern Mississippi, many of them in the thick pine forests of Neshoba County, where the Ku Klux Klan in the 1960s was in the midst of a murderous reign of terror. The worst of it came in the first half of the decade, especially 1964—"Freedom Summer," the civil-rights workers called it—when they set out to register black people to vote. The Klan responded by firebombing churches, and then by kidnapping three young workers—Michael Schwerner, James Chaney, and Andrew Goodman—whose bodies were eventually discovered in a dam. Before they were found, some Choctaw fishermen located their car, the burned-out shell of a Ford Fairlane, in a swamp not far from the holiest of places—a thousand-year-old mound called Nanih Waiya, the ancient center of the Choctaw Nation. Not long after the recovery of the car, a Mennonite mission to the Choctaws was bombed, serving notice to the Indians to remember their place.

In the nineteenth century and much of the twentieth, the Choctaws' response to the hostility of their neighbors was to retreat more deeply into the Mississippi forests, turning in on themselves, minimizing their encounters with the outside world. For a time, they paid a price for that approach—an unemployment rate that even as late as 1980 hovered somewhere around 75 percent. It was true that their culture was essentially intact. Most were full bloods, most spoke the language. But the Choctaw Reservation was a slum, full of run-down houses and broken windows, and most people were way behind on their rent. It is different today. Since 1980, the tribe and the federal government have built a thousand new units of housing, and under the leadership of Chief Phillip Martin, the tribe has emerged as an economic force, transforming not only its own reservation but the economy and the mood of east-central Mississippi. The Choctaws operate more than a dozen enterprises—a mail-order house, manufacturing plants, and, most recently, a casino. Their unemployment is down to less than 15 percent, and for the blacks and whites who live in the area, the tribe has provided a ready source of jobs—becoming, early in the 1990s, the tenth-largest employer in the state of Mississippi.

As models for economic development, the Choctaws and Creeks have been as aggressive as any tribes in the country, and their efforts have instilled a new sense of pride.

KLAN ROBE, NESHOBA COUNTY, MISSISSIPPI, 1997

"Oh my, yes," says Ruthie Mae Rackard, as the memories flash across her face, "lots of things are getting better all the time."

To understand the magnitude of the difference not only for the elders but the young people, too, it is necessary to go back in time. For a century and a half, the intertwining histories of the Choctaws and Creeks were as painful and hard as any the Indian people have known. The turning point in their story was a war that began in the summer of 1813—on a hot August day in southern Alabama—when a band of Creeks attacked Fort Mims, killing nearly all the settlers inside. The retribution that followed was brutal and swift, sealing not only the fate of the Creeks but that of the neighboring tribes as well. The Indians—even some of those who took part in the fight—were afraid that it would be that way. But they knew that history had a mind of its own, and all they could muster in the end was the hope that the time of troubles would one day subside.

William Weatherford, who led the fateful

PHILLIP MARTIN, CHOCTAW CHIEF, PHILADELPHIA, MISSISSIPPI, 1997

attack on the fort, was one of those who clung to that hope. In the Indian world, he was known as Red Eagle—a mixed-blood chief whose father was a Scot. For most of his life, he argued passionately against war with the whites—even when the great Tecumseh had come south seeking to build a coalition of tribes capable of driving the white man to the sea. Red Eagle was impressed with Tecumseh's oratory. In 1811, the Shawnee chief cut a terrifying figure on his visit to the Creeks. His face was daubed with black war paint, and his straight, dark hair was shaved at the temples, and a pair of crane feathers hung from his crown. But Weatherford thought that Tecumseh was a fool. There were too many whites for the Indians to fight, and at the council of chiefs in the Creek town of Tukabatchee, he rose to speak against Tecumseh and his plans.

People disagree about his change of heart. Some say he was the Indians' Robert E. Lee, opposed to war but casting his lot with his people when it came. Whatever the case, this much is clear. On the night before the attack on Fort Mims, he ordered the warriors who made up his band to spare the lives of women and children. He and Tecumseh agreed on that. It was foolish and cruel to desecrate the innocent, but on August 30, 1813, that is precisely what the Creek army did. In a surprise attack in the middle of the day, they rushed through the open gates of the fort and began to slaughter anybody they could find, hacking, scalping, slashing even the women and children into pieces.

In the days that followed, outrage spread along the frontier. The legislature in the state of Tennessee commissioned Andrew Jackson to go and "exterminate the Creek nation," and several armies were arrayed for that purpose. There were troops from Georgia and the territory of Mississippi, and even many Indians volunteered for the cause—the Cherokees, led by Chief Junaluska, a Choctaw army under Pushmataha, as well as a major contingent of Creeks. The hostile forces were quickly subdued in a scorched-earth war that ended with the Battle of Horseshoe Bend. In Jackson's mind, there was only one piece of unfinished business—to find William Weatherford and make him pay for his crimes.

He didn't have long to wait. A few days after the battle at the Horseshoe, Weatherford appeared at the general's tent, riding in alone on his gray horse, Arrow. He was tall and muscular, a light-skinned man bare to the waist, with buckskin trousers and a pair of moccasins that had seen better days. "General Jackson," he said, according to one historian's account, "I'm Bill Weatherford. I understand you are looking for me."

Jackson was astonished by Red Eagle's courage, though at first he simply sputtered with rage. "How dare you show yourself," he demanded, "after having murdered the women and children at Fort Mims?"

But the two of them sat and began to talk,

and Weatherford made an eloquent plea for peace. He admitted that the Indian people were defeated, and that their only course now was to seek to live as neighbors with the whites. "I am in your power," he told General Jackson. "You can kill me if you desire." But before that happened, he asked for mercy on the women and children and, if the general would permit it, a chance to speak once again to the Creeks, who still believed in the possibility of war.

So impressed was Jackson that he agreed to set William Weatherford free, and Red Eagle proved to be a man of his word. He preached his gospel of peace to the Indians and then moved back to his Alabama farm, living with a stoic dignity and pride in the midst of neighbors he had once tried to kill. Jackson, of course, moved on to the White House, where one of the cornerstones of his presidency was his decision to remove the Indian people from the East—even those who had fought at his side.

The Choctaws were first on his list, agreeing in the Treaty of Dancing Rabbit Creek to give up 10 million acres of land. In less than a decade, the Cherokees, Chickasaws, Seminoles, and Creeks all made the terrible trip to Oklahoma, their death toll rising to at least ten thousand, and by 1840, the deed was accomplished. The Indians who remained were those who had fled to the swamps or the Blue Ridge Mountains, plus a favored few who had gotten land grants. There were Choctaws and Creeks in the latter category, and though they clung to a remnant of the homeland, they did not prosper for the next hundred years.

In Alabama, the Creeks' land base kept slipping away, and the people were left to huddle in the hamlets, trusting only each other. By the 1940s, most were poor, eking out a living the best way they could, and formal education was hard to come by. Their own schools ended in the sixth or seventh grade, and though they were permitted to continue their education in Atmore, the nearest town, they understood clearly that they were not welcome there. For one thing, there were no school buses provided for the Indians—a fact that was galling to Calvin McGhee.

Calvin was a farmer, one of the most successful of the Alabama Creeks, raising his hogs and cattle, peanuts and corn—a man of ambition who wanted to see better things for his children. His younger sister, Ruthie Mae Rackard, remembers his fury—or at least his air of soft-spoken resolve—when it came to the obligations of the school bus. Calvin thought it should stop for the Indians, and he made that case to the powers in the county. "He just told 'em," recalls Ruthie Mae, " 'You're gonna stop, or I'm gonna know why.' "

The officials tried at first to coopt him. Keep the issue to yourself, they said, and we'll give your children a ride every day. The McGhees, after all, were more light skinned that some of the others—less likely, in the end, to give much offense. But Calvin refused. He was concerned about all of the children, he explained, not merely those who bore his own name or lacked the copper-colored skin of their cousins.

So the issue went to court, and Calvin began to raise his sights, moving from the modest issue of a school bus to questions that had even broader implications. It was a pattern that became commonplace in the South—grass-roots leaders of racial minorities asking for the simplest things at the start, then learning from the sting of official rebuff exactly what kind of war they were in. Over in South Carolina, for example, as Calvin was waging his fight in Alabama, blacks in Clarendon County were also asking for a bus for their children. They, too, were denied, and they, too, decided to raise the stakes, demanding an end to segregated schools. Their case soon made its way through the courts, and the Supreme Court heard it along with four others, ruling in 1954 that segregated schools were unconstitutional. It was a landmark moment for blacks in the South, and it gave hope to other minorities as well—a belief in the possibility of change.

It was true, of course, that the Indians' struggles were less publicized, overshadowed for a time by the civil-rights movement and the great southern drama of black and white. But the issues they were raising were equally vast. Beginning in 1948 and continuing until the end of his life, Calvin became part of a national demand that the federal government honor its treaties with the tribes. It had not

done so in the case of the Creeks. At the end of the war of 1813, the Indians had met with Andrew Jackson and surrendered their claim to 25 million acres. In return, they were promised some payments of cash, which were never made—until Calvin McGhee and the Creeks of Oklahoma asserted their claims in the 1940s. For Calvin, the principle overshadowed the money. He regarded his own people as forgotten, and he wanted simply to say that they were there.

In that pursuit, he made frequent trips to Montgomery and Washington, meeting with Presidents Kennedy and Johnson, members of Congress, and assorted bureaucrats from the BIA. For an astonishing span of twenty-two years, he pursued a settlement of the Creeks' land claim, sustained by a vision of the future of his people and also, apparently, by the power of his faith. There is a story told often among members of his tribe about the time he was waiting for a meeting at the White House—nervous, perhaps, about how an Indian from Alabama might fare in such a bewildering and high-powered environment. So he pulled out a pen and an old envelope and began to scribble on the back, repeating while he waited the most reassuring line from the Twenty-third Psalm: "The Lord is my shepherd . . ."

The same verse appears on the stone at his grave, where the Poarch Creeks gather every year in his honor. Calvin died in the summer of 1970 on his way to a funeral, the victim of a heart attack at age sixty-seven. He was deeply in debt, having borrowed against his farm to finance much of his mission for the tribe, and the irony of it was that he never saw the tangible results of his work. There were buses, of course, for the Creek school-children, and he knew the land-claim settlement—probably in the neighborhood of $4 million—was coming. But it remained for the next generation of leaders—Eddie Tullis, Buford Rolin, and some of the young ones—to build on his struggles and create a different way of life for the tribe.

That's the most remarkable part of the story—that the second generation was equally as strong. Its leader was Tullis, an affable man, shrewd and energetic, with the air of a rural politician about him. Like Calvin, he was deeply committed to his people, but he seemed more comfortable in the corridors of power, reveling in the rush of getting things done. In 1978, he won his first election as tribal chairman, a position he has held for more than twenty years. His first major challenge was federal recognition—official acknowledgment from the BIA that the Poarch Creek Indians in fact were a tribe. It was a piece of lunacy that they still had to prove it, having won a land claim of $4 million precisely on the basis of their Indian ancestry. But such was the nature of the federal government—a byzantine world in which the bureaucrats made their arcane distinctions. Descendants were one thing, a tribe was an-

other, so Tullis and the others set out to demonstrate that they had been a functioning community all along.

Working with J. Anthony Paredes, an anthropologist at Florida State University, the Creeks put together a systematic case for the "social and political continuity of the tribe," as it is known in the language of the BIA. The case was built on the scholarship of Paredes and also on the work of Gale Thrower, the tribal archivist, who carried a good part of the story in her head. She knew that in the 1700s, her ancestors had moved to the southern boundaries of the Creek Nation, where they often found work as interpreters and guides for whites who were beginning to drift into the area. They had fought on the side of Andrew Jackson and received land grants in return for that service, and although much of the land had slipped away, the Creeks themselves had stayed where they were.

Gale had heard stories at the family dinner table, and shelling peas with her grandmother Zeffie Gibson, about how the community had functioned through the years. The people were close and often rallied to each other's defense. A case in point was the story of John Rolin, Zeffie's father, who had killed another Indian around the turn of the century and was tried for the crime and sentenced to prison. Soon, however, he was pardoned by the governor at the urging of the other members of the tribe. Rolin, they said, had done what he had to. His victim, William Colbert, had gotten drunk at a party and was cursing some women when Rolin intervened and ordered him to stop. In the escalation that followed, Rolin slashed Colbert across the stomach with a knife—"a gut-cutting," one Indian called it—but the consensus was that Colbert had it coming.

Having heard the story for most of her life, Thrower searched out the written records of the pardon and the petition submitted to the governor by the Creeks, and they became pieces in a much larger case that the tribe had made collective decisions all along. There were other anecdotes to support that view, other records that Thrower and Paredes pulled together, and in 1984, the word came down from the BIA that the Alabama Creeks were officially a tribe.

Eddie Tullis moved quickly to build on the victory. He knew that housing was a critical need, and with the federal money that was now available, they could build infrastructure as well—roads and sewers, a tribal headquarters, a new health clinic—plus a hundred new houses. From there, they could work on the economy and education, creating new jobs, persuading the young people to remain in school, and soon it would be a different kind of place. No longer would the Indians have to leave to get a job, and those who had drifted away in the past would now find a reason to come back home.

Such was the dream of Eddie Tullis, and most of it has happened in exactly that way.

The Creek Reservation, carved from the low-lands of southern Alabama, is a flourishing place with broad, green fields stretching toward the stands of timber in the distance. There are housing developments and well-paved roads and plenty of places for the people to work—a restaurant, a bingo palace, and farms. Veronica McGhee was worried at first that it would be too quiet. She was one of those who came home from the city, a single mother who returned to care for her invalid parents. Before the effects of diabetes took a toll, the McGhees had traveled together as a family, performing the traditional Creek Indian dances, taking part in a revival of interest in the culture. Veronica still shares that preoccupation. Now in her twenties, she has always been proud of the Indian blood in her veins, and after she returned to the Poarch Creek community, there was something reassuring on Saturday nights about the sound of the Indian drums in the distance. The traditionalists gathered once a month in a clearing, dancing sometimes until it was almost dawn. But even in a time of cultural renewal that seemed to spring from a new sense of pride, perhaps the most striking thing was the quiet.

"I wasn't sure at first," says Veronica today. "But that's what I love about it the most. There's a feeling of peace."

She is not alone in that. All through the community, there are people who speak of their affection for the place and their pride in what their leaders have accomplished. But in the minds of some, there is also a worry, a fear that something is about to be lost. "Hard times held this community together," says Billy Smith, a longtime member of the tribal council. He wonders what the Indians' modest prosperity will bring. Will it weaken the bonds that helped them survive? There are some signs—more petty crime than in the past, more problems with drugs, more chances for their children to drift into trouble. But many people say there are good signs, too—more young people in college today than there were in high school a decade ago, and more opportunities to keep them at home.

Eddie Tullis believes the old ties can survive, with progress replacing desperation as the glue. But whatever happens, one thing is for sure. Almost nobody wants to go back. "Lord no," says Mabel Jackson, a tribal elder who remembers how it was. "I sure wouldn't want to get down in that rut."

They feel the same in rural Mississippi, where the changes, if anything, have been more dramatic. Chief Phillip Martin has seen to that. He grew up hard in the tiny Choctaw community of Tucker. His father was killed when he was eleven, run down by a car, leaving Phillip's mother with six young children, and one day in 1939, she was faced with an agonizing decision. She wanted her children to receive an education, and Phillip was at a critical age. He was thirteen—too old for the schools in the Choctaw community, which ended at the elementary level, yet barred from the other schools in Mississippi because of the unbending codes of racial segregation. But there was an alternative. The local superintendent from the BIA appeared at the Martins' house with an offer. He intended to take a group of Choctaw children to a boarding school in North Carolina, a facility on the Cherokee Reservation, and he intended to leave on the following morning. Phillip had until then to make up his mind. At first, the boy was full of excuses. He didn't have the clothes or a good suitcase, but the superintendent promised to help him with that, and Phillip decided to go.

Because of the distance and the condition of the roads, it was almost impossible to go back home for the next five years. But Phillip adjusted to his new surroundings. The mountains were pretty, and his teachers were committed, and when he graduated at the age of eighteen, he thought he could make his way in the world. He joined the air force and rose through the ranks, and he believed for a while that Mississippi was behind him.

"I knew I'd come back to visit," he says. "But I had no plans to stay."

All of that changed because of his wife. In 1954, he married Bonnie Kate Bell, and the following year, they returned to Mississippi, where she took a job with the BIA. She liked being home and wanted to stay, and soon her

BILLY SMITH, FORMER CREEK COUNCIL MEMBER, POARCH, ALABAMA, 1997

husband was committed to it, too. In 1957, he ran for the tribal council and won, and on that body, he joined chairman Emmett York and others in pursuing a better life for the people. The needs were obvious—there weren't any jobs in Choctaw country, the housing was bad, the schools inadequate. In 1959, Martin and several other leaders from the tribe made a trip to Washington. Martin says today it was the first delegation since Chief Pushmataha in 1824. But if the meeting at the BIA was historic, it didn't seem to change anything in the short run. A few weeks later, a letter arrived. "The bottom line," says Martin, "was no money, no help."

Gradually, however, he learned to play the game—an education that lasted the better part of twenty years, as Martin emerged as a leader in the tribe. He was chairman of the council, and then, in the Great Society years, director of the Choctaws' War on Poverty. He absorbed the lessons of each of those jobs, and by the 1970s, a new understanding was taking shape in his mind. He thought he saw how the future might be—how the Indians could build a whole new economy, not only for themselves but for the blacks and whites in central Mississippi. They could start with a new industrial park, inviting in companies that could see the advantages—a cost of living that was under control and a pool of labor that was hungry and large.

The Choctaws, of course, had never attempted anything of that scale, but Martin began writing to CEOs, and for more than five years, the answer was the same. "Thanks but no thanks," he says with a smile. But then one day, another letter came. Packard Electronics, a division of General Motors, was looking for a place to build a plant. It made wiring harnesses, electronic circuitry for cars in Detroit, and Martin eagerly embraced its proposal. He had just been elected chief of the Choctaws, and now he saw the possibility of a breakthrough, an escape from the poverty his people had endured.

His elation, however, proved to be short-lived. Barely two years after the new plant opened, it was clear to Martin that it was about to go under—the victim of management problems at the top. The chief could hardly believe it at first, and he wondered sometimes in his darkest moments if the people at the BIA were right. They had been skeptical of the industrial park all along, through all those years when it stood there empty, a pitiful gash in the red-clay earth, and suddenly, in fulfillment of all those doubts, the Choctaws' first major industry appeared to be failing. Martin is not a man to bare his soul, and many years later, he was cautious and reserved when a stranger asked how he felt at the time. It was clearly a difficult moment, he said, and all he could do, all his pride and ego would allow, was to keep pushing forward.

He made a call to Lester Dalme, an impressive young executive at Packard Electronics, and asked him to come and take over the plant. He was careful not to beg, to make no appeal to sentiment or guilt or the white man's burden. It was strictly business—"A new plant, good equipment, and a good labor force," Martin said at the time. Dalme was left to weigh that pitch against the other realities he would have to confront—an operation in desperate financial trouble, with fifty-seven workers in the middle of nowhere.

In the end, he decided it was too good to pass up, a challenge of monumental proportions where the stakes were greater than the corporate bottom line. It didn't take him long to turn things around. By the summer of 1997, employment in the Choctaw electronics industry had risen to a thousand workers, who produced annual revenues of $42 million. There were other successful ventures also—a tribal shopping mall and, of course, the casino, which opened in 1994 and within a year paid off its note of $32 million. Three years later, it was paying dividends of $1,000 each to more than eight thousand members of the tribe, but that was just a small percentage of the profits. The rest was invested in the future of the people—building new schools, improving the curriculum, sending Choctaws to college. Under the terms of the tribal scholarship program, any Choctaw student who can get into college—any college—will have his education paid for.

As remarkable as all these changes have been, the new prosperity didn't end with the Indians. From the start, Phillip Martin was convinced that the way to improve the racial climate of Mississippi was not to make demands but to create jobs—to end the perpetual state of recession in the poorest area of the poorest state in the country.

"I always figured," he says today, "if *we*, instead of *they*, could provide new jobs, that would change a lot of things."

So far, it has. But it's also true that despite his energy and the things he's accomplished, Phillip Martin is not universally admired. One of his critics is Kennith York, the first Choctaw in modern times to earn his Ph.D. York is principal of a Choctaw school, a friendly and unassuming man who believes that Martin has too much power, that he rules sometimes with an iron hand, and that his vision is impaired by his need for control. Among other things, York has demanded better checks and balances in the Choctaw government and greater diversity in the economic structure—more emphasis on entrepreneurs, for example, instead of the tribe providing all the jobs.

"I think when he started," York says of Phillip Martin, "he had the best interests of the people at heart. But then somewhere, he lost that vision."

There are other critics who make the same case, sometimes more harshly, but they also know they are in a minority. On three occasions, Kennith York has run against Martin for chief, and on each of those occasions, he lost. For the Choctaw people, it's easy to compare. They remember how it was less than twenty years ago, when there weren't any jobs and the reservation was a slum, and almost nobody wants to go back. And yet there are those—even among the ranks of Phillip Martin's admirers—

who worry about the future. Melford Farve is one. His father, Elbert Farve, was a school-bus driver who served for years on the tribal council. When Elbert's health declined in 1994, Melford was appointed to fill out his term, and later was elected on his own. He believes in the general direction of the tribe, especially the recent history of economic development, which he sees as a "godsend." But he wonders sometimes if it is moving too fast.

Now in his thirties, Farve has strong feelings for the Choctaw culture, a pride in the fact that most of the people still speak the language. He remembers the time a few years ago when a group from Oklahoma, descendants of those who survived the Trail of Tears, came back to Mississippi for a glimpse of the homeland. They made a pilgrimage to Nanih Waiya, the sacred mound of the Choctaw people, and sang their Indian hymns at the summit. It was a reminder to Melford, if one were needed, that their traditions were born in the soil of Mississippi, and that it is simply unthinkable to allow them to die. But he knows it could happen. More and more children in the Choctaw community speak English more easily than their native tongue, a product in part of the television age, and studies conducted in the 1990s indicate clearly that the language is slipping.

In 1997, Pat Kwachka, a nationally known linguist working for the tribe, asked to meet with Phillip Martin. She had bad news. She had done some testing on the children, she said, and the things she learned had come as a shock. Among those getting ready to enter the schools, fewer than 50 percent spoke Choctaw. Many more understood it, but if they no longer spoke it as a matter of habit, it could be the death knell—a crumbling of a cornerstone of the culture.

Chief Martin's response to the news was immediate. "Let's do something," he told Pat Kwachka, and the result of his declaration was a grant—money allocated by the tribal council for a pilot program of summer immersion. For a six-week period, small groups of children spoke only Choctaw as they studied the history of their people and their culture. They did woodcarvings and listened to stories handed down in the tribe and, at least for the moment, withdrew from the world pressing in around them. Nobody can say how well it worked. The Indians live, after all, in the country of Nahollo, a Choctaw word often used for whites, translating literally as "someone who is grasping after things." But if it's true the children will have to deal with that world, Pat Kwachka and others take heart in the fact that the little ones are open—eager for another kind of knowledge as well.

"Their interest level in their culture is increasing," says Roseanna Nickey, a Choctaw teacher who coordinated the summer language program. "There is hope in that, but we need to do more."

Nickey believes it's a critical time. She knows that the Choctaw culture is strong, with basket

MALLIE SMITH, CHOCTAW BASKETMAKER, CONEHATTA, MISSISSIPPI, 1997

makers and stickball players and most of the people still speaking the language. But the isolation that once reinforced it has crumbled with the dreams of Chief Phillip Martin and must now be replaced by something more deliberate. Nickey believes it is likely to happen, believes the tribal school system, for example, is sensitive to the needs of the children who attend it.

"They need to compete," Nickey says of her students, "but they also need to know who they are. I think that is where we are headed. But there is work to be done."

The elders, meanwhile, are doing their part. Out in the hamlet of Conehatta, Esbee Gibson works most days at her baskets. She is frail and shy, a tiny woman in her eighties who dresses in the old way, with hand-stitched aprons and cotton dresses reaching to her shoe tops. She weaves her baskets with strips of river cane, which is fast disappearing in central Mississippi, but the weavers still find it on the edge of the creeks. Esbee doesn't cut her own anymore; she is too old now, but her hands are sure when a new batch arrives. She colors the strips with handmade dyes, and then she begins to work on the shapes, and when the baskets are done, she sells many of them at Rose Bryan's store—a cluttered little market in the town of Freeny, where many of the Indians once came to barter. They traded their baskets for a week's worth of food, and

Rose invariably was impressed by their art. She also discovered it was good for her store. The market for Choctaw baskets was brisk—and has become more so in the 1990s with a revival of outside interest in the culture. Rose thinks there may be a lesson in that, a reminder that the Indian ways can survive.

J. Anthony Paredes, the anthropologist and scholar who has worked with the Poarch Creek Band in Alabama, believes that, too. He believes the Indians' identity is getting stronger and that the key to their cultural strength is economic. Deprivation may have served in the past—all those years of segregation and poverty that forced the Indians to turn to each other. It may have kept old traditions alive— the language and the baskets in central Mississippi, the sense of community among the Creeks in Alabama. But in the end, the price was simply too high, and their survival depended on a different kind of strength.

That is certainly the view of Phillip Martin and his Alabama counterpart, Eddie Tullis. There is always a risk in an era of change, a chance for precious things to disappear. But there is also the hope, the article of faith, that with pride and prosperity and a good education, the Indian identity of the next generation will survive more easily than it has in the past. For Tullis and Martin, who remember how it was, there is no other vision that makes any sense.

They know that time will tell if they are right.

ESBEE GIBSON, CHOCTAW BASKETMAKER, CONEHATTA, MISSISSIPPI, 1997

WILFORD "LONGHAIR" TAYLOR, MOWA CHOCTAW CHIEF,
MT. VERNON, ALABAMA, 1997

CHAPTER FOUR
The Quest for Recognition

THE WILD TURKEYS SCATTER at the passing of a car. They are accustomed to solitude in these hills, which rise from the lowlands of a dark river delta, home to the alligator and the bear. There are Indian people who live here, too—the Mowa Choctaws, they are called today, a stubborn group of mixed-blood survivors whose painful story has long been obscured not only by the other racial struggles of the South but by another piece of Indian history as well.

Their home in the woodlands of southern Alabama was also the site of a military post—the place where Geronimo was held captive. In April 1887, he and his band of Chiricahua Apaches, captured finally after a long and bloody war in Arizona, were shipped to a fort on the Mobile River. The Apaches found it a terrible place, the trees so large they blotted out the sun, and some of the men became so morose, missing the wind and the wide-open spaces, that they climbed through the spindly limbs of the pines merely to catch a glimpse of the sky. Even worse, there were

unknown fevers that rose from the swamps, and Geronimo himself was taken ill more than once, and was treated in a rustic wood-frame building that stands today on the Mowa Reservation.

The building will soon become a museum, for the chief of the Mowas, Wilford Longhair Taylor, feels a kinship with Geronimo's suffering—and perhaps even more with his spirit of defiance. Following his election in 1995, Chief Taylor embarked on a frustrating mission. He is seeking recognition for the Mowa Choctaws, an official declaration from the BIA that his people meet the definition of a tribe. He remembers the words that his grandmother gave him—the bits and pieces of the Choctaw language—and the stories handed down from the nineteenth century.

Nobody denies that at least since the days when the Europeans came, there have been Choctaw people in Mobile County. They fished the waters of the Mississippi Sound and traded their furs in the town of Mobile—a ragged outpost on the Alabama coast with a brick-walled fort and a cluster of huts. In the early years, the Choctaws were strong, and they traded as equal partners with the French, who controlled Mobile until the 1760s. But their status changed in the next hundred years, and by the time of the white man's War Between the States, they lived in poverty on the fringes of the town—a remnant band that escaped the Trail of Tears.

A British visitor to the Alabama coast wrote of their "wretched" cluster of wigwams, and of the women who shuffled through the streets of the city selling chumpa, or chips of pine, used for starting fires. "They speak to nobody, rarely smile, or take the smallest interest in anything going on about them," the visitor remembered.

But the Choctaws endured, their presence recorded in old cemeteries, their stories preserved and handed down by the elders. Wilford Taylor remembers being told that one of his early ancestors was a chief—Piamingo Hometah, his grandmother said, a man born in the days when the people were strong. But there was another message he absorbed through the years, and it came down to this: As far as the larger community was concerned, the Indians were now an invisible people. There was once a state trooper who told him when he applied for a driver's license that he had to be registered as white or black because there weren't any Indians in Alabama anymore.

For Taylor, who is visibly, indisputably an Indian, with his dark, copper skin and long,

braided hair, it was part of a barrage of insidious denials that has plagued his people for the past hundred years. In recent times, they have tried to fight back. They formed an elected tribal government that was officially recognized by the state of Alabama, and in 1980, they put on a powwow—a gathering of Indians from all over the country who danced and sang and dressed in regalia. They affirmed for each other the basic truth in their hearts, that despite all the suffering their people had known—Apaches, Comanches, Choctaws, and Creeks—the good news was that they had managed to survive. Their culture was not what it had been in the past. In the case of the Mowas, the language had dwindled to just a few words. But a feeling persisted that was hard to explain, and Wilford Taylor could see it in the children as they danced with the elders to the rhythm of the drums.

"I love being an Indian," said Heather Wilkinson, a fourteen-year-old Choctaw girl dressed in a long, flowing dress made by hand in Philadelphia, Mississippi.

Taylor smiled at the young woman's words. Identity, he said, is the key to the future—the sense of Native American pride that carries with it the strength for dealing with the world. But the Mowa Choctaws, like many other remnant groups in the East, have felt the sting of the federal government's denial—an explicit finding by the BIA that they simply don't qualify as a tribe. With his election as chief,

Taylor was determined to deal with that view, to present a petition for federal recognition that would persuade the bureaucrats once and for all. He hired some scholars to help him with the task, and they submitted a report in 1996. It was a mixture of evidence—old documents sprinkled with Choctaw names, pictures of graves where Choctaws are buried, and census records from the turn of the century, including a few pages from 1910, when racial identifications had been scratched through except for people who were black or white.

In the view of the scholars who examined the evidence, the Mowa Choctaws were "a persistent people" who refused to disappear despite the best efforts of the world around them. "The evidence is here," wrote Dr. Richard Stoffle, an anthropologist at the University of Arizona, "and the time for federal recognition has come."

Wilford Taylor was pleased when he saw the report, but he knew the Mowas faced a hard road ahead. For one thing, the line in front of them was long. Back in 1979, the BIA established a formal procedure for federal recognition, and by March 1992, more than 130 tribes had submitted their petitions. Some of the criteria were clear and precise. An Indian group could be recognized if it had a treaty with the United States government or had been named as a tribe by an act of Congress. After that, it was a little more fuzzy. If a particular group had been treated as a tribe by other federally recognized bands, and if it exer-

cised political authority among its members and demonstrated a history of social solidarity, then it might be entitled to recognition as well. In the end, it depended on the BIA—on judgments made in the District of Columbia by people who were serious about their jobs but who worked for an agency that few people trusted, based on its shabby track record. And the worst part was, the stakes were enormous.

For the Burt Lake Band of Ottawas and Chippewas, the stakes were approximately $8 million. In 1997, they lived near the village of Brutus, Michigan, just south of the narrow passageway of water separating Lake Michigan from Lake Huron. They were a struggling community of 650 whose problems had started with Andrew Jackson. Back in 1836, the Ottawas and Chippewas, including those at Burt Lake, had signed a treaty with the United States government ceding nearly 14 million acres in response to President Jackson's policy of removal. In return, they were promised both money and land—but for the Burt Lake Band, the land never came. Instead, the people used their treaty allotments to purchase a small reservation of their own, where they were able to live until the turn of the century. But then a timber speculator appeared, a white businessman named John McGinn, who seized their land in an illegal sale, a scam over taxes, and a few days later, he and the local sheriff, Fred Ming, burned the Indian village to the ground.

Even then, the Burt Lake Band refused to

CHRISTEN BEACH, MOWA CHOCTAW DANCER,
MT. VERNON, ALABAMA, 1997

SIERRA RIVERS, MOWA CHOCTAW DANCER,
MT. VERNON, ALABAMA, 1997

disappear, and for nearly a century, its leaders have tried to work out a settlement. In 1903, they rejected an offer from the state of Michigan for a swampy piece of land they found uninhabitable. In the 1930s, there were new negotiations with the federal government—new hopes raised and subsequently shattered, as the government declared that it simply couldn't help. And then came the nineties and a federal offer of $72 million for all the Ottawa and Chippewa bands who had signed the treaty of 1836 but were never compensated in return. The Burt Lake people were entitled to a share, perhaps as much as $8 million, if they were officially recognized as a tribe. But the BIA was unsympathetic.

"The fact that a recognized Burt Lake Band existed at some earlier point in time does not automatically mean that a tribe presently exists," declared Assistant Secretary Ada Deer, speaking to a writer from the *Detroit News*.

Whatever the reasons for those official doubts, the recognition issue was still unresolved in the spring of 1998. Gary Shawa, the executive director of the Burt Lake Band, says his people will have to keep on pushing. They've been at it now for the better part of a century, having started long before there was any money at stake, and according to Shawa, they have received the support of other Chippewa communities—some of which have also been through the wars.

The Chippewas are one of the largest tribes in the country, their villages scattered from Montana to Michigan. Most are east of the Mississippi River—seven bands in Michigan and six in Wisconsin, all of them living near their ancestral homes. In the twentieth century, they have struggled to restore their shrinking land base, much of which was taken away by fraud, and to preserve their fishing and hunting rights, as well as the cultural traditions of the tribe. Recognition is critical to all of those efforts and is important also in their strides toward economic development. Most bands have enjoyed federal status since the thirties, but there are others whose struggles have been more prolonged.

In 1980, the Grand Traverse people—Ottawas and Chippewas living on the eastern shore of Lake Michigan—became modern pioneers in the recognition process. After years of frustration, they were the first tribe in the country approved by the Branch of Acknowledgement and Research, a controversial division of the BIA. The branch was established in the 1970s to examine the claims of unrecognized tribes. A few more were approved—the Mohegans in Connecticut, the Jena Choctaws in northern Louisiana, and the Gay Head Wampanoags on Cape Cod. But the process was arbitrary and slow, and after fifteen years, there were only ten tribes that had managed to survive it—just enough to tantalize the ones left behind.

"The whole thing is political," says Greg Richardson, a Haliwa-Saponi from North Carolina who has studied the federal process carefully. Richardson serves as executive director of the North Carolina Commission of Indian Affairs, which has a recognition procedure of its own. It is similar in intent to the BIA's—a chance for any group of Indians to prove who they are. Do they have an identity and a tie to a place? A sense of community? A history they can trace? Have they governed their own affairs through the years? If the common-sense answer to those questions is yes, then Richardson believes they ought to be a tribe, officially recognized by the government. But with the BIA, it's never cut-and-dried, and one of the frustrated bands is his own, its recognition battles still unresolved.

The Haliwa-Saponis are a remnant collection of Indian nations that began coming together in the 1600s, settling in eastern North Carolina. There are tribal members who can trace their family trees to those times, and the tribe overall has been known as a clannish people with a deep sense of place. Kay Ensing is a Haliwa who was born in Richmond, Virginia, where her parents had gone in search of better jobs. They were in close touch with other Indians there, but every weekend, the family went home, driving five hours on the country roads to reconnect with their cousins in North Carolina.

As an adult, Kay chose to live in Virginia. She started an Indian cultural center and developed strong ties to the tribes in the state— the Rappahannocks, Chickahominies, and Mattaponis—but in the end, the pull of her home was too strong, a home, in fact, where she had never lived. In 1997, she packed her things and once again headed south, to the rolling fields of tobacco and corn and the scrubby pine forests of Halifax County. She found it pretty much as she remembered. Many of the three thousand Haliwas were poor, more than half of them earning less than twenty thousand dollars. But she found great strengths in the community as well. The people worked hard. There were carpenters and factory workers and merchants and at least a few who still tilled the land, raising tobacco as they had for generations. "It gets in your blood," said Alston Richardson, a Haliwa farmer with an easy smile and a sun-wrinkled face. But the thing that was clearly in the blood most of all was a surge of Indian identity and pride.

Some people say it began to take shape in the 1940s—and certainly by the 1950s, when the Haliwas' leader, W. R. Richardson, came home to live and was chosen almost immediately as chief. He had spent twenty years in Philadelphia, working in the shipyards during the war, but he missed his home and the wide-open spaces, and so he returned. In 1954, he toppled some pines with his crosscut saw and built his house on a rural highway—a warm and inviting two-story place with a garage and gables and half-moon arches on the doors inside. Then he set about building a school. There were facilities in the county for the blacks and the whites, but the Indians had long been neglected by the state, and

KAY ENSING AND DAUGHTER RACHAEL,
HALIWA-SAPONI, HALIFAX COUNTY, NORTH CAROLINA, 1997

Richardson decided that if that was the case, the Haliwas would simply build a school for themselves. It became a benchmark for the Indian people, an event that is celebrated even now.

"I remember when I was two or three years old," says Barry Richardson, now the executive director of the tribe, "my mother and father would leave me with an aunt so they could go and build that school."

There have been other moments in the past forty years, other landmark achievements for the tribe. In the 1970s, the Haliwas were the force behind a rural health center regarded as one of the finest in the state. They built new housing and started a powwow, the oldest such gathering in North Carolina, with dancers and artists from all over the country.

They also supported craftspeople of their own, including Pat Richardson, who had moved to the Haliwa community with her husband. She was born a Coharie in the town of Clinton, North Carolina, and grew up in a close-knit Indian community. Her father was a farmer, and her family lived in a wood-frame house with three brick chimneys and the kitchen set apart in a building by itself. It was a cozy place, and fifty years later, her memories are fond. But as a young girl, she wanted to escape—to pull away from the farm and the small-town South and see what was waiting out there in the world. After high school, she boarded a train, just herself and a cousin, giddy with the notion of new possibilities.

They used lipstick for the first time in their lives, dabbing on color for the ride to New York, but the city in the 1950s was a shock. People kept asking her about her background. Was she Hispanic, perhaps, or maybe Italian? And when she told them that in fact she was Native American, there were often more questions that she simply couldn't answer—questions about her Indian identity and culture.

"I remember thinking to myself, 'Oh my. It's time I learned about my people,'" she says.

As expressions of her new curiosity, she started doing beadwork, and then making baskets, and somehow it all came naturally to her, as if the old knowledge was already inside her. A few years later, she met a man at the Indian center in New York City, a Haliwa-Saponi named Arnold Richardson, who played the flute in the Indian way, with soft, haunting sounds that got in her blood, and they decided to marry and move back south.

She has lived since then in the Haliwa community, where she has met other artists like Senora Lynch, a potter whose work she regards as superb, and hundreds of others who are not as gifted but nevertheless seem eager to learn. She has taught bead making and made at least a part of her living from her crafts, and it pleases her especially that the young people have noticed. They have gone to powwows and learned the native arts, and most of them are working hard in their schools. In 1997 in Warren County, where many of them live, there were fifteen Indian graduates from the high school—thirteen of whom went on to college.

Earl Evans is part of the new generation, a role model for his peers. He took his degree in Indian studies from the University of North Carolina at Pembroke and then went home to work for the tribe. He has long been fascinated by tradition—by the elders and the artists and the old-fashioned healers like Allie Richardson, who could cure anything from a hangnail to AIDS simply by the power of his words and his touch. That was what people said, and Allie's driveway was often full of cars. He never charged anything for his work, and if people tried to pay, he gave all the money away to the church. That was the way it had to be—the way it had been for four hundred years. A healer understood that his power was a gift, not a source of profit, and Earl Evans came to believe in that power—not in the claims of its infallibility but simply in the notion that God, the Creator, often moves through the world in mystifying ways, and that the Indian people have their own understandings.

On a hot August day in 1997, Earl led a pair of visitors to the woods, down a rutted clay path that cut through the pines, to a sacred place well hidden from sight, where the sweat-lodge ceremonies are held. Several times a year, the traditionalists gather for a process of purification and prayer. It has become a part of Earl Evans's life, a reconnection with the native spirit of his people, but there is more.

With his friend Marty Richardson, another of the promising young men in the tribe, he has also set about learning the language—the ancient Tutelo tongue that has fallen from use. They hope to restore it in the next several years, perhaps by the start of the new millennium, and even if only a few people know it, there are others who will learn some words here and there.

It is one more reminder for Evans and the others that Indian identity has a life of its own. There are times when it sleeps, when the pressures of the outside world are too vast, but still it survives, and given that fact, it is hard for the Haliwa people to understand why their petition for federal recognition is a problem. They submitted it first in 1989, and a letter came back the following year citing "deficiencies" in the work they had done. The Haliwas are trying to address those issues, even though some of them wonder if it's worth it.

But in the end, they say, it comes down to resources. More money is available to the recognized tribes—more for housing and health and other pressing needs—and in the case of the Haliwas, the needs are too great to allow them the luxury of turning away from the struggle.

If they need a reminder, they can find it every day in Halifax County, just a few miles from the tribal headquarters. Nestled against a rolling field of tobacco, there's a back-roads community known as White Rock, a cluster of shacks with tarpaper siding, and doors ajar,

EARL EVANS, HALIWA-SAPONI, GRADUATION DAY,
PEMBROKE, NORTH CAROLINA 1997

and plastic covers on missing windowpanes. "It's nearly Third World," says one tribal leader, though he admits that some of the people seem content.

"It's what you're used to," says James Lynch, a White Rock resident who was working one morning with a group of friends, building new steps for a neighbor's mobile home.

Still, the physical needs are apparent, and are a challenge to the leadership of the tribe—a symbol of investments yet to be made. But for Barry Richardson, the executive director, there is another dimension to the recognition question—less tangible, certainly, but equally real. In the minds of many native leaders, there's a stigma that attaches to tribes like his own, a second-class status that only the BIA can erase. Richardson is amazed sometimes that it comes down to that—that the Indian people have granted such power to the white man's government, the power, in effect, to decide who is real.

But if that's the irony they confront every day, he says his people will play by the rules, believing that eventually, perhaps sometime in the next several years, justice will prevail and the Haliwa-Saponis will take their place among the ranks of the federally recognized tribes.

There are other groups that are less optimistic.

The Chicora-Siouan Indian Nation consists primarily of four hundred people and a tiny storefront headquarters in the town of Andrews, South Carolina. It sits not far from a historic site—the place where a group of Spanish explorers landed on the coast in 1521. It was one of the first North American expeditions, and the Indians they met that day were Chicoras.

Gene Martin has claimed that history as his own. He is the elected chief of the modern-day Chicoras—a descendant, he says, of those bewildered warriors who confronted the Spaniards at Winyah Bay. The problem is, there is no way to prove it without a thorough written history of the tribe. Even the oral tradition is incomplete, but in the case of Gene Martin, it comes down to this: he was born in the low country of South Carolina and lived in a community where the people were different—certainly not black, but darker skinned than their neighbors who were white.

Every now and then, somebody would notice, and not very often in a positive way. When he joined the army at age seventeen, his corporal declared that he was not white. "You're an Indian," he said with disdain, and for Martin, the slur had the sudden ring of truth. He decided to ask his father about it, and James Clarence Martin, a low-country farmer with dark brown skin and even darker hair, told him it was true. They talked for a while about the history of the family—how the Martins had lived in the area for two hundred years, perhaps even more, and how the whisper of the Indian ways still survived. In

BILLBOARD NEAR CHICORA-SIOUAN HEADQUARTERS,
U.S. HIGHWAY 521, SOUTH CAROLINA, 1997

GENE MARTIN, CHICORA-SIOUAN CHIEF, ANDREWS, SOUTH CAROLINA, 1997

the grandparents' time, the women made baskets, and when somebody was sick, they found their medicines deep in the swamp. The family farmhouse faced east, an Indian tradition, even though the road on which it stood cut through the woods and the fields to the west.

In the years after that, Gene Martin looked harder at the family photographs—at the high cheekbones, and the shape of the eyes, and the hair that was almost always dark—and he studied the Indian history of his place. The pattern was clear. Decimated by wars and disease, the coastal tribes had splintered into pieces, sometimes coming together again in small and unobtrusive communities hidden away in the swamps. Often, there were people from several different tribes who adopted English as their common language and became united in a single resolve: to keep as low a profile as possible. In the late twentieth century, there were other small groups in South Carolina—the Edistos and Santees down near the coast and the Peedees on the border with North Carolina.

But Martin was interested in the ancestral people—the Chicoras who lived in the sixteenth century and spoke in a language much like the modern Sioux. He set out to learn that language on his own, making several trips to South Dakota, where he met the descendants of the great Sioux chiefs. They called him a brother and made him welcome at their sacred ceremonies, some of which he began to practice in the Bible Belt country of South

Carolina. Seeing his resolve, they also gave him an Indian name—Igmu Tanka Sutanaji, which translates roughly as Great Cougar Stands Strong.

They said he would need all the strength he could muster, given the improbable mission of his life. He was determined, he said, to rebuild the tribe—complete with recognition from the BIA—and to reclaim an Indian identity for his people. There were times when his path was crooked and hard. He had an upholstery business to run, and there were nights when he drank and played music in the bars—just another honky-tonker from the country. But over time, he says, the pieces fit together.

He developed a following among people like himself, and the tribe incorporated in 1992, with four hundred members by the end of the year. He admits that federal recognition is a long shot—impossible, by the standards of the BIA. There are simply too many holes in the record. But maybe that will change. Maybe a genealogist will learn something new, or perhaps the government will alter its procedure. But even if it takes the Chicoras a century or more, Martin has decided that at least they can start. They can establish a government, and strengthen their community, and build a new history. That is work enough for the current generation, and a legacy for those not yet born.

In the meantime, the Chicoras' struggle is one more piece of the Indian story, the saga of a people who nearly disappeared. It's different from the history of many of their neighbors, whose journeys are documented and clear. Those people are lucky, in Gene Martin's view, for despite the problems they've encountered through the years, at least their identity is beyond dispute.

In Virginia, for example, the Pamunkeys and their neighbors, the Mattaponis, are eligible for federal recognition anytime. They live on the oldest reservations in the country, with treaties going back to 1646, and they are quite literally the people of Pocahontas—the first to encounter the Jamestown settlers. Their leader was Powhatan, a tall, imposing, sour-faced man turning gray at the temples who had built a confederacy of three dozen towns. His empire receded with the coming of the English, but the Pamunkeys survived in an area of wetlands forty miles north of the Jamestown colony.

Even according to the white man's records, they have governed themselves for nearly four hundred years, and at least until late in the 1990s, they never saw a need for federal recognition. "We don't need the BIA to tell us who we are," says Warren Cook, assistant chief of the tribe, and Cook has ample reason to know. His father, Tecumseh Deerfoot Cook, was probably the last of the old-time chiefs, a hunter and trapper who didn't give it up until the 1990s, when he was closing in on a hundred and the regimen was finally becoming too hard. Tecumseh's father was also a chief,

a solemn-looking man named George Major Cook who wore eagle feathers and spoke with an eloquence that made people cry. He collected artifacts from the history of the tribe—tangible reminders of a story going back more than ten thousand years, when the Pamunkey ancestors hunted woolly mammoths.

In 1979, Warren Cook took the treasures handed down in the family and helped build a museum. He believed in the collective memory of his people and didn't want it lost, and he also knew that the past lived on if you knew where to look. The Pamunkeys still hunted and grew their corn, as they had since the days of the Jamestown settlement, and there were tribal potters who knew how to use all the modern techniques but sometimes worked in the old way as well. All of those things were important and real, but the thing that held them together most of all was the unrelenting pressure of the outside world. The Pamunkeys had tried to make their adjustments. They had long ago abandoned the Algonquian language, and except for a few ceremonial occasions, they dressed pretty much like most of their neighbors. But they believed in the sovereignty of their own reservation, and that fact often brought conflict. In the 1990s, they found themselves battling with the state over fishing rights and the building of a dam that would inundate some of their ancestral sites.

Because of those battles, they reluctantly decided to consider the possibility of federal

TECUMSEH DEERFOOT COOK, RETIRED TRAPPER AND PAMUNKEY CHIEF,
PAMUNKEY RESERVATION, VIRGINIA, 1997

recognition, hoping against hope that the BIA would prove to be a better ally than the state. They were still not sure, but there was encouraging news from other parts of the South—for example, the story of the Tunica-Biloxis, who had been chasing recognition for as long as any other tribe in the country. Their effort began in the 1920s and didn't succeed until 1981, and between those times, they had sent innumerable delegations to Washington. The first was led by Eli Barbry, the chief of the tribe, who made the trip in a Model T Ford. Fifty years later, his grandson Earl kept the struggle alive with a greater sense of urgency than ever before. The Tunicas were involved in a complicated battle with a Louisiana graverobber, and without official recognition as a tribe, they had no standing in the fight.

The story began in the 1700s, when the Tunicas were a band of entrepreneurs. They traded with the French in the Mississippi Valley, supplying two things that the Europeans needed—horses and salt. For those commodities, they were paid in treasure—an astonishing array of trinkets and cookware from all over Europe, much of which ended up in the hands of the chief. His name was Cahura-Joligo, and when he was murdered by a band of Natchez Indians, many of the treasures were buried in his grave. They stayed there from 1731 until 1968, when a prison guard named Leonard Charrier, having studied old maps, began a search for the tomb. He found it in

the summer, and after what one writer called "a haphazard mutilation of the Tunica mausoleum," he offered to sell the artifacts to Harvard. A court case followed to decide whether Charrier was in fact the owner, and the Tunica Tribe, appalled by the blatant act of desecration, sought to overturn what it said was a theft. The problem was, the legal status of the tribe was unclear, for despite its long and traceable history and its close-knit community in eastern Louisiana, it had never been recognized by the government.

But all of that changed in 1981. With the official announcement of federal recognition, the case was decided in favor of the Tunicas. The treasure was returned and placed on display at the tribal museum, which is regarded as one of the best in the country. The museum is built in the form of a burial mound, with earthen sides and a grave at the center, where the human remains from the original tomb were reinterred. The treasure is now on permanent display in a setting as tasteful as the Tunicas can make it.

"Federal recognition is key," explains Bill Day, the tribe's director of historic preservation. "But things are not automatic. You have to work for them."

So far, it is clear the Tunicas have. In addition to securing the return of the ancestral treasure, they were able to build a casino, which gave them resources not available from any other source. Dirt roads have been paved on the small reservation, a health center has been established, and many of the shacks with no indoor plumbing have been replaced by new houses air-conditioned against the Louisiana heat.

All in all, the Tunica experience is what the other unrecognized tribes hope for, from the Mowa Choctaws to the Chippewas on the shores of Burt Lake. Every group is different. The Pamunkeys are not the Haliwa-Saponis, the Chicoras are not the Mattaponis. But there is a thread of aspiration that ties them together—a belief in the future that is rooted in the past, an identity they say has long been ignored.

They know the road ahead of them is hard, but they also live in an era of hope. From Louisiana to Maine, from Wisconsin to the coastal plains of Carolina, the world of the Native Americans is changing. They don't want to be the people left behind.

BARRY AND LAURIE DANA, MOMENTS BEFORE 100-MILE
CEREMONIAL CANOE JOURNEY, OLD TOWN, MAINE, 1997

CHAPTER FIVE

The Battle for Maine

THEY GATHER AT DAWN in the drizzling rain, circling the fire and praying in the language their ancestors used. Some of them are afraid, for this is the day of the sacrificial journey—a hundred miles by canoe against the flow of the river, or on foot through the forests of evergreen and birch. It is a mirror of the ancient patterns of the people, the annual migrations of the Penobscot Indians, who hunted in the shadow of Mount Katahdin and lived on the river. They traveled by canoe from the mountains to the sea, moving with the seasons, keeping their bargain with the salmon and the shad, stalking the caribou and the moose. They made their canoes out of birch and their baskets out of ash, and they built an alliance with the tribes all around—the Micmacs and Maliseets to the north and the Passamaquoddies down near the coast.

Butch Phillips knows that it must have been hard. For six months a year, the winter winds blew in from the Arctic, testing their strength, but the land provided what they needed to survive—the fish and the game and the clear blue water—until sometime early in the seventeenth century, when the world of the Indians began to come apart. Those were the days when the white men came, though it didn't seem so bad for a while. They traded their guns and trinkets for furs and looked to the Indian people for advice—the keys to survival in a hard, new land. But they kept on coming, and soon it was clear that they had a different idea about the earth. They believed they could own it, that the Creator's gift—which was there for the people to nurture and preserve, to share with the fish and the creatures of the forest—could become their possession, and by the late 1830s, it had. The Penobscots' territory was gone, reduced to a ribbon of islands in the river, and the Passamaquoddy people to the east were crowded onto two peninsulas of land, where they did their best to eke out a living.

That was how it was until the 1950s, when the Indian men came home from the wars and began to consider the idea of justice. They had heard about the struggle in the American South, where the civil-rights movement of Martin Luther King had stirred new hope not only for the blacks who followed in his path but for people all the way to the north woods of Maine. The Indians decided it was time to make a stand, and beginning in the sixties and seventies, they did it with a boldness that took their adversaries by surprise.

Butch Phillips was one of the leaders in the fight, a Penobscot traditionalist who served as lieutenant governor for the tribe. He was proud when the Penobscots joined a Passamaquoddy crusade—an ancestral claim to two-thirds of Maine. He was even prouder when they won, for that was certainly how it appeared when they negotiated a settlement of $81 million and began to buy back the land they had lost. Their accomplishment reverberated through the country, as Indian people from Alabama to Alaska applauded their example of tenacity and courage. In the season of hope that followed in the eighties, the Penobscot people began a new tradition. They started their sacred journey to the mountain, an annual event in the last days of August, when the leaves are beginning to turn in the forest and the hunters are waiting for their chance at the moose.

For Phillips and the others, it is a time to celebrate and remember, to give thanks for the native culture that has survived. They sing their songs and offer up prayers, and one by one, they pass by the fire to lay their sweet-grass tufts on the coals.

"We carry our ancestors' spirit to the mountain," says Phillips. "We remember their suffering, their endurance through the years, just to ensure there would still be native people on the river." And then they are off, some in canoes gliding swiftly through the shoals, while others set out on a hundred-mile run.

In 1997, the oldest of the runners was Sam Sapiel, one of the most respected elders in the tribe, who made the journey at the age of sixty-six. It took him four days. At the end, his face was covered in sweat and his gray hair matted as he completed the equivalent of four marathons. But he said it was worth it.

"I run for my people," he explained as the last of the miles slipped away. "I come to the mountain to talk to the Great Spirit. I have that knowledge. I understand how He works. I ask Him to take all the sickness away."

Sapiel didn't say any more after that, but the Indian people understood what he meant. These are troubled times in the state of Maine, and the Indian celebration now has an edge— a fear that even in a time of possibility, when the tribes are stronger than they've been in many years, the same old problems refuse to go away. In the 1990s, the Penobscot people continue to die of cancer, the result, they believe, of a chemical infestation of the river— dioxins from the paper companies upstream and the leftover filth from a century of misuse. The Passamaquoddies, meanwhile, face issues of their own, chief among them the right to fish unimpeded by the state. For both of the tribes, the issues of the nineties go straight to the heart of their Indian identity. For six thousand years, the Penobscots have tied their survival to the river—the cold, dark waters for which they were named. And in the Passamaquoddy language, their name means, literally, "the people who fish."

"It's who we are," says Passamaquoddy governor John Stevens, the man who launched the tribe's claim to the land. And the terrible irony his people now face is that the land-claim settlement, which seemed at first to be such a triumph, has proven in the end to be murky and flawed, pushed through in a hurry and containing loopholes that the state can exploit. Maybe it was destined to be that way. From the earliest days, the officials of Maine have never done very well by the Indians, and as the battle rages on toward a new millennium, the final outcome is not yet clear. But whatever the problems the tribes now face, their resolve is stronger than it's been in the past—more powerful, certainly, than forty years ago, when they first decided it was time to take a stand.

John Stevens was the spark. He came home from the war with a new understanding. In the snows of Korea, he saw the children without any food, and it was a painful reminder of the conditions at home. He had seen people die on his small reservation, pregnant women who were so undernourished that they were unable to make it through the rigors of child-birth. There were children who starved to death in the winter, and even the lucky ones who survived were living in a world without any hope. Like their Penobscot brothers to the west, the Passamaquoddies were wards of the state, many with incomes of less than three hundred dollars a year. Their schools were degrading, staffed by nuns who were quick to punish not only for ordinary misbehavior but for the offense of speaking in the Indian tongue. And the white people kept encroaching on the land. Stevens remembers when his father was arrested—charged with cutting wood on a white man's land, even though the property was owned by the tribe. The day finally came in the 1950s when the Passamaquoddies could no longer stand it.

"I started to attack," Stevens says today, "but at first, I didn't know what to attack."

He found a mentor, however, to help him—an old man who had stayed for thirty years in Detroit but had finally come home to live as an Indian. His name was George Francis, and his counsel was always steady and wise. He and Stevens set about the task of creating jobs and improving the schools, and later they organized demonstrations, particularly when the owner of a lakeside resort wanted to get rid of his Indian neighbors. He wanted the shoreline clear for development, even though the land was the Passamaquoddies'.

JOHN STEVENS, PASSAMAQUODDY GOVERNOR,
PRINCETON, MAINE, 1997

For Stevens, it was the breaking point in his patience, and in the late 1950s, he suddenly discovered a way to fight back. He had always heard that the tribe had a treaty, an agreement signed in the 1790s confirming its right to the reservation land. But nobody seemed to know where it was. Stevens had searched through the state archives and queried the officials he thought ought to know, and for the first several years, he had come up with nothing. But then he began to search through a trunk handed down to him by the widow of a chief. The old woman, Louise Sockabasin, told him there were papers he needed to examine. Stevens had put it off for a while, but then he decided to open up the trunk and see for himself. He found a packet inside, tied together with a ribbon and strands of sweet grass taken from the marsh, and carefully he began to sort through the stack. The paper was old, and some of it began to crumble at his touch. But then he saw what the ribbon had contained. "Holy God," he whispered to himself, for it was the treaty signed in 1794—an agreement between his people and the state of Massachusetts, of which Maine was a part until 1820, providing clear title to twenty-four thousand acres of land. There was also a letter to the Passamaquoddies sent by their friend and father, George Washington, giving thanks for their support in the Revolutionary War. The tribe had been a buffer, helping to turn the British out of Canada, and General Washington promised that in return for that service, their hunting grounds would never be disturbed.

Stevens was astonished. How could such agreements have gone unacknowledged? Why had they never been a part of the record, or at the very least a starting point for discussion between the tribe and the state? Whatever the answers, the bad faith was clear. Over the years, more than six thousand acres had been lost to the whites, and when the encroachments continued in the 1960s, Stevens decided it was time for a lawsuit. But he soon had the feeling he was lost in a swamp, a legal morass that was so complicated it was almost more than his tribe could comprehend.

He hired a young attorney named Tom Tureen, a recent graduate of George Washington University who had developed an interest in Indian law. Several years earlier, he had worked at a boarding school in South Dakota, an institution run by the BIA. It was a brutal place, in Tureen's estimation. The children who came were cut off from their families and were punished if they spoke in their native tongue. One of the teachers carried a club on his belt and didn't hesitate to use it if he heard a conversation in Crow or Lakota.

"It was a pivotal experience," remembers Tureen. "I was a middle-class kid from suburban St. Louis. I decided that summer that I wanted to do something useful."

So he accepted the Passamaquoddies' land case, and if he was new to that particular corner of the law, he made up for it with passion and commitment and a mind that proved to be aggressive and bold. He spent two years trying to figure out the case. What were the laws that applied to the tribe? Was its status any different from that of the western Indians who had signed their treaties with the United States government and were recognized by the BIA? All over the East, he was starting to discover, there were Indian communities that lacked legal recognition, and their problems, incredibly, were even worse than those in the West. But did it really have to be that way?

The more he studied, the more certain he was that the answer was no. The Indian communities on the first frontier, where the contact with Europeans had begun, were bruised and battered after three hundred years, but remarkably enough, they had managed to survive. It was a testament to the strength of the Indian spirit, and with the native reawakening in the seventies, the tribes in the East seemed to be getting stronger. Tureen saw hope in the reemergence, and as he continued his study of Indian law, John Stevens set out in search of allies. He traveled from Maine to Alabama and beyond, meeting with the remnant people who had made it. He put together a nonprofit group, the Coalition of Eastern Native Americans, and the leaders of the tribes began to talk about their problems.

Tureen, meanwhile, was busy in Maine. He had developed a whole new theory of the case, with a conclusion so astounding that when he presented it to the assembled members of the tribe, they stared back at him in silent disbelief, as if their young and energetic attorney had taken leave of his mind. But Tureen seemed certain of what he was saying. He explained that along with their Penobscot neighbors, the Passamaquoddies had a claim to 12 million acres—nearly two-thirds of Maine—and he said he thought it was a case they could win.

His theory was based on an ancient law, the Indian Non-Intercourse Act of 1790, which declared that no one could buy or take control of Indian land without the approval of Congress. The legal assumption in the past had been that the law applied only to the western tribes. But Tureen couldn't find any basis for that—nothing in the statute or the legislative history to compel a federal court to reach that conclusion. The treaty that Stevens had found in the trunk had never been ratified by Congress, which was actually good. Instead of suing for the six thousand acres they had lost since the treaty went into effect, the Passamaquoddies could claim a thousand times that amount—every acre they had hunted when the whites first started to take away the land.

But there were some problems. Maine was one of a handful of states that had never waived the right to sovereign immunity, which meant, essentially, that it could not be sued except by a government. And since the tribal governments in Maine were not recognized by the BIA, there was a chance that the case might never be heard.

Tureen, however, saw a way around the problem. The federal government, he decided, should sue the state on behalf of the tribes. It was a federal law, after all, that had been ignored. The question was whether the government would do it, and Tureen found an early ally in the cause. He was Louis Bruce, a Mohawk Indian from the state of New York who had recently been appointed by President Nixon as the new director of the BIA. Nobody expected anything very radical. Bruce was simply a Republican Indian—an endangered species in much of the country—who had been active all his life in Indian affairs. He was exactly what the Nixon administration was seeking—a man with solid, unimpeachable credentials who had never made a habit of rocking the boat.

Bruce, however, proved to be a surprise. An aggressive reformer almost from the start, he waged his guerrilla war from the inside on the stubborn bureaucrats of the BIA. He surrounded himself with like-minded people, many of them young and full of native pride. There was Sandy McNabb, a Micmac from Maine, and Leon Cook, a Chippewa from Minnesota, and together they were battling a paternalistic history that had been unbroken since the founding of the country.

It was in that spirit that Bruce took the side of the Passamaquoddies, recommending to officials up the line that the United States

government go to court against Maine. Slowly but surely in the months after that, the land-claim issue began to look a little different. In the capital city of Augusta, the people who had scoffed at the theories of Tureen were now getting worried. Was it really possible that the case would go to court—this preposterous allegation that two-thirds of the largest state in New England still belonged to the Indians? It was not an easy thing to imagine, but the mere possibility was cause for alarm, particularly to the timber companies in the north. They owned much of the land in question, and nobody believed they would simply give it up.

The Nixon administration was worried also, and for a while, the officials just above Louis Bruce did nothing at all. They offered no response to his memo recommending a federal lawsuit, hoping, apparently, that the statute of limitations would expire. As the stonewalling continued, Tureen decided to force their hand. He filed a petition in federal court—a lawsuit to force the federal government to sue. He knew it was a highly unusual procedure, and he was grateful for the fact that the federal judge assigned to the case was Edward Gignoux, a conservative Republican appointed to the bench by Dwight Eisenhower. Most people agreed that Gignoux was the best, a believer in the law who refused to shirk its inconvenient implications. In the case of the lawsuit filed by Tureen, he sifted his way through the multiple layers of technicalities, and on January 20, 1975, he ruled in favor of the Passamaquoddies, declaring them a federally recognized tribe and upholding their right to take their claim to court. It was now that the real confrontation could begin.

John Stevens remembers the sound of the gun. It cut through the night as he was headed toward home in his pickup truck, a shiny red Ford he had owned for a year. The threatening calls were coming every day, and now as the bullet ripped through the roof, Stevens knew they were serious. The mood was turning ugly in the state of Maine. Governor James Longley was fanning the flames. An antitax populist whose ascension to office came in 1975, Longley spoke often of the threat the Indians posed to people's homes. Again and again, the tribes had been explicit on that point: they had no intention of taking any homes. The land they wanted was undeveloped, a place where their people could hunt and fish, preserving a critical tie to their past. But the governor's rhetoric played well across the state, and the anti-Indian fervor that began to take hold was not very different from the mood in the South a decade earlier, as the civil-rights movement had hit its stride.

At the very least, it was a difficult environment for settling the case, which had been Tureen's intention all along. He knew that if a court were compelled to decide it, both sides ran the risk of disaster. Already in Maine, there was a threat to the integrity of municipal bonds because of the shadow the land claim had cast. It was hard to imagine the implications if the Indians really won back 12 million acres, or anything close. But what if they lost? What if the antiquity of the claim worked against them, or the fundamental unorthodoxy of the case? Would things be worse than when they had started?

Tureen understood that when the stakes were huge and unpredictable, rational people had incentive to settle. He hoped the people of Maine would agree, and he had an ally in that point of view. Jimmy Carter, the former governor of Georgia, won the presidency in 1976 and emerged as a strong proponent of a settlement. But he also made it clear from the start that the Passamaquoddies and their Penobscot allies, like Indian people all over the country, were entitled to justice. On February 17, 1978, he came to Maine to present that message, appearing at a community meeting in Bangor where whites outnumbered the Indians ten to one.

"I thought he'd never make it out of the state," remembers John Stevens. He was impressed with the president's courage that night, his ability to absorb the hostility of the crowd and still hold fast to the things he believed. Stevens, like the other Indians, saw Carter as a friend, and that perception had a life of its own, becoming a critical ingredient in the story. As the negotiations dragged on through the rest of the decade, the Indians had the feeling that time was running out.

PENOBSCOT ROOT CLUB, INDIAN ISLAND, OLD TOWN, MAINE, 1997

Butch Phillips remembers how it was. He was one of the negotiators for his tribe, part of a committee of a dozen people appointed by the Passamaquoddies and Penobscots to try to find a final solution to the issue. The Carter administration was a part of that effort, trying to broker a deal, and as the 1980 election approached, a terrifying notion began to take shape in the minds of many of the Indian people. They were afraid that Jimmy Carter would lose—and that if he did, the pressure from the federal government would dissolve, leaving the Indians negotiating with only the state. It was a prospect that no one relished, for Maine at the close of the 1970s was like Mississippi nearly twenty years before—aflame with racial demagoguery and hate. Indian children were beaten in the schools by classmates caught in the mood of the times, and the governor had drawn his line in the sand. Perhaps, he said, they could work out a deal, but he felt the Indians were seeking much more than they deserved—and whatever the decision about money and land, the Passamaquoddies and Penobscots would be subject to the legal jurisdiction of the state. They were citizens, after all, like everybody else.

What it meant in the autumn of 1980 was that a chasm of misunderstanding remained on the most critical and complicated issue they faced. Indian people in many parts of the country had struggled to preserve their legal status, a mixture of citizenship and sovereignty. In certain respects, they were, in fact, like everybody else. They could vote in elections, and they paid federal income taxes, and they were subject to the criminal laws of the country. But their tribal governments had a standing of their own, an authority to regulate their reservations, to oversee hunting and fishing by their members, to operate their police departments and courts, and to wield other powers that were not very different from those of a state.

The Indians of Maine were determined to preserve those powers for themselves, and that was their final sticking point with the state. There had been some progress on the land claim itself, an agreement that the federal government would provide more than $80 million for the Indians to buy back the land they had lost—or three hundred thousand acres, at least, which was an impressive amount for two small tribes. For those who had been in the trenches since the sixties, it was difficult to pass on that kind of offer, particularly when they knew it might be their last. With conservative Republicans—people who had shown no sympathy in the past—headed for the White House, the Indians' most likely alternative seemed to be the courts, a strategy that was full of uncertainty and risk. So they signed.

Butch Phillips remembers the outcry at home—how members of his family were among the dissenters who believed they had given away too much. There was a phrase tucked away in their agreement with the state that left many of the Indian people uneasy. It was Section 6204, an affirmation that the laws of Maine would apply. But what did that mean? Was it merely a broad and general affirmation, or was it a club for the state to use in battles over the rights of the tribes in the future?

For the first few months, everything went well. The Penobscots set about the task of buying land, and within two years, they had amassed a base of nearly 190,000 acres. The Passamaquoddies proceeded more slowly. They bought a blueberry farm in the north, and using their settlement money as collateral, they also bought a cement company. It turned out to be a remarkable investment. The purchase price was $25 million, and they sold the company five years later for $60 million. But despite such tangible measures of progress—the satisfying fruits of their battle for the land—the problems of the Indians did not go away.

The Penobscot River was still unsafe, the waters so polluted from industrial waste that the cancer rate among the Penobscots was nearly twice that of the state as a whole—and higher than the rate for other tribes in the country. The Indians began crusading for reforms. Using standards approved by the EPA, they tested the waters and took samples from the fish, and they were able, they said, to pinpoint the problem. The Lincoln Pulp and Paper Mill, located just upstream from Indian Island, the place where most of the Penobscots lived, was producing dioxins as a part of its process, and the deadly carcinogenic wastes were found in the water and the tissues of the fish. There were great, dark stains on the surface of the river, and according to the state's environmental scientists, the fish were no longer safe to eat. But a succession of governors and other state officials resisted the Penobscots' efforts at reform. The Indians' case was really very simple. A treaty they had signed in 1818 gave them the right to fish in the river as long as the waters continued to flow, and that treaty was affirmed in the land-claim act of 1980. But their rights, of course, were essentially irrelevant if the fish in the Penobscot River were poisoned.

If the logic was clear and straight to the point, it proved for years to be no match for the political realities that existed in Maine. The paper companies had money and power, and the state continued to approve their exemptions, a series of permits that allowed the steady discharge of waste as long as the level of dioxins was reduced. With the land claim settled, the Indians now were merely an irritant, no longer a force to be taken seriously. That, at least, was how it seemed to John Banks, the Penobscots' director of natural resources.

According to Banks, throughout the struggles of the past thirty years, the state had been jealous of its own jurisdiction, determined to bring the Indian people into line. And in recent years, the most explosive test of that resolve began on the afternoon of November 2, 1995.

At three o'clock, Fred Moore got a call. Moore is a leader among the Passamaquoddies, the nation representative who, among other things, speaks for the tribe in the state legislature. Moore was deeply disturbed by the call. An Indian fisherman had been threatened with arrest—a Passamaquoddy named Donnell Dana, who had come of age on the coast of Maine digging clams with his hands. Sometimes as a boy, he had left home in the morning for a day on the water and not come back until well after dark, finding all the food he needed from the sea. As a man, he had made his living from the fish, just as his ancestors had for generations. He had never carried a license from the state; like others in the Passamaquoddy Nation, he never saw any need for laminated proof of his right to the fish the Creator had provided. He understood, of course, that they were not his alone. His brothers in the towns of East Port and Calais, the whites who also dug for the clams or cast their fishing nets on the water, had as much right to the bounty as he did. It was theirs together to protect and preserve, and he understood clearly that the conservation measures of the Indian people were nearly identical to those of the state. They were, after all, the result of a careful meeting of the minds, of many months of compromise and discussion.

But the arrests kept coming in 1995, and the issue had little to do with conservation. It was simply a matter of the state's jurisdiction, a matter of principle for the governor and others who wanted the Indians to abide by the laws—to carry a license like anybody else and accede to the regulations of the state.

The Passamaquoddies were enraged. They had never compromised on their right to fish, a way of life much older than Maine, and in meeting after meeting for the next several years, Fred Moore made it clear that his people never would.

On September 2, 1997, he stared across the table at Evan Richert, a representative of Governor Angus King, and delivered a short extemporaneous speech. Moore was dressed in a red flannel shirt, in the style of the commercial fisherman he is, his hair unkempt, a flash of anger and determination in his eyes.

"In the strongest terms," he declared, "I have to state that under no circumstances will the Passamaquoddy submit to the jurisdiction of Maine on saltwater fishing. We will fight to the man to preserve the rights of our people to harvest from the sea. This is an area where we will not give ground. We are not going to subject ourselves to the state of Maine—ever. We would like to avoid conflict if we can. But we will not back down."

"Does that mean," said Richert, "that there is no need to talk?"

"Oh, no," said Moore, "we are happy to talk. We can be sworn enemies and I would still talk. But this is our way of life. This is who we are. We have our backs to the edge already."

As the standoff continued into the fall, John Stevens looked back on the battles with regret. The aging governor of the Passamaquoddies knew there were phrases in the land-claim settlement that gave the state ammunition for the fight. He knew the Indians had rushed through the weeks when they were afraid that Jimmy Carter might lose, when they were struggling to work out some kind of settlement. He remembered his own mental state at the time. His life had been threatened as a matter of routine, and one night, his wife got a call that he was dead. His marriage eventually fell to pieces from the strain, and for Stevens, at least, after paying such a price, it was simply unthinkable to let the land-claim agreement slip away. "Maybe," he says, "the old war-horse was tired."

But John Banks believed that if the final settlement was flawed, it also contained the seeds of a triumph. In addition to the restoration of their land, there were explicit confirmations of the treaties—and of the fundamental notion that Indians have a right to govern their affairs. "Land and natural resources acquired by the tribes . . . shall be managed and administered according to terms set by the tribes." It was all right there in black and white, and by the end of 1997, Banks thought he saw a new hint of progress. From the clergy in Maine to the state legislature to the United States Department of the Interior, the pressure was mounting on the governor's office to work out some kind of truce with the tribes.

"We're going to win this fight," Banks said in the fall. "We are going to win it because we are right."

Stan Neptune didn't know about that. He had never been a fan of the land-claim settlement. He thought the Indians had given away too much. As a traditional woodcarver among the Penobscots, he tried to keep his distance from the battles with the state—and the capricious interference of the people in control. Instead, he spent his days with the wood, remembering the lessons that had been handed down. Neptune was part of a cultural renaissance that ran parallel to the battle for the land. In the 1970s, he began an apprenticeship with an elder—an eccentric old man who was known as Senabeh. Some people thought that Senabeh was odd, a little too fond of the bottle, perhaps, but Neptune was fascinated by his wisdom. The old man was skeptical of Indian politics and predicted a time of internal division that would come in response to pressures from the state. He had no use for that kind of thing. His mission was to keep the old ways alive, and he turned to his eager pupils like Stan, teaching them bits and pieces of the language—Penobscot, Maliseet, and Passamaquoddy—and helping them to see the beauty in the wood. Their carvings were the most traditional kind—root clubs made from the wood of the birch, once the most primitive instruments of war but now considered to be great works of art.

Stan Neptune emerged as a master, carving

out the faces of the Indian people in the delicate twists and turns of the birch. Soon, he was also teaching his son, Joe Dana, who had established a reputation as a painter, and together they began to assume their place in the front ranks of traditional Indian artists.

But there are others. Theresa Hoffman is a basket maker who helped put together a state-wide alliance. She moved to the village of Indian Island, the Penobscots' home in the middle of the river, after getting her master's degree in geology. She remembers the visits when she was a child, how her grandmother Mildred Akins was an Indian dancer who wanted the young people to learn all the steps, and how her great-grandmother Philomene Nelson made the traditional Penobscot baskets. In 1988, Hoffman began to take up the craft, studying under one of the tribal elders and working with molds handed down in the family. There was a connection she felt building baskets out of ash, some ornate, others intended for everyday use, and beginning in 1992, she worked with artists from four tribes—the Micmacs, Maliseets, and Passamaquoddies, as well as her own—to try to make certain that the craft didn't die. She admired the work of Mary Gabriel, a Passamaquoddy who was still going strong at the age of ninety, and Fred Tomah, a Maliseet artist whose worked seemed perfect until you looked at it hard and found every time an intentional mistake.

"Only the Creator," he said, "makes perfect baskets."

The first president of the basket makers' alliance was Donald Sanipass, an aging Micmac who lived in the woods of northern Maine and worked with Mary, his wife of forty years, to make potato baskets for the farmers. They had amassed their share of memories through the years, not all of them pleasant. They were born in Canada and sent away to a Catholic school in Nova Scotia, where they were beaten by the nuns for speaking Micmac and where Mary was forced on at least one occasion to eat her evening meal from the floor. When she refused, she was beaten with a stick and then force-fed by one of the nuns, who had accused her of spilling the food from her plate.

Many years later, after they had moved across the border to the United States, where they scratched out a living selling baskets for a dollar and working the potato fields in the fall, their teenage son, David Sanipass, also battled his way through school. At the public high school in the town of Presque Isle, he relied on the boxing lessons from his father to defend himself against the taunts of his classmates. Those were the days of the land-claim struggle, when racial hatred was spreading through the state—and though the Micmacs were not a party to the claim, the distinction was lost on many of their neighbors.

But the Sanipass family survived the ordeal—unembittered, from all indications, and committed to living in the Indian way. Today, they make regular trips to the forest—to the

MARY GABRIEL, PASSAMAQUODDY BASKETMAKER AND WINNER OF
NEA NATIONAL HERITAGE AWARD, PRINCETON, MAINE, 1997

DONALD SANIPASS, MICMAC BASKETMAKER POUNDING BROWN ASH,
PRESQUE ISLE, MAINE, 1997

low, swampy areas down near the creek—to
search out the ash they can turn into baskets.
The prices are better than they were in the
past, and David Sanipass is now in demand
as a teller of traditional Micmac stories. They
worry sometimes that the old ways are dying,
but they often feel better when they simply
look around. There are people from every tribe
in the state who are working to keep the In-

dian culture alive, and Theresa Hoffman,
among many others, believes it's stronger today than it's been in many years.

If that is true, some people say the land-
claim settlement—the battle to achieve it and
the frustrating controversies that have followed—may have played a major role in the
change. Wayne Newell, a Passamaquoddy
educator and linguist and a longtime political

DAVID SANIPASS, MICMAC CRAFTSMAN AND STORYTELLER,
PRESQUE ISLE, MAINE, 1997

leader in the tribe, is one who now subscribes to that theory. He says the identity of the Indian people has been reinforced by the bittersweet process of standing for their rights. The settlement agreement may have been flawed, but Newell believes they are braced for the fight—more sure of themselves than they have been in the past, ready for the struggles in the century just ahead.

Nobody doubts that the struggles will come. There are too many issues that are still unresolved. But even in Maine, Newell says with a shrug, where the battle with the state has raged for thirty years, the spirit of the Indian people has survived.

BULLET-RIDDLED SIGN, TUSCARORA RESERVATION, NEW YORK, 1997

CHAPTER SIX
Iroquois Troubles

TOM PORTER DREAMED of leading the Mohawk people back home, back to the valley where the pale blue mountains rise in the distance. The prophets had always said it would happen, and he heard all the stories—the collective memories of the Iroquois past—while growing up in the long house. As the elders understood it, there had once been a time of turmoil and fighting—fratricide among the nearby tribes more horrible than anything they had known. But then, at last, the Peacemaker appeared, a man of vision and great spiritual power who traveled the country with his young assistant, Hiawatha, and together they worked out the Great Law of Peace. Partly, it was a diplomatic arrangement, a confederacy of five independent nations with interests that were inextricably intertwined. But for all of those nations—the Oneidas, Senecas, Cayugas, Onondagas, and Mohawks—the Peacemaker's vision and the splendid metaphors he used to explain it—the laws giving

shelter like the branches of the pine—were also a way of understanding the world. The Indian people were a part of creation, not the culmination or the focus, and they gave thanks every day for the corn and the trees, all those gifts from the Creator's hand that enabled the Iroquois people to survive.

The message took root in the Indian heart, and by the time the white man arrived on the land, the peace had lasted for a century or more—the Iroquois scholars say five hundred years. Whatever the dates—and the oral tradition, of course, is imprecise—the confederacy was ancient when the Europeans came, and the newcomers were astonished at how well it worked. The journals of the French, the British, and the Dutch—and later the Americans, who came with the torch—are filled with descriptions of the great fields of corn and the silos brimming with the fruits of the harvest and the people who lived in sturdy wood houses.

Benjamin Franklin was particularly impressed. Like other colonial leaders, he was beginning to grapple with the idea of freedom, and on his frequent visits to the Iroquois nations, the abstractions from the Magna Carta and John Locke began to take on a shape. Soon, however, his country was at war with the Indian people, who were attempting to chart an independent course in the bewildering world of European diplomacy. Forced to pick a side, many of them chose to fight for the British at the fateful moment of the American Revolution, and General John Sullivan, one of George Washington's least-favorite lieutenants, set out in 1779 on a scorched-earth assault, burning whole villages and silos of corn. The suffering of the Iroquois people wasn't new. Already, they had died by the thousands from disease, and around the time of the American Revolution, the Mohawks—the "Keepers of the Eastern Door" of the confederacy, who felt the pressures of invasion most acutely—left their homes in the Mohawk Valley and moved to the hunting grounds to the north.

"They needed a rest," explains Tom Porter, and so they came to the land of Akwesasne, which they named for the beating wings of the partridge—a symbol of the new abundance they had found. But for centuries, they talked about their return, and Porter was one of those who listened. Born in 1944, he was raised in a time of receding oppression, when the Indians felt freer to speak their minds.

"I was lucky," he says. "In the Mohawk world, there was a vein of tradition just under the ground. But there were other veins, too. I was touched by the right uncles, the right grandmother. I came along at just the right time."

Taught by the elders to revere the heritage of the Mohawk people—the language, the ceremonies, and the history—Porter was caught in the 1970s in the militancy that swept through the Iroquois world. He came to admire the traditional chiefs—an old Mohawk named Ira Benedict and a trio of charismatic Onondagas, Irving Powless, Oren Lyons, and Leon Shenandoah. These were men who lived on the edge, the frontier of revival for Native American people nationwide. Early in the decade, there was a road project that threatened the Onondagas' territory, a widening of Interstate 81 as it cut through the hills of central New York. Chief Shenandoah drew a line in the sand precisely at the border of the Onondaga Reserve. "The United States stops here," he declared.

A standoff followed for the next two months, as the Onondagas blocked the construction site with their bodies. There were rumors that the police were preparing to attack, but instead they were called to the Attica prison, which was then in the middle of an inmate rebellion. With the troopers already in the mood for a fight, the Attica confrontation turned bloody. One Onondaga, after reading the newspaper accounts of the battle,

OREN LYONS, TURTLE CLAN CHIEF, ONONDAGA NATION, NEW YORK, 1997

declared in a somber moment of reflection, "Those bullets initially were intended for us."

Despite the dangers that went with the times, and despite the activism that he regarded as essential, Shenandoah was a man who preferred not to fight. The message he preached to Indian people was that theirs, fundamentally, was a mission of peace.

Donna Chavis, a Lumbee activist from North Carolina, remembers a time in the 1980s when her people were engaged in a battle with the state. There were bitter allegations of police brutality, and a Lumbee lawyer named Julian Pierce was running for the office of superior-court judge. It was a campaign of enormous symbolic importance, and Pierce seemed almost certain to win. But one night not long before the election, he was murdered in the living room of his home. About the same time, two armed militants invaded the local newspaper office, and a respected leader in the Lumbee community was killed in a car wreck. Shenandoah came down to "help with the healing," as Chavis later put it. He had little to say about politics or strategy. Instead, he built a sacred fire in the park, and the people all gathered in a circle around it, offering their prayers for a better day ahead. It was a reminder to Chavis at a critical time that the native renaissance in the twentieth century had to be a spiritual movement at its heart.

That was the message of the Iroquois chiefs. The work they were doing was merely their duty—a moral imperative with roots tracing back to the Peacemaker's vision, handed down to the people in 1000 A.D.

But there are other, more modern antecedents as well. In 1909, the members of an aging Iroquois family—Oneidas, as it happened, who lived just east of the city of Syracuse—were roughly and abruptly removed from their home. Their land had been appropriated by whites, who simply assumed, in the climate of the day, that there would be no resistance. According to one eyewitness account, the policemen gathered up Mary Shenandoah and dragged her out of her house to the street. She got up slowly and returned to the house. Several more times, they carried her away, finally throwing her to the street with such force that she gave up the fight. It was only the latest encroachment, and an Oneida chief, William Rockwell, decided at last that he had had enough. He took the Oneidas' case to federal court, and thirteen years later, the Supreme Court ruled in favor of the Indians, affirming their ancient title to the land.

Others stood up in the years after that. A Cayuga chief by the name of Deskaheh carried the case to Geneva, where he asked for an audience with the League of Nations in defense of the Indians' eighteenth-century treaties. It was a heartbreaking mission in many respects. The Europeans had other things on their minds, and Deskaheh returned to the

United States convinced that the rest of the world was indifferent. It was true that he had met some sympathetic people who were touched by the desperation of his message. But the officials who had come together in Geneva refused to let him speak.

Eventually, he decided to go back to his home, only to discover that he couldn't. He lived on the Canadian side of the border—that international abstraction that cuts a slash through the heart of Iroquois country—and despite the treaty of 1794, which assured the Indians unimpeded access, the Canadian government refused to let him in. He died soon after at the home of Clinton Rickard, his friend and ally, who was already enraged at the treaty violations. Rickard was a Tuscarora chief, a leader in the newest of the Iroquois nations, which had joined the confederacy in the 1700s after a disastrous war in North Carolina. Enraged by the treachery and encroachments of the whites, the Tuscaroras had attacked in 1711, often torturing and mutilating their victims. The whites fought back, supported by an army of Indian allies, and after a bloody two-year stretch, the Tuscaroras were defeated.

Clinton Rickard's granddaughter, Jolene, remembers the stories handed down in the family—how the ancestral people were trying to escape, and one small band was swimming in a river, their presence hidden by a clump of driftwood as they tried to slip past a military outpost. There was a child in the group who began to cry, and the Indians had to drown it

to avoid being found.

There were stories of more modern vintage also, told most often by Eli Rickard, Jolene's father, who had great respect for the oral tradition. His voice would rise at the family dinner table as he remembered Clinton Rickard's crusade for open borders. It was a matter of principle as well as practicality, for the treaties of the 1700s were clear, and if they were cast aside in the twentieth century, then the Indian people didn't have any rights. Clinton Rickard was tenacious in pushing that case, leading frequent demonstrations at the border, and on one occasion, he was jailed in Quebec, locked in a dungeon without any heat. According to Eli, the Canadian authorities refused to give him food, then appeared one day with a steaming plate.

"Chief, it's poison," said the prisoner across the aisle. But Rickard was starving and the food smelled good, and despite his misgivings, he began to eat. Soon, he noticed the world turning black, the single light bulb on the ceiling of his cell shrinking to a tiny pinprick of light. The prisoner across the hall kept screaming, telling him to vomit, to cast out the poison or soon he would die. He lay there retching, but a short time later, the authorities found him still clinging to life—and, after his recovery, still ready for the fight. Eventually, he won. In 1928, his organization, the Indian Defense League of America (IDLA), secured open borders for the Indian people and began a tradition of militancy and protest that extends to the Iroquois leaders of today—to Tom Porter, Oren Lyons, and all the rest who were inspired by the courage of Rickard and his peers.

For a while, Porter thought that the current era would be the culmination, a legacy of identity that was rooted in the past, in which every generation built upon the last. Together, they had managed to preserve the confederacy—the Haudenosaunee, as the Iroquois called it—and Porter was convinced the best days were ahead. There were so many people of his own generation who were caught in the spirit of Indian renewal—Senecas, Mohawks, Tuscaroras, Onondagas, people from practically every tribe he could name. But something went wrong in the 1980s, a tragedy of such stark and monumental proportions that Porter has days when he still can't believe it.

By the end of the decade, some of the people with whom he was raised—allies in the struggle for Iroquois rights—had transformed the principles of Indian militancy into a shield for their own criminality and greed. They were engaged in smuggling, a massive operation involving everything from cigarettes and drugs to automatic weapons—even human beings who were trying to make their way across the border. Akwesasne—a Mohawk reservation that straddled the divide—seemed to offer the greatest opportunity. It was a small piece of land that skirted the fringes of New York State and the Canadian provinces of Ontario and Quebec—"a jurisdictional nightmare," says Ed Smoke, the chief executive of the Mohawk Band. Smoke and his parents, Edward and Selena, understand exactly how confusing it can be. The elder Smokes go to bed every night in Canada and eat breakfast every morning in the United States. The international border comes in their front door and goes out the back, and the Smokes, like everybody else at Akwesasne, cross it freely anytime they choose. Twenty years ago, remembers Ed Smoke, there was a sleepy official from United States Customs who spent his days in a small white building not far from the line, reading his paper and nodding occasionally at the people passing by. Eventually, the customs official retired, and the vacuum in law enforcement was complete.

That, at least, was how the smugglers saw it, and the Mafia, among others, understood the opportunity—the gash in the border created in part by the Iroquois passion for crossing the line unimpeded. As the forces of crime gained strength in the eighties, there were Iroquois leaders who spoke out against them. Two of those were Oren Lyons, the Turtle Clan chief of the Onondagas, who had emerged as an international figure in the seventies, and his friend Tom Porter at Akwesasne, who opposed what he saw as a great perversion—the terrible mutation of militancy and rage into the most destructive movement the Iroquois had ever seen. There was a warrior class that emerged in the eighties,

EDWARD SMOKE, CHIEF EXECUTIVE, ST. REGIS BAND OF
MOHAWKS, AKWESASNE, NEW YORK, 1997

speaking in the language of protest and pride but working for the smugglers—and armed very often with automatic weapons. On October 30, 1980, Tom Porter's house was burned to the ground, and the violence quickly escalated after that. The opponents of organized crime were slowly but surely pulled into the fray, and by 1990, the reservation was in a state of civil war.

Doug George saw the whole thing coming. He was a Mohawk journalist, an editor at *Akwesasne Notes*, one of the most respected Indian publications in the country. He was born on the banks of the St. Lawrence River at about the same time the engineers moved in and dredged out a seaway, transforming the swift and free-flowing river into what amounted to a series of lakes capable of accommodating great ships. The life of the Indians changed after that. The pollution that came with industrial development virtually destroyed the Iroquois fisheries and left the Mohawks scrambling to survive.

Doug George was one of those who left, at least for a while, but he came back home in the 1970s and took his place in the great reawakening—the revival of Indian identity and spirit. Like Tom Porter, he thought the people were heading toward a whole new era, a glorious rebirth of the Mohawk Nation, fulfilling the ancient predictions of the prophets. But then came the smugglers, claiming profits of a million dollars a day, and as George began to write about the warriors' betrayal—the twisted nationalism they proclaimed—the threats on his life became more serious. His newspaper office was burned to the ground, and finally in April 1990, he found himself in a gun battle that lasted four days. He was one of the few who decided to remain as the gunfire became a daily occurrence and many of those who were opposed to gambling fled the reservation in fear of their lives. He moved in with his brother, Dave George, who was one of those people—men and women—who had blocked the roads leading into Akwesasne in a futile attempt to interdict the gamblers. At the end of April, the George brothers and nine other people, including two journalists who had asked to be there, braced themselves for a steady bombardment of ten thousand rounds of machine-gun fire. All over the Akwesasne Reserve, the houses of traditional Mohawk people—those who opposed the descent into crime—were consumed by flames as the warrior faction asserted its control.

Two people died in the course of the shootout, and only then did the combined police forces of Quebec, Ontario, and New York State move in to restore some semblance of order. Incredibly enough, Doug George was accused of one of the murders, and although the charges against him were dropped, it did little to relieve his deep sense of gloom. He had the feeling of being overrun—a sense that the Peacemaker's message, those ancient principles handed down through the centuries, had

WARRIORS' WARNING, AKWESASNE, NEW YORK, 1997

been subverted and destroyed in his own generation.

"It's the greatest tragedy of our time," he declared then. "I'm not optimistic."

But things are better now for Doug George. He moved away from Akwesasne, where it still seemed clear that his life was in danger, and married a beautiful Oneida woman who shared his passion for the Iroquois traditions. Joanne Shenandoah was emerging as a star—a Grammy-nominated entertainer and singer who had performed with Jackson Browne and Willie Nelson and gained a following among Native Americans for the beauty and serenity of her Iroquois songs. Together, they spent some time with the music and tried to put as much distance as they could between Doug and the terrifying days at Akwesasne. But it was hard to pull away. The issues, in the end, were too important, and George continued his work as a writer, trying to sort through the things that had happened.

He was not alone in that undertaking. In Indian communities all over New York, there were leaders and scholars with their own explanations. Some of them blamed the problems on the Mafia, which had become such a presence in much of the state that it was hard to do business outside of its web. "Where does it start, and where does it stop?" demanded one Tuscarora. "There is no clean business. . . . Money is blood."

Rick Hill agreed in part with that assessment. He was a Tuscarora scholar, a gray-haired man with sharp, friendly eyes who

hadn't thought much in the early years of his life about the Iroquois traditions on which he was raised. His family planted corn every year, but he seldom thought about the miracle of life, which was the reason the Creator had given the seeds. But then one day, he met Oren Lyons, the stern and eloquent Onondaga chief, who helped him to look at the ordinary things and to see the gifts that were scattered all around. The prophets had warned that the people would forget. As early as 1799, a Seneca by the name of Handsome Lake had spoken of the day when people would move at an unruly speed in wagons that no longer required any horses. The white man would come with his dubious gifts—the rum and the deck of cards and the fiddle—and the Indians would dance to a whole different tune. Now, of course, the prophet's metaphors were becoming concrete. There was hardly an Indian family in America that didn't have an alcoholic in its ranks, and gambling was a cornerstone of the economy, and gratitude—which had been at the heart of the Iroquois prayer— was crumbling in the face of a new form of greed.

"A lot of young people were bitten by the gold bug," said Oren Lyons. "The government, the state, the corporations, Wall Street—they are trying to access Indian country again, and the spear point now is our own people."

Lyons was worried about the smugglers, of course, including twenty-one criminals indicted in the summer of 1997. But he knew that the story was more complicated. Within the Iroquois communities, there was also a raging debate over values—a struggle for the hearts and minds of the people in which the winners were not yet clear.

To Lyons and others, one of the most disturbing figures in the battle was Ray Halbritter, a charismatic Oneida who had emerged as the most powerful leader of his nation. Nobody denied that Halbritter was brilliant. He was a graduate of Syracuse University who had gone from there to Harvard Law School, where his Iroquois pride became intermingled with a new understanding of the white man's world. Halbritter had come to the resolute conviction that money is power, and that there are no substitutes, and in 1993, he helped to establish the first Iroquois casino to operate legally in New York State. Almost immediately, the numbers were impressive. According to the tribe, the casino employed more than 2,000 people, the majority non-Indian, and had a weekly payroll of $1 million. It was pulling in 2 million visitors a year, who were spending nearly $12 million in the area—and because of the money that was now rolling in, the Oneidas discovered a new kind of strength.

"We had tried poverty for two hundred years," explained Halbritter. "We decided to try something else."

One of the most prominent of Halbritter's admirers is an Indian leader by the name of Keller George, an Oneida who served in the 1990s as the president of USET, the United South and Eastern Tribes, one of the most respected Indian organizations in the country. George grew up with his great-grandfather, an Oneida elder who was born sometime around 1850 and lived to the age of 101. Partly because of the old man's stories, George says he believes in the Iroquois traditions—the language, the ceremonies, and the songs that are part of what it means to be an Oneida. But he also believes in building for the future, and he is proud of the things Halbritter has accomplished. The Oneidas have a cultural center today, and a college tuition program for their students, and late in 1997, they were working on a center for children and elders that appeared from the plans to be state of the art.

The critics, however, are easy to find, and many of them are afraid. "We could lose our jobs," says a young Indian who works for the Oneida Nation. "We have to be very careful what we say."

Halbritter's opponents describe him as dictatorial and greedy, a man who has amassed great personal wealth from the position of power he holds in the tribe. That power traces back to the 1970s, when Halbritter and two other men were appointed by their clans as nation representatives—a triumvirate that was soon reduced to one when the other men died. Many people were impressed in those early years, seeing Halbritter as energetic, bright, and genuinely committed to the interests of the tribe. But Doug George, among many others, believes Halbritter may have absorbed too deeply the combative lessons from his classes at Harvard—an Ivy League lawyer's conception of the world as an arena where battles are won and lost and survival inevitably belongs to the fittest. Whatever the reasons, Halbritter has emerged as a leader who believes, as he said in a Canadian television program, that "he who has the gold makes the rules."

It is a view that has spread through Iroquois country, and everywhere, it seems, there are entrepreneurs pursuing their version of the American Dream. To the most traditional of the Iroquois leaders—Tom Porter, Doug George, and Oren Lyons—that is not good news. It may be true that many of the business people are honest, working within the letter of the law, trying to build better lives for themselves and their families. But the traditionalists see danger in a new set of values. They have little use for the capitalist assumptions that have now taken root among the Indian people. In the past, it was never every man for himself. There were no class fissures in the Iroquois world—the kind that became such a blight on America, where some people grew rich and others had nothing and everybody seemed to be grasping for more. But now, that appears to be where they are headed—some of the Indian people, at least— and there is something else also. The profits they are making in Indian country have introduced a final complication to the story: the

issue of taxes, which, potentially at least, is a threat to the fundamental status of the tribes. In New York State, it is generally agreed that Indians doing business in their own territory should pay no tax on sales to other Indians. But for sales to tourists and non-Indian visitors, the courts have ruled in the past twenty years that those transactions are subject to tax. In 1996, New York's governor, George Pataki, announced that he was planning to go after the money.

The Indians reacted with bitterness and rage—particularly the Senecas, whose treaty was clear. In an agreement signed in 1842, they were promised immunity from any form of state tax. Michael Schindler, among many others, is determined to see that principle defended.

Schindler is a handsome man with soft, steady eyes and shoulder-length hair, an ironworker until a few years ago, walking the beams of embryonic skyscrapers in cities all the way from Buffalo to Dallas. In November 1996, he was elected president of the Seneca Nation—a political novice who won overwhelmingly on the strength of his personality and convictions. He was an emerging leader in the Seneca majority that was opposed to a reservation casino. He said he had done some thinking through the years, reflecting on the values of white society and those of his own, and the materialism he saw all around seemed to be at the heart of everything that was wrong. The question was whether the

MICHAEL SCHINDLER, PRESIDENT, SENECA NATION,
CATTARAUGUS RESERVATION, NEW YORK, 1997

Senecas could find a way out, and it was, he thought, the most critical issue that they still had to face. What values would guide them at the end of one century and the beginning of the next? But in the meantime, there was the state of New York and the taxes it apparently intended to collect.

As the tension mounted, there were demonstrations in April 1997. On consecutive Sundays, the Senecas shut down the New York Thruway as it passed through their Cattaraugus Reservation. Michael Schindler was there in the middle. He knew there was a point that had to be made, a principle they needed to defend, but when the violence came, nobody was surprised.

At the first demonstration, there was pushing and shoving and a visible increase in the level of rage, and on the following Sunday, everything broke loose. Policemen were trying to negotiate with the Indians when an angry mob closed in around them. Dwayne Sylvester was one of the people who was caught in the melee. An Iroquois artist known to his friends as an even-tempered man, he says the whole scene was suddenly aswirl with policemen swinging their clubs and batons, and sirens screaming, and demonstrators smashing the state troopers' cars. Sylvester remembers a woman with a flagpole who managed to hit one trooper in the head. The policeman turned and grabbed for the pole, and the woman hung on, flopping like a doll, as Sylvester immediately rushed toward

the spot. "Things moved fast," he remembered much later. He grabbed for the pole, which broke in two, and the policeman hit him across the thumb with his club. Sylvester's last memory is of raising the jagged remnant of the pole, not knowing for sure if he intended to swing it—but according to police, the videotape confirms that he did.

It was a moment of insanity that could have been worse, and as the tensions continued to mount in the spring, the traditional chiefs tried to work out a settlement. In the end, they failed. Their tentative tax agreement fell apart, and despite the fact that it protected the tribes from any form of state tariff, the militants denounced Oren Lyons and the others for even attempting to cut a deal with the governor. Everywhere, there was division and chaos, and the warriors found new hope in the rage. They put up signs on the reservation borders denouncing the enemies of the Indian people and asserting their claim to the whole hemisphere.

Rick Hill, the Tuscarora scholar, summed up the fears of many of his peers. "Somebody," he said, "is going to get killed."

In the darkest days, when almost everyone was waiting for the worst, Tom Porter knew it was time to pull away. His heart, quite literally, was ready to explode. The chest pains hit him at Onondaga, and he was rushed immediately to the nearest hospital. He had been brooding, he says, about the betrayal—the men his age who had grown up with him in the Indian movement, who had attended all the sacred ceremonies and proclaimed their allegiance to the Iroquois people. In the end, they were liars, selling their heritage for $800 million in smuggled cigarettes and uncounted more in drugs and guns and illegal aliens. Perhaps it was still a form of warfare, a measure of their hatred for the United States government, or perhaps it was simply a matter of greed. "We got tired of being poor," one of them said, but whatever the reason, the crime was incomprehensible to Porter.

"They took a brand-new baby," he says, "the Mohawk Nation, and aborted that baby before it was born."

During his time of recovery, Porter found himself thinking again about the ancient prophecies on which he was raised—the prediction handed down since the eighteenth century that the Mohawk people would return to the valley where they had once been "Keepers of the Eastern Door." He found a piece of land to the northwest of Albany, on the banks of a river where a long house had stood in the ancestors' time, and where his great-great-grandmother had once given thanks. He decided that the time had come to return. He gathered together a small group of people, perhaps a dozen members of his clan, and they made the trip south from Akwesasne and set up a farming community in the hills. They raised their traditional Iroquois crops—the corn interspersed with the beans and the squash—and spoke the language and practiced the ceremonies of the tribe. The community grew slowly. Jonathan Wagers was an early recruit—a troubled teenager who met Tom Porter after traveling across the country in search of something he couldn't quite name. He says he found it on the Mohawk farm, where life was uncluttered and the people were kind and the cupboards even in the winter were full.

For Porter, for a while, all that was enough. They were bearing witness to the traditional Iroquois way and living out the prophecy on which he was raised. But after a year or two of the quiet, he began to have other plans, to feel a restless need to do something more. He had long been worried about the death of the language, which, for almost all of the Iroquois nations, no longer seemed to be far away. There were only a handful of Onondaga speakers and even fewer Tuscaroras, and Porter thought the answer was a new kind of school. He liked to call it "Carlisle in Reverse," after the boarding school in Pennsylvania where many generations of Indian children were stripped of their native identity and language. Porter had visions of an Iroquois immersion—young students coming to the school with their parents, whole families learning the traditional ways.

In 1998, he set off boldly in search of the funds, and his sermon to anybody who would listen was a curious mixture of apocalyptic

JONATHAN WAGERS, MOHAWK, CANAJOHARIE, NEW YORK, 1997

warnings and a spirit of fatalism and patience. He spoke of the possibility of extinction and the catastrophic events of the 1990s. "It will take us," he said, "fifty years to get back on our feet." But the implication seemed to be that they will do it.

Certainly, it is clear there are people who are trying. There are the traditional chiefs like Oren Lyons, who stands firm against the pervasive ideology of greed, and elected officials like Michael Schindler, who shares a reverence for the Iroquois culture. There are Doug George, the writer, and Rick Hill, the outspoken Tuscarora scholar, and there are others whose names are less well known. Peter Jemison is an artist, a Seneca who works with Indian students at a time when many of them are confused. Francis Hill is a Mohawk who works every day in inner-city schools, and Harvey Longboat is a spiritual leader who presides over ceremonies at the long house.

But perhaps most important, there are also the people like Tammy Bluewolf, a mother of four who raises her children in the Iroquois way. For Tammy, it could have been a lonely undertaking. Her husband, Charles, was a handsome young artist, and they were deeply in love. He came from a Chippewa clan in Minnesota, some thirty miles east of the Mississippi River, but his family moved around a lot when he was young—a military life where home was merely a temporary notion. As a teenager, he was feeling rootless and alone in the schools of Charlotte, North Carolina, un-

til he finally fell in with the right group of people. One of those was Rosa Winfree, a Lumbee educator in Charlotte who caught a glimpse of his talent, buried somewhere in the layers of doubt. In Winfree's experience, it is a common condition for Indians in the city, especially the young ones, who have never had reason to be sure who they are. She and Charles began to talk about it, and after a while, his identity began to appear in his art—in the paintings and sculpture that soon became the focal point of his life.

"When he connected with his culture," says Tammy today, "that's how he defined himself as a man."

By the time they met, Tammy herself had been through some changes. There had been an evolution in her teenage years from taking her Oneida identity for granted to a passionate study of exactly what it meant. She wrote papers about it in high school and college, and as she and Charles began their twelve-year marriage, there was no disagreement about how things should be.

"We wanted to be a native family," she says.

They wanted little children who were courteous and proud, respectful of the elders, and able to move comfortably in the Indian world. They wanted to practice the traditional ceremonies and become fluent in the language, and for a while, their life together was exciting. But then one night on his way home from work, Charles Bluewolf lost control of his car. Suddenly, in a split-second blur, he was gone,

CIARA RAINSONG BLUEWOLF, AGE 3,
DAUGHTER OF TAMMY BLUEWOLF, ONEIDA, NEW YORK, 1997

leaving Tammy and four young children with a loss more terrible than they thought they could bear.

Tammy's aunt, Maisey Shenandoah, was an Oneida clan mother who knew what to do. She went to the spot where the crash had occurred and burned the ceremonial tobacco and invited the spirit of Charles Bluewolf to come home and rest. There was a journey ahead, a difficult passage to the unknown place where the Creator waited. But first, the family needed time to adjust—a ten-day period of mourning and grief when the members of the clan all moved in together and at least one person was always awake, making certain that the spirit never had to be alone.

Tammy wasn't sure how much she believed it, all these tenets of the Indian faith, but she discovered in the course of the next several days that they gave a structure and a meaning to her grief and enabled her to func-

tion. Finally, she was able to say good-bye, to reassure her husband that she knew he had to go and that she understood now, more clearly perhaps than she had in her life, her purpose and her reason for being on the earth. She knew she could raise the children by herself, and that whatever happened, the Bluewolf family was going to be fine.

In the years since then, there have been some moments of depression and doubt, but they have always passed, giving way to the feeling that her life makes sense, that it is now a part of a much bigger story. For the Iroquois people who cling to that faith, there is a sustaining patience in the difficult days. For those who have lost it, there is only the moment in which they are living, when the desperate struggles are not yet resolved and the divisions that threaten to tear them apart only grow deeper and more dangerous by the day.

SAM SAPIEL, PENOBSCOT ELDER, ARRESTED
AT PLYMOUTH DAY OF MOURNING, 1997

CHAPTER SEVEN
Days of Mourning

SAM SAPIEL WAS READY TO LEAVE. He had put his drum in the car and was standing by the door when he heard the screaming in a nearby street. He rushed to the spot and saw the police of Plymouth, Massachusetts, their uniforms a vast sea of blue, wrestling the Indian people to the ground. Sam was startled at first by the sight. He hadn't thought there would be any trouble. The protests now were a Plymouth institution—a ritual that played out every Thanksgiving as the Indians gathered at the statue of Massasoit, the honored sachem of the Wampanoag people who had enabled the Pilgrim invaders to survive.

It was, of course, a calculated gamble. From the day they arrived at the tip of Cape Cod, paddling ashore in their frail wooden dinghy, the Pilgrims had stolen everything they could find. On November 15, 1620, a scouting party under the command of Miles Standish found several baskets of Indian corn, which it seized and carried away to the ship. Two weeks later, the Pilgrims returned and plundered the food supplies at a village—the beans and the corn

that the Wampanoag people had put away for the winter. It was a bad way to start. But Massasoit knew a little bit about the English. For fifteen years, their slavers had visited the shores of New England, kidnapping Indians and spreading diseases for which the people could find no cure. The English, however, seemed to be unaffected, and Massasoit could only marvel at their power.

He was encouraged in that by an ambitious young brave whose name was Tisquantum, a victim of the slavers who had been taken from the Indian town of Pawtuxet and sold to the Spaniards. It was a miserable journey across the cold, gray waters of the North Atlantic, but Tisquantum soon learned the language of his captors and somehow managed to escape from the Spaniards and make his way to England. In 1619, he was picked as the pilot for a transatlantic crossing, and he was back in New England when the Pilgrims built their village at Pawtuxet. By then, the Indian community was gone, wiped away by disease, and the Pilgrims called the new place Plymouth.

Tisquantum soon emerged as their friend, teaching them the basics of native agriculture, and on March 22, 1621, he led Chief Massasoit to the settlement and helped negotiate a treaty of peace. For a while, at least, it was a useful alliance. The first fifty years of the seventeenth century were a turbulent time in the New England forests. The powers of Europe—the English, French, and Dutch—were staking their claim, battling for supremacy in a virginal land, and the Indian nations were doing much the same. The Wampanoags and their neighbors were part of a political and economic competition in which warfare was only one measure of strength.

There was also the growing trade with the Pilgrims. The Indians most often bartered wampum or fur for the sparkling new wares of the European settlers. Tisquantum—or Squanto, as he was known to the English—understood from his travels that the supply of such goods was nearly inexhaustible, and he was proud of his knowledge and the power that it gave him. Massasoit, too, saw advantage in maintaining peace with the British, and in the centuries that followed, his loyalty has been steadily enlarged into myth. He and Squanto were the Thanksgiving Indians, embracing the Pilgrim fathers as their friends.

In the official understanding of Plymouth, Massachusetts, the rest of the story was put out of mind—for instance, the memories of Massasoit's younger son, King Philip, who saw the English people growing strong, their numbers swelling to more than fifty thousand. Within a half-century of the landing of the Pilgrims, the English established more than ninety different towns, and their arrogance seemed to keep pace with their power. They were hungry for land and took what they wanted, and King Philip decided that enough was enough. After building an alliance with the neighboring tribes, including the Narragansetts to the west, he declared his personal war on the English. In 1675, he attacked, killing nearly a thousand of the whites. But in the winter, his army was ravaged by disease, and the English regrouped, and the following year, the rebellion fell apart. King Philip was killed, and his head was severed and impaled on a pike and displayed in Plymouth for twenty-five years.

At a Thanksgiving celebration in 1970, a Wampanoag teacher by the name of Frank James wanted to talk about some of those things. He had been asked by a committee of Plymouth's city fathers to deliver a speech on Thanksgiving Day offering a native perspective on the story. James was only too happy to oblige. He prepared an address about the theft of the land and the injustice to the Indian people through the years, and declared that Massasoit's welcome of the Pilgrims would go down in history as "our greatest mistake." But the good news was that the spirit of the Indian people wouldn't die: "The Wampanoags still walk the lands of Massachusetts."

Looking back on it now, many people say that if James had been allowed to deliver that speech, whatever the momentary ripples of surprise, the moment would have passed. There would have been no controversy or rage, no insult or modern provocation to be added to those handed down over time. But that was not how it happened. The officials at Plymouth asked to see a copy of the speech in advance, and once they read it, they said they were shocked. Such words, they said, would not be allowed to mar their public celebration of peace.

But James wouldn't quit. He took his address to the statue of Massasoit just up the hill—a steep, grassy knoll where the Wampanoag sachem stood watch on the harbor, naked except for his loincloth and feather, the great muscles rippling in his legs and his arms, a symbol of strength. According to one eyewitness that day, James read his speech to a small group of people, but the word went out in Indian country, and over the next several years, the crowds grew larger.

The American Indian Movement created an event called the Day of Mourning. It struck a chord with Indian people nationwide, this counter-celebration of a national holiday. It was a moment of awakening, the kind of symbolism and drama that were rapidly becoming a trademark of AIM. One of the masterminds was Russell Means, an Oglala Lakota who grew up in Oakland, where the Black Panther Party had shot it out with police. At first, AIM seemed like an Indian version of the Panthers. The organization was born in the streets of Minneapolis, led initially by Dennis Banks and a group of city-bred Anishinabes, or Chippewas, who had grown tired of a pattern of police brutality. They began to patrol the Indian ghettos, confronting the police, but their mission soon spread from the heart of the city and embraced the cause of native people everywhere.

For Shirley Mills, a Wampanoag leader in the Plymouth demonstrations, the leaders of AIM were modern-day warriors—these aggressive young men with their long, flowing hair and steely resolve and impressive understanding of the nature of the struggle. For Means and Dennis Banks, the stakes were greater than the issue of civil rights. The question was whether Indian people would survive, whether they could find a way in America to reassert their cultural identity and pride, to be who they were.

To Shirley and others in the Wampanoag community, the issue was familiar. In the 1950s, her husband, Earl Mills, had presided over a Wampanoag reawakening, trying to continue what the elders had begun. As early as the 1920s, the Wampanoag community in the town of Mashpee, hidden away in the forests barely twenty miles from the village of Plymouth, had begun holding powwows. These were festive, inspirational occasions with Indian delegations from all over the country—the Rappahannocks from Virginia, the

Iroquois from New York, even the Catawbas from South Carolina. They smoked and prayed and listened to the drums, and after the tradition was interrupted by World War II, Earl set out in the fifties to restore it. He had just been picked as the Wampanoag chief, a young man who had spent many hours with the elders—including the medicine man, Billy James—and who understood the traditions that had made the Wampanoags a people. He rekindled the powwows and other ceremonies, then set out to restore their old meeting house. Built by the Quakers in 1684, it was a place where the Indian people had worshiped, flanked by the graves of a tribal cemetery, the history of the Wampanoags written into stone.

Chief Mills was happy with the spirit of renewal, the revival of the customs and institutions of the tribe. But in the 1960s, the outside world began closing in. Subdivisions and country clubs were built on the western end of Cape Cod, and as the tax rates soared with the new flood of wealth, the Wampanoags began losing land. There were not as many places to hunt anymore, and the pollution that came with the wave of development began to take a toll on the shellfish beds.

In the seventies, the Wampanoags were angry. It was part of the passion of the Plymouth demonstrations, and with many of the issues still unresolved, the protests flared once again in the nineties. As a matter of record, they had never really stopped. Every year since the first, when Frank James tried to deliver his speech, the Indians had gathered at the Massasoit statue to proclaim a new meaning for the Thanksgiving season. It was a ritual for the Native Americans of southern New England, accepted by most of the people of Plymouth until a flutter of tension in 1995, when a small group of Indians dumped a load of sand on Plymouth Rock. The following year, 1996, they disrupted the parade. But 1997 was the worst.

"There were more police than I had ever seen," remembers Shirley Mills.

She assumed there would be no march, for like most Indians who gathered that day, she had little interest in a battle for the streets. Sam Sapiel assumed the same thing. A Penobscot elder sixty-six years old, he had moved to Massachusetts and married Shirley after she and Earl Mills had divorced. On this particular Thanksgiving Day, there were family members who were waiting at home, and Sam and Shirley were getting ready to leave when a woman's voice rang out from the crowd: "Let's take back the streets!"

Suddenly, there was chaos, everybody screaming and fighting with police, as Sapiel rushed from his car to the street and ordered the Indians to get back on the sidewalk. For a moment, at least, the people obeyed. In the Indian world, Sapiel carries weight—a Native American straight from central casting, with his long, gray hair and the lines of wisdom that are etched in his face. He has spent his life bringing Indians together, forging alliances

WAMPANOAG MEETING HOUSE, BUILT IN 1684,
MASHPEE, MASSACHUSETTS, 1998

RUSSELL PETERS, WAMPANOAG, BOSTON, MASSACHUSETTS, 1998

among native people in the East, and when his voice rang out above the Thanksgiving riot, almost everybody did what he asked.

"There," he said, turning to the police. "Things are all right now. If anything happens, it's your fault."

As Sapiel remembers it, the captain in charge, a skinny-looking man maybe fifty years old, motioned to the officers who were standing nearby and told them simply, "Arrest that man." For the next several minutes, everything was a blur. The police surged forward and threw Sam to the ground, and many of the demonstrators rushed to protect him. Instead, they almost managed to crush him. Sapiel was at the bottom of the pile trying to breathe when the policemen began to use the pepper spray. The burning was awful on the side of his face, but he could tell from the cries of pain and disbelief that the people above him were hit even worse. He thought of Mississippi, or Selma, Alabama, as the policemen dragged him away to the wagon, the handcuffs choking the blood in his wrists.

He knew it was a day that would not be forgotten—another provocation, as if one were needed, for the Mashpee Wampanoags to endure. All over southern New England, in fact, there were Indian people struggling for their rights. At least one tribe, the Mashantucket Pequots, had made great progress, but for many of the others, it was an uphill battle—a struggle against problems that were rooted in the past and in the eco-nomic forces all around. Whatever the future of the Thanksgiving protest—and most people assumed there would be more trouble—it was only one skirmish in their war to survive.

As the 1990s drew to a close, it was difficult to tell sometimes if they were winning.

It's been thirty years since Russell Peters decided to come home. He left for the army during World War II, then got his degree and went to work for Honeywell in Massachusetts. He did well enough in his career in computers, but a part of him envied the people left behind, the young men his age who lived on the land, hunting, fishing, growing what they needed, as the Wampanoag people had done since the start. His father had long been a leader in the tribe, and his brother, John Peters, was the medicine man, and one day late in the 1960s, Russell realized that he had gotten homesick.

He also knew that the Wampanoag people were facing a crisis. There were non-Indians who were moving to the cape and taking control of the land, which they were able to do because of a decision made by the commonwealth of Massachusetts. In 1870, the state had converted the Mashpees' land—a wooded tract of thirteen thousand acres that the native people had held in common since it was granted to them in 1666—into a town like any of the others on the cape. The land now belonged to individuals, and over time, some of them agreed to sell. Others discovered that they had no choice when the tax rates rose and they simply couldn't pay. But the crisis didn't come until the 1960s, when the Mashpees found themselves outnumbered. Until that time, they had controlled the government of the new township, and although their language had slipped away and some of the Wampanoags had intermarried, mixing their blood with the blacks and the whites who lived in the area, there was a sense of Indian identity that survived. Part of it was simply the way they lived—close to the land, hunting, fishing, raising what they needed, viewing the earth in much the same way that their ancestors had.

In the words of anthropologist Jack Campisi, this identity was "a spiritual entity, not a commercial asset," and that was the way they wanted it to stay.

But the developers, of course, didn't see it that way. They were building their resorts on the south end of Mashpee, handsome waterfront communities like New Seabury, and Russell Peters and others on the tribal council saw the writing on the wall. Soon, there would be nothing left for the Indians—no place to hunt, no waters that were clean enough for the fish. But Peters also thought there was hope. He knew that the Indian tribes in Maine were pursuing their ancient claim to the land, and when he met with their lawyer, Tom Tureen, the attorney thought the Wampanoags had a case.

Tureen, in fact, was meeting with other Indian leaders as well. On the tip of Martha's Vineyard, an island off the southern shore of Cape Cod, there was another community of Wampanoag people whose history was essentially the same as the Mashpees'. In 1870, they, too, had seen their holdings transformed, converted from communal land to a town, and one of their elders, a commercial fisherman named Alfred Vanderhoop, still had a copy of the petition of protest that the Wampanoag leaders had submitted at the time. A hundred years later, he shuddered sometimes when he thought about the future. He was afraid the Indians' way of life would disappear.

Vanderhoop was one of many in the tribe who had always made his living from the sea. His uncle, Amos Smalley, had once harpooned a great white whale and served as a consultant for the movie version of *Moby Dick*. Vanderhoop never had that experience. But as whaling declined in the twentieth century, he did the next best thing. He fished the waters from Cape Cod to Nova Scotia harpooning swordfish, and dragged the bays for shellfish and lobster, and even in his eightieth year, he wouldn't stop.

But he knew that things were beginning to change. Even in the tiny community of Gay Head, where the Indians lived, the outside world was closing in fast. Developers were searching for prime real estate, and the Indians were determined to save what they could—to reassert their claim to the historic

ALFRED VANDERHOOP, WAMPANOAG FISHERMAN AND
TRIBAL COUNCIL MEMBER, GAY HEAD, MASSACHUSETTS, 1998

places where their people had lived for ten thousand years. There was Herring Creek, where the fish came in from the sea to reproduce, and the cranberry bogs, where the fruit grew wild and the Wampanoags gathered in the autumn for the harvest, and the great, rugged cliffs at the end of the island, a sacred place where Gay Head artists like Gladys Widdiss found the veins of clay to use in their pots.

The Wampanoags were determined to save those places, to reclaim them for the generations still to come, and the same impulse was also at work among the Narragansett people to the west. On the southern coast of Rhode Island, a medicine man named Lloyd Wilcox understood that his people had struggled through the years. During the time of King Philip's War, they joined the fight and suffered the consequences of defeat. They were pushed to the fringe of the Rhode Island forests, the scraggly thickets that grew near the sea, and their land base continued to shrink over time. Part of it was the fault of their own leadership. There were chiefs who sold big pieces of land to pay off debts they had built for themselves. But in the 1880s, the state of Rhode Island tried to finish the job, seizing the last of the tribal land, a tract that covered some nine hundred acres.

Looking back on the history, Lloyd Wilcox thought it was part of a pattern. Back then, the Indian wars were nearly over in the West— the Sioux were beaten, and even Geronimo

was in trouble. And now in the East, the whites were taking the land and teaching the children in the Rhode Island schools that there had once been Indian people in the state. But the Narragansetts knew they were not yet extinct. In the 1970s, there was a new generation that was coming of age, future leaders like Matthew Thomas, who would later be chief, and Randy Noka and Hiawatha Brown, who would take their places on the Narragansetts' council. These were people who knew who they were, and Wilcox thought there were better days ahead. But what the Narragansetts needed was land, a place to be a tribe, and they, too, met with Tom Tureen and filed a claim for more than three thousand acres.

And so it happened in the 1970s that the Wampanoags and their Narragansett neighbors, along with several other tribes from Connecticut to Maine, all set out on the same path together. They would pursue their ancient titles to the land as a cornerstone of tribal restoration.

The Mashpees' case was the first to go to court, and the Indians were aggressive in pursuing their claim. Before the trial in 1977, two of their leaders, Earl Mills and Russell Peters, met with officials at the Carter White House, and William B. Gunter, an old friend of Carter's, asked what it would take to settle the case: "A million, two million, or what?"

Peters said the Indians were not after money. They wanted their land—all thirteen thousand acres of it that the commonwealth of Massachusetts had converted to a town. But the claim of the Wampanoags was startling. Unlike the native people in Maine, who had set their sites on undeveloped land, or the other tribes whose claims were small, the Mashpees were demanding the return of parcels—and a significant number—that included people's homes. "We were prepared to go against individuals, corporations, the state of Massachusetts," remembers Russell Peters, and not surprisingly, the response of their non-Indian neighbors was intense—"almost violent," says Peters today.

It may have been possible to work out a settlement, but not in the climate that prevailed on Cape Cod. Until their lawsuit, the Mashpee Indians were not taken seriously. "Our ideas," said one developer, "reflect what modern Americans are thinking. The Mashpees can go along or not. It won't make any difference."

After the suit, the atmosphere was different. The Indians were taken seriously, all right, but they were also reviled—hated by the economic powers on the cape. Even the judge in the Wampanoags' case, Walter J. Skinner, regarded the Indians' demands as extreme. "You know," he told the lawyers at the trial, "the remedy you are seeking is a very radical remedy."

Against that backdrop—a volatile mixture of public hostility and a feeling of skepticism by the judge—the hearing began in October 1977. The first question for the federal jury to decide was whether, in fact, the Mashpee Wampanoags were a tribe. If the answer to that pivotal question was yes, the courts had ruled in the case of other tribes that their land was protected by federal law. It could not be taken without the explicit consent of Congress, and that consent, quite clearly, had never been given.

In defense of the tribal status of their clients, the Wampanoags' lawyers marshaled an impressive array of experts—Wellesley anthropologist Jack Campisi, Smithsonian ethnologist William C. Sturtevant, and historian James Axtell of William and Mary. They also brought in Vine Deloria, one of the most respected Indian scholars in the country. Deloria was a Sioux who had taken a special interest in the struggles of the Indian tribes of the East, and he testified that without any question, the Mashpee Wampanoags were a tribe. They could trace their lineage to the people who met the Pilgrims at the boat, and they had managed to survive for more than three hundred years pretty much in the place they had always lived.

"What you are talking about," he said, "is a group of people who know where they are."

For Skinner, however, it was not that simple. The judge was convinced that the Mashpees bore the burden of proof and must demonstrate clearly that they had lived as a tribe since the 1600s. He also noted that the Indian people had intermarried through the years, and the question now for the jury to decide was whether "this influx of outsiders was such as to change the character of the group from an Indian group to a mixed group." The jury came back with a curious verdict. It found that the Mashpee Wampanoags had lived as a tribe at various times in their history but not at others, and that they were no longer a tribe in 1976, the date when their federal lawsuit was filed. The Indians appealed but lost once again, and their defeat sent a chill through the ranks of other tribes.

The Narragansetts were the first to cut a deal. In the winter of 1977–78, the tribe, the federal government, and the state worked out an agreement under which the Indians were granted federal recognition, along with eighteen hundred acres of land. Half of that land was a state-owned swamp, but the Narragansetts took it, plus settlement money of $3.5 million, which they used to buy the other nine hundred acres.

The Gay Head Wampanoags also managed to work out a settlement. But theirs was a long and arduous process complicated by the bitter opposition of their neighbors and the prevailing myopia of the BIA. At one point, their petition for federal recognition was denied, prompting a blistering letter of support from one historian who lived on the island. Francis Jennings, author of a book on colonial history, *The Invasion of America*, had been coming to Martha's Vineyard for the better part of forty-five years, and he said that everybody understood that the Gay Head Wampanoags were a tribe. But when their land-claim case was headed for the courts and a battery of lawyers stepped into the picture, everything went fuzzy. People made distinctions that didn't fit the facts, much as they had done in the Mashpees' case, and the BIA became caught up in the deliberate distortions handed out by the lawyers.

"I have never heard the Gay Head Indians mentioned as other than a tribe," Jennings wrote to officials at the Department of the Interior, "until those hired guns, the lawyers, appeared on the scene. That they can make white appear black should surprise nobody; it is their lucrative livelihood. But that a government agency proposes to adopt such malevolent distortions and falsehoods is shameful."

Other noted scholars took up the cry, and the Gay Head Wampanoags pushed ahead, winning federal recognition in 1987 and a land-claim settlement of $4 million. Even then, however, their frustrations didn't end. Like the Narragansetts to the west, they could see the value of federal recognition. There were new programs in housing and health and new opportunities for building their economy. But there were also ongoing battles with the state—jurisdictional disputes on issues ranging from fishing rights to casinos, even the building codes for their houses.

Since the 1970s, the New England states from Rhode Island to Maine have sustained

their attack on the notion of sovereignty—
the idea that the federally recognized tribes
have a governmental status much like their
own. The Indians know the law is on their
side. Despite occasional setbacks, there has
been a succession of federal-court decisions
affirming the right of the tribes to govern their
affairs. But the states are resisting.

"When the law finally became available to
us," says Lloyd Wilcox of the Narragansett
tribe, "I never heard such complaints from the
outside world. It made me ashamed."

There has been, however, at least one exception to the story of frustration, and it came
in a place that would have seemed unlikely
even as recently as twenty years ago. The
Mashantucket Pequot people have lived for
centuries with an elemental terror, a memory
of suffering that was so overwhelming it almost caused the tribe to disappear.

In 1637, an army of Puritans attacked a
Pequot settlement called Mystic Fort, not far
from the southern shores of Connecticut. It
was the culmination of three years of tension
that had begun with the murder of a Pequot
chief and escalated into all-out war. Just before dawn on May 26, the Puritan commanders set fire to the fort, and as the Pequots—
mostly women and children and a few old
men—fled to escape from the flames, the colonial army quickly cut them to pieces. The
victims lay dying in the shadow of the blaze,
their bodies charred and slashed by the swords
of the Puritan soldiers.

"Great and doleful was the bloody sight . . . ,"
wrote the English captain John Underhill, "to
see so many souls lie gasping on the ground,
so thick, in some places, that you could hardly
pass along."

Underhill conceded that some might wonder at the nature of the slaughter. Was it necessary to kill every Pequot person they could
find? The captain concluded that the answer
was yes. The Puritans, in a way, were like King
David, turning their wrath on the enemies of
God, and sometimes women and children had
to die. The precedents were clear in the Scrip-
tures, he said: "We had sufficient light from
the word of God."

And so it was that the Puritan fathers set
out from the fort on a mission of death, tracking down the survivors from May 26, killing
off most of the Pequot warriors, and turning
the rest of the people into slaves. "God's hand
from heaven was so manifested . . . ," wrote
one of the Puritans in defense of the geno-
cide they performed, "that the name of the
Pequots is blotted out from under heaven,
there being not one that is, or at least dare
call himself, a Pequot."

For many years, that was almost the case.
The Pequots retreated to the hills, rocky ra-
vines, and low-lying swamps of Connecticut,
where they tried not to call much attention
to themselves. Betty Fayerweather remembers
growing up in the 1960s not really certain who
her ancestors were. Her father, Edward Williams, was a cranberry picker who would

BETTY FAYERWEATHER, PEQUOT,
NORTH STONINGTON, CONNECTICUT, 1998

sometimes take his children aside, all fourteen of them, and tell them not to forget that they were Pequots. Betty didn't know what to make of that advice. She remembers being told many times in her life that the Pequot Indian people were extinct, casualties of the wars of the seventeenth century. But later, she came to understand the truth. The Pequots survived because of people like her father, their history preserved in the whisper of the ancestors drifting through the years, handed down at the start by people who were literally afraid for their lives.

By the twentieth century, they were almost gone. There were two communities—the Eastern Pequots near the Rhode Island border and the Mashantuckets twenty miles to the west. Their leaders knew the painful history of the tribe, how it had clung to the land, and how the Connecticut colony had appointed overseers for its affairs. Some of these men were honest and fair, but others were not, and the tribal land base began to erode, and many of the Pequot people moved away, often into indentured servitude. By 1935, there were forty-two Mashantucket Pequots, nine of whom lived on the tribal land, which had dwindled to 178 acres. Their leaders, however, were defiant and proud. Two half-sisters, Elizabeth Plouffe and Martha Ellal, demanded better housing for the Indian people and protection of their land and their status as a tribe, and when the state continued to ignore their pleas, the women turned

angry. One anthropologist wrote of a time when trespassers were driven from the reservation at gunpoint. But through it all, the Pequots survived, and in the past twenty years, their fortunes have changed—more dramatically, perhaps, than any other Indian group in the country.

Looking back on it now, the turning point came in 1975, when the tribe picked Richard Hayward as chairman. He was the energetic grandson of Elizabeth Plouffe, a man who believed in the history of his people and the stories that held them together as a tribe. But he also believed in the Pequots' future, and he set out on a plan for economic development, selling tribal firewood and maple syrup, clearing the land for a community garden, constructing a hydroponic greenhouse. In the beginning, of course, everything was a guess. There was no way to know what would work and what wouldn't, but there was hope in the flurry of tribal enterprises, and there was also the matter of getting back the land. The Pequots, too, hired Tom Tureen, the lawyer from Maine who was working with other New England tribes, and after negotiations that were sometimes bitter, they worked out a settlement in October 1983. In exchange for renouncing all future claims, the Pequots were granted federal recognition and $900,000 to buy back land that the state of Connecticut had failed to protect.

They continued to develop other tribal enterprises, and in February 1992, their crowning achievement was the Foxwoods Casino, a gambling hall that rose improbably from the wooded hillsides near Interstate 95. It is an easy drive from roughly 10 percent of the nation's population, and as the people and the revenues poured in, even the Pequots had to be astonished. By 1996, gross receipts totaled nearly $1 billion. The slot machines alone raised $600 million, a quarter of which went to the state of Connecticut under an agreement negotiated by the tribe. The rest of the money belonged to the Pequots, a group that now numbered five hundred members.

Some people say there's a downside to the story—that for many of the Pequots, the sudden affluence sometimes carries its own set of problems. There are social workers from other tribes in the country who worry about the example the Pequots are setting. "Indian welfare," one of them calls it—casino money in six-figure amounts coming to the tribal members twice a year. There's a new stereotype growing out of all that, a national backlash of hostility and confusion that assumes that Indians are the nouveau riches. Several times in the nineties, congressional legislation has been introduced that would abolish the special trust status of the tribes and the social programs of the BIA, on the theory that the Indians no longer need them.

The Pequots reply that it simply isn't true. Poverty still haunts much of Indian country, and nowhere else in the Western Hemisphere is there a casino as grand and successful as their own. In addition to that, most of the money that the tribe is bringing in has been invested in the future, not spent by the members. From shipbuilding enterprises to pharmacies, the Pequots have established a network of businesses and created a total of twelve thousand jobs. They have contributed $10 million to the Smithsonian's Museum of the American Indian and have opened a research center of their own, valued at $350 million.

Other tribes have been inspired by the Pequots' example. On Martha's Vineyard in 1998, the Gay Head Wampanoags were working on a plan for high-stakes bingo. The tribal chairman, Beverly Wright, can picture in her mind all the possibilities that would come with the money. Wright is an interior designer by trade, a woman who was raised in the Gay Head community but left it to pursue another life in the city. She remembers how her grandfather used to tend sheep, working white people's farms for $.50 a day, and how the Gay Head people spent their lives in rustic isolation, lacking electricity until early in the 1950s. She thought for a while that she could do better, but the salt air beckoned all the way in New Jersey, and eventually she returned, taking her place on the Wampanoags' council. At the tribal headquarters, built after federal recognition in the eighties, she lined the walls with photographs of the elders, the people who kept the community alive, and in the nineties, she and the others began building new houses and working on a plan for college scholarships. They are also trying to revitalize the culture, holding language classes and raising seed money to build a $3.5 million museum.

Heading the cultural committee is Berta Welch, a Wampanoag woman who is part of the new generation of leaders. She lives with her family in a house just east of the cranberry bogs, where the winter wind swirls across the final spit of land. For some time now, her husband, Vernon, has been engaged in a search, a quest to discover who his ancestors were. It is said that his father was part Cherokee and his grandmother was an Indian from South Carolina—perhaps an Edisto or Chicora—but the records of the family are difficult to find. Vernon only knows that he feels at home in the land of Aquinnah, which is the Wampanoag word for the Indian place. His spirit is stirred by the beauty of the moors and the waves that pound at the base of the cliffs and the subtle interplay of the Indian clans. There are factions in the tribe, tensions that come and go with the times, depending on the pressures of the outside world. But through it all, there is a sense of extended family that survives, and Vernon and Berta want their two young children to feel it. They know that Giles, their twelve-year-old, has the sea in his blood, and they want him to listen to his great-uncle's stories—how he fished the Atlantic waters with his crew, and how the

rusty harpoon in his old fishing shack found its mark in the days when the swordfish ran near the cape.

For Berta, this is home, and she wants the cultural center they are planning to be a place where the Indian people can gather—not only to study the language and the crafts and the physical reminders of the Wampanoags' past, but to feel that sense of community and pride that has held them together. She knows that the challenges now are more subtle. Their rural isolation is a thing of the past, and along with the multiple environmental threats that have come with the population growth on the island, there is the inevitable pull of a new way of life. Some of it is good. It is hard to argue with the material improvements—better houses and cars and a little bit of money to spend on themselves. But she also believes that there is something important that has to be preserved, the same old attachments to each other and a place that seem to be a part of their DNA. For centuries now, they have been unmoved, and along with their Wampanoag cousins in Mashpee, they are determined to resist the temptations and the threats, no matter what form those forces might assume.

Peter Hendricks remembers when the game warden tried to take away his gun. It wasn't very pleasant. Hendricks is a Wampanoag hunter from Mashpee. He and his cousin, Earl Mills, Jr., the son of a chief, have roamed the

VERNON AND BERTA WELCH, WAMPANOAG COMMUNITY,
GAY HEAD, MASSACHUSETTS, 1998

forests since they were little boys. Even to-day, they build their lean-tos out in the woods much like their ancestors did in the past and go hunting for days—not for recreation or even for the love of being near the land. They are putting meat on the table for themselves and their families, killing only what they need to survive. They don't believe they require anybody's permission—no hunting license handed out by the state to do what the Wampanoags have always done. There's a price to be paid for that point of view, and Hendricks, especially, seems willing to pay it. With the veins of rage popping out in his neck, he tells the story of the ill-fated warden who tried to take his gun. Hendricks simply refused to give it up, threatening instead to use it on the warden in defense of his aborigi-nal rights. There seemed to be little doubt that he meant it, and for the moment, at least, the warden let it drop.

On another occasion, in 1984, Hendricks took a similar issue to court, winning a ruling on behalf of his tribe to allow the people to hunt and fish as they chose. But there is a larger controversy still unresolved. Given the pace of development on the shores of Cape Cod, will there be any animals left for the hunt? Any deer or bear? And will there be any fish? Already, the scallops are disappearing from the bay, and even the berries in the woods are unsafe.

"It's a clash of cultures," says Earl Mills, Jr., "one that cares about the land as it is, that thinks it's just right, the other that thinks it needs to be tamed."

For now, in Mills's estimation, the Indian people are losing that fight, not because they are wrong but because, once again, they are outnumbered. But Mills maintains that it's a matter of time, that the Creator who gave them the land in the first place will not let it die. And more practically, perhaps, they are working to develop new tools for the fight.

Mashpee administrator Jim Peters is pursu-ing federal recognition for the tribe, which was denied when its land-claim case went to court. He is hoping that once the people are armed with that status, they can buy back land and restore the shellfish beds in the bay. But he also knows it's an uphill battle. In 1998, there was talk of a new shopping center in the area that could quadruple the level of sewage in the water. The Indians will do what they can to prevent it, but whatever happens, it's what the Wampanoags say they expect—develop-ment that threatens their existence as a tribe.

"America is America," says Peters with a shrug. "It started here."

And so it is that in the village of Plymouth, less than twenty-five miles up the road from Mashpee, the demonstrators gather every Thanksgiving morning to record their own understanding of the day. The Indians come from all over the country to protest the as-saults on the native way of life, and the Wampanoags have taken their place at the front. They know that the news is not all bad.

MASSASOIT STATUE, PLYMOUTH, MASSACHUSETTS, 1998

There is a new prosperity among a handful of tribes, including the Pequots just to the west, and among many of the others, there's a new sense of pride and a renewed commitment that they bring to the fight. But it makes them angry that it won't go away. In New England especially, the Day of Mourning has turned into rage, fueled by history and the modern disappointments that have yet to be resolved.

BETTY MAE JUMPER, FORMER SEMINOLE TRIBAL CHAIRMAN,
SEMINOLE RESERVATION, HOLLYWOOD, FLORIDA, 1998

CHAPTER EIGHT

Seminole Winds

THE INDIAN COMMUNITIES are scattered through the swamps—from the saw-grass country in the southern Everglades to the cypress groves along the Tamiami Trail, then north to the shores of Lake Okeechobee. There, the marsh gives way to a prairie, and the cattle herds gather on a summer afternoon, seeking shelter in the meager shade of the palms.

For Ted Underwood, there is something elemental about this place—this peninsula where his people have managed to survive. Underwood is a Seminole from Oklahoma, an activist who came of age in the seventies and was willing, in those days, to take up a gun. With his fellow Oklahoman Tom Ahaisse, he joined the American Indian Movement and gathered supplies for his brothers at the Battle of Wounded Knee.

The bitter symbolism was nearly overwhelming—militants in 1973 digging in at the site of the terrifying massacre, where the Indian holocaust of the nineteenth century had finally come to an end. Then Congress took over where the cavalry left off, passing a stream of insidious legislation to make the native people disappear—to make them give up the land that they held in common and fade away quietly into the mainstream created by the whites.

For Underwood and thousands of other young Native Americans, AIM was the antidote to those policies. It represented a demand for civil rights and the freedom from bigotry that other American minorities were seeking. But there was another dimension to the struggle also—a proclamation, when they picked up the gun, that the culture of the native people wouldn't die. Their tactics began to change over time. The briefcase took the place of the rifle, but the passion was the same—the vision that was slowly taking shape in their minds of a day when the Indians would rise up together, overcoming the divisions that history had imposed.

At the very least, it was Underwood's hope for the Seminole Nation. He understood the factions that developed over time, for he knew the story of the Seminole people, how they had fought three wars with the United States government without ever signing a treaty of surrender. Nine different commanders were sent in to fight them, and the worst part came in the 1830s, when Andrew Jackson was the president and was determined to move the Seminoles to Oklahoma. They were able to mount a resistance in the swamps, which had long been a haven for the runaway people. For more than a century, the remnant survivors all the way to Carolina had made their way to the Everglades country. Yamassees, Yucis, Oconees, Creeks, and even a trickle of runaway slaves had joined the indigenous people of Florida and were determined now to hold onto the land. They were skillful fighters led by Micanopy, Osceola, and Jumper and inspired by the medicine man Arpeika.

But eventually, of course, it began to go badly. With forty thousand troops and $20 million to spend on the war, the Americans were winning the battle of attrition. In October 1837, they captured Osceola, the renegade Creek born in Alabama who was known for his ego as well as his courage. Some say he had finally grown weary of the fight and was ready to work out a deal with the whites. Whatever the case, he was captured just south of St. Augustine, taken ignobly by the United States Army despite the protection of a white flag of truce. It was an act of treachery that made him a hero even in Charleston, South Carolina, where he was sent as a prisoner. He died in 1838 from a throat infection compli-

cated by malaria, and the attending physician, Dr. Frederick Weedon, cut off his head and kept it for a while as his own souvenir.

Meanwhile, in Florida, the fighting continued, and the majority of Seminoles were defeated. They were eventually captured and shipped to the West, where they arrived with nothing and had to adjust, to rebuild their society in a land where the winds blew cold in the winter. Even the medicine men were confused. The healing herbs didn't grow in Oklahoma, and almost nothing seemed to be the same. But they stayed together on land just west of the Cherokees and Creeks, who had also lived through the Trail of Tears, and just east of the Chickasaws and Comanches.

Back in Florida, there were a handful of holdouts who retreated so deeply in the sawgrass country—the land of the alligator and the panther—that the United States Army finally gave up the search. There was another brief skirmish in the 1850s, followed by a curious period of reprieve. It was as if the Indians had suddenly gone back in time—to an era when the white people left them alone. There are Seminoles today who can still remember their first encounter—perhaps with a trader who came to the swamps to barter for the plumes or the alligator skins. They hunted and fished and lived in chickees made out of thatch until sometime late in the 1920s, when they could feel the world begin to close in around them. The turning point came with the Tamiami Trail, a highway slashing west from Miami, connecting the coasts. The developers began to drain the Everglades for suburbs and farms and warm-weather resorts, and soon the Florida land boom was on.

The Indians did get part of that land, some eighty thousand acres that have since been expanded into seven reservations. But there were very few places to hunt anymore, or to fish in waters that were unpolluted, and by the 1950s, most of them knew that their life had to change. They began to meet near Hollywood, Florida, a committee of leaders, to decide what to do. They gathered most often at the base of an oak—a tree still standing in the 1990s, a shady oasis in the middle of the sprawl. At the time, it was quiet, a place for contemplation and debate, and Betty Mae Jumper, a member of the group, was impressed by the spirit of the Seminole leaders.

"I don't remember any hollering or yelling," she says. "It was all very easy. The hardest part was getting people together."

Betty Mae herself is a symbol of the changes that the tribe had to face. She was raised in a chickee out near the lake, a little girl who knew she was lucky to be alive. Her father was a man she saw only once—a white man who came to visit one day and seemed out of place in the Indian world, where the people would gather at night around the fire and Betty Mae's grandmother, Mary Gopher Tiger, would talk about the legends and the history of the tribe. Betty Mae's mother, Ada Tiger, was a woman of medicine, a tribal midwife who also hunted alligators in the swamp and helped tend a herd of five hundred cattle.

Life wasn't easy back in those days, and even the warmth of the Indian family was disrupted by the superstitions of the people. As Betty Mae remembers it, she was five years old when a group of full bloods came to her family's camp and told them that Betty had to die. She was the evil one, they said. Her Indian blood had been mixed with the whites', and the Seminoles couldn't survive that way. They were few in number, and their ways were sacred, and it was simply unthinkable for the bloodline to fade. But Jimmie Gopher, her grandmother's brother, rejected that talk. He had been a medicine man himself, but he was also a convert, a Christian who knew there were changes in the wind, and in any case, he loved Betty Mae and drove her accusers away with a gun.

Her life was never the same after that. Her family moved closer to Hollywood, Florida, just before the coast was beginning to develop, and as her mother took work on the white people's farms, Betty Mae decided she wanted to go to school. She had met a girl who was reading a book, and Betty Mae was fascinated by the thought—all those symbols that were leaping from the page. She knew she wanted that knowledge for herself, but it was not an easy thing to arrange. The schools in Florida were still segregated, and there were none at all for the Seminole children. She thought about going to school with the blacks, for there was a woman her mother had met in the fields, an African-American who was sure that Betty Mae would be welcome. But she was not.

"She isn't black," the principal explained, and so, eventually, at the age of fourteen, Betty Mae left home for North Carolina and a boarding school run by the BIA. She still spoke "Indian," as she puts it today—both the Miccosukee language of the people to the south and the Muskogee, or Creek, imported by the refugees from Alabama. She also knew a little bit of English, which was the only language permitted at the school, and she proved to be a good student—the first in her tribe to earn a high-school diploma.

After graduation, she moved to Oklahoma, where she studied at the Kiowa Indian Hospital, then came back home to work as a nurse. By now, it was late in the 1940s, and Betty Mae was convinced that it was time for the Seminoles to adjust. It wasn't that she wanted to give up the old ways—not entirely, at least. She came from a line of Seminole healers, and she knew that traditional medicine had a place. But there were children, including one of her sisters, who were dying every day from the white man's diseases, and the medicine men were helpless to prevent it. So she set out on her personal mission of healing—and was threatened more than once at the point of a gun by traditionalists who thought she was leading them astray. But she kept on pushing.

She knew that the road ahead of the Seminoles was hard. They were entering a time when everything was changing—their economy, their medicine, their view of the world—and some of the Seminoles didn't make it.

"We saw suicides," she says, "and people turning to bottles. In the old days, they used to kill the deer and fish and turkeys. They had no money. They would trade furs and alligator skins for grits and coffee and those kinds of staples. It was a very different life."

The amazing thing was that for the majority of the Seminoles in Florida, it lasted well into the twentieth century, and some of them haven't given up on it yet. But Betty Mae was sure that things had to change, and she and the others would gather in the comfortable shade of the oak, talking about what to do. By the late 1950s, they had fashioned a rough blueprint for the future. On August 21, 1957, the tribe adopted a new constitution, and ten years later, Betty Mae was elected tribal chairman, replacing Billy Osceola. In the past, there were women who had played that role, who had emerged as leaders, but in modern times, Betty Mae was the first—a woman of stature in the Indian world who was also respected nationwide. Within the tribe, she followed her predecessor's example and pushed for better education and health care. Outside it, she worked to build coalitions among tribes in the East.

All in all, it was a progressive agenda that the Seminoles followed—independent and bold. Betty Mae's successor was Howard

Tommie, a chairman who believed in "self-determination," as the Indian people often put it in the seventies. They were tired of the control of the BIA and determined to build an economy of their own—a source for the money that they needed to survive. Tommie came forward with a simple idea. As a federally recognized Indian nation, the Seminole Tribe was essentially a government entitled to raise money for the needs of its people without paying taxes to the state of Florida—no more than Florida would pay them to Georgia. The question was how to raise that money, and one of the answers was the white man's vices—not a noble approach, to be sure, but one that proved effective through the years.

They began with smoke shops, bringing in enough money from their bargain cigarettes (as well as other tribal enterprises) to make small cash payments to every member of the tribe. Soon, they began to experiment with bingo. Under Tommie's successor, James Billie, a swashbuckling veteran of Vietnam, they began a high-stakes game that grew into the most profitable component of the Seminoles' economy in the eighties. It was also the most controversial. Within two years, the tribe was bringing in $5 million, and a backlash followed—as it does so often in Indian country at the first sign of progress. Florida decided to enforce its statutes, which restricted bingo to charitable organizations and limited the pots to $250 per session. The Seminoles went

to court, and in October 1981, the United States Circuit Court of Appeals affirmed the sovereignty of the Seminole Tribe and its right to choose its own path to the future.

In the years since then, the Seminoles have expanded their gaming operations, and there are other tribal enterprises as well, ranging from citrus groves to vast cattle herds. Under James Billie, the tribe operates its own departments of construction, recreation, and health, its own libraries and tribal museums. There are cultural preservation efforts also, led by Seminole teachers like Loreen Gopher, who work at every level from Head Start to high school to teach the Seminole language to the children.

"We are paddling upstream as fast as we can," says Patricia Wickman, an ethnohistorian who works for the tribe. Wickman knows that the job isn't easy—preserving traditions and culture when the world around them is changing all the time. But the Seminoles are "quick learners," she says, and under James Billie, they are beginning to achieve a level of prosperity that they dreamed about more than forty years ago.

Sitting in the shade of the great council oak, they used to imagine, perhaps half-seriously, a day that would come sometime in the future when there would be Seminoles who were driving Cadillacs. That day has arrived, says Betty Mae Jumper—with some BMWs thrown in as well. But there are people who see a downside to the story. The tribal newspaper, the *Seminole Tribune*, reported in the autumn of 1997 on a meeting at Big Cypress, one of the Seminole reservations. Parents were worried about a new form of predator—the drug dealers who descended on their children, particularly, it seemed, on the days when the dividend payments were made. When the tribal enterprises first showed a profit, the dividend for every Seminole was a check for three hundred dollars twice a year. By 1997, those payments had increased to two thousand dollars a month, and some parents were worried about the effects. Melissa Sanders, a mother of three, said she often saw the dealers trying to flag down cars on dividend day. In addition to that, there were children who decided to drop out of school. Why study, after all, when their future was assured? Some people argued that the dividend payments ought to be tied to classroom attendance, but whatever the solution, it was clear that this was a new kind of problem.

Lottie Huff can feel it in her bones. She runs a gift shop on the Brighton Reservation, selling Seminole dresses and palmetto dolls, mostly to the tourists who wander in and out. Behind her shop, she has set up a camp—a collection of chickees made out of cypress, exactly like those in which she was raised. As a child, she lived in the saw-grass country, where almost everybody spoke Miccosukee, and she misses those days of extended family—the people gathering together in the camps, telling their stories at night around the fire. She knows that things are better in some ways. She wouldn't trade her house for the palmetto thatch and the mosquitoes buzzing just beyond the nets, but she knows that many of the changes were imposed. There weren't enough animals for the hunt anymore.

But if she has made her adjustments like everybody else, there are days when she allows herself to remember—when she goes to the chickees out in the yard and cooks her meals at the center of the camp, just as her family did when she was a girl. She also speaks in the Indian tongue—to her husband and neighbors, and her grandchildren, too, if they show any interest. But she is afraid that someday the language will die.

"First the language," she says, "and then the blood. I don't like the way the young people are going."

There are too many, she says, who are battling with drugs, and too many more who forget who they are. Not completely, perhaps, but their struggle is real, and so she worries about the years just ahead. It is true that her people have done better than most. They have had strong leaders, and the culture isn't dead, and there are people, in fact, trying to keep it alive. But there is also a sadness that flickers in her eyes.

With everything they have gained, there is also a loss, and they have to wonder sometimes if it's worth it.

LOTTIE HUFF, SEMINOLE DOLLMAKER AND SEAMSTRESS,
BRIGHTON RESERVATION, FLORIDA, 1998

Buffalo Tiger saw the whole thing coming—these dilemmas that the Indian people would face. As a boy, he lived just west of Miami in the Everglades country, where they kept to themselves. "When I was a little guy," he says, "we were afraid of the white-skinned people. They had guns." But as a man, he knew they couldn't be avoided, which made him angry sometimes. He saw what they did, all the devastations they brought on the land, all the changes they wanted to impose, and sometime late in the 1950s, he set out on a personal mission of resistance. He became a spokesman for the Miccosukee people, the traditionalists living in the southern Everglades who hunted and fished in the River of Grass and wanted nothing more than to be left alone. They were skeptical of many of the Seminole leaders, who were adjusting their ways too quickly to the whites, and in the 1960s, they asked for separate recognition as a tribe. The BIA resisted them at first, but Buffalo Tiger came up with a plan. In 1961, he flew to Cuba with other members of his group and asked for diplomatic recognition from Castro. The Cuban leader was warm and sympathetic, and Buffalo Tiger was able to use that leverage to receive his acknowledgment from the BIA.

His purpose from the start was to preserve what he could of the Indian way, of the Breathmaker's vision for living with the land, and as the elected leader of the Miccosukee people, he gave it his best. But it appears that the years have left him disillusioned. The Everglades' waters are no longer clean, and the minds of the Indian people also have been seduced and polluted by a new set of values. But what could they do? It wasn't that most of them gave in completely. They still spoke the language and knew who they were, but it was simply impossible to live as they had. There was not enough land anymore to support them.

That, at least, was the way Tiger saw it, and he tried to find someplace in between. Still fiercely independent, his tribe was one of the first in the country to contract with the United States government to operate its own reservation school. The money still came from the BIA, but the Miccosukees were the people in control, a pattern that has become more common nationwide. They built new housing along the Tamiami Trail, slowly but surely replacing the chickees, and many of the four hundred members of the tribe, including Tiger himself, gave up hunting and fishing for a living and began to seek other ways. Some of them have gone to work for the tribe, which generates money from its bingo hall and a handful of other more modest enterprises. Others make baskets or patchwork dresses or have experimented as entrepreneurs, wrestling alligators or running airboat tours in the swamp.

Buffalo Tiger has chosen that course. In the spring and summer, his airboat company is open every day, taking the tourists from the

BUFFALO TIGER, FORMER MICCOSUKEE TRIBAL CHAIRMAN,
MICCOSUKEE RESERVATION, FLORIDA, 1998

Tamiami Trail through the saw grass stretching as far as you can see. There are still the alligators swimming in the shallows—a mother and her babies, a young male who paddles toward the boat—and out in the distance, there's an Indian hammock, a small rise in the land where a family of Miccosukees once lived in a camp. The sagging chickees have now been abandoned and serve as a home to a family of raccoons, who have learned that the tourists will toss them some bread.

Sometimes, Buffalo Tiger will come here alone, or he will guide his boat even deeper through the swamps and cut the engine and let it drift in the wind. "I know the Glades pretty well," he says. "I like to come here and think." He is worried these days about the River of Grass, the polluted waters and the mutilating force of the white man's development, and on behalf of his people, he is worried about the compromises they have made. Every departure from the old ways comes with a price, played out in the social problems of the tribe—especially the young people struggling with the drugs.

"They tell us to go to school," he says, speaking in English, a language that's still a distant second to his own. "They say, 'Learn, protect yourself.' But the minute you go to school, you think like a white man. Traditional feelings and traditional learnings are walking away from us. That says so much. That says everything."

Now pushing eighty, Buffalo Tiger knows that he, too, is different than he was. He drives a car and lives in a house, and his airboats roar through shimmering grass.

But even if all this is true, he says with a shrug and a glimmer of defiance still in his eyes, "I will not walk away from my heart."

As the twentieth century draws to a close, Buffalo Tiger is not alone in that vow—there are others, in fact, whose commitment seems to be more complete. Bobby C. Billie is a medicine man, part of a line going back to the wars and the holy man Arpeika, who stirred the Seminole troops with his words and refused to compromise with the whites. Coming of age in the 1950s, Billie heard the stories about how it was, an oral tradition passed along in the camps. There were memories that each generation preserved—of flights from the soldiers in the heart of the swamp, and chilly nights on the hammocks without any fire, and the crying baby that had to be drowned when the white man's army was passing nearby.

It was easy enough for a young boy to envision, for even in the middle of the twentieth century, his family still lived in the Seminole way, in a tiny village hidden deep in the marsh—a peaceful place until the night the white men came with their guns. As Billie remembers it, it was almost dawn, and he was a boy of no more than eleven when the drunken hunters stumbled into the camp. The Seminole men were away at their jobs, working in

BOBBY C. BILLIE, SEMINOLE MEDICINE MAN, EVERGLADES CAMP, 1998

the fields or on the crews building roads, and when the shooting began—perhaps out of sport—the women and children had to run for their lives. Billie says the bullets were splashing at their heels, and the only thing a boy could conclude at the time was that the white men were crazy. Certainly, they had no respect for the Indians, who wanted only to be left alone.

In many ways, that is still Billie's desire. He is part of a community of traditional Seminoles who have built their village in the western Everglades. Their chickees are made out of cypress and thatch, and they live as independently as they can. Officially and politically, they are not Miccosukees or members of the Seminole Tribe of Florida. They have never sought recognition from the federal government, nor are they willing to accept any money. They call themselves the Independent Traditional Seminole Nation, and Bobby C. Billie is their spiritual leader. He says there are fewer than two hundred people who have chosen the path of Seminole tradition, a way of living that assumes that human beings— Indian, white, and any other kind—are the caretakers, not the masters, of the world, which is far more fragile than many of them think. The alternative point of view, he believes, is the path of ecological disaster, the beginnings of which he can see all around.

In the early nineties, he met Shannon Larsen, a white Floridian and environmental activist who was struck, she says, by the power and the eloquence of Billie's understanding. He would talk about the ancient Seminole ways— how the elders would apologize to the cypress whenever they had to cut it for their homes, and to the deer and the fish that they took for their food. His English most often was broken and frayed. He was almost forty when he began to learn it, and even then, he wouldn't learn to read.

"Our elders," he says, "told us not to touch the papers and the pens. They would slap our hands."

Some people, of course, think that is archaic. The traditional Seminoles are like the Ghost Dancers—the Paiutes and Lakotas of the nineteenth century who proclaimed that the son of God had returned, bringing a new dance to the Indian people. It was one that would summon the ancestors' spirits and usher in a time when the earth, treated so badly by the whites, would be made whole. No wars of resistance would be required this time, no shedding of blood, just the dancing to proclaim that the spirits were alive.

Whatever the parallel to those times, this much is clear: In the mystic vision of Bobby C. Billie, the Seminole people have a message for the world. The time has come to pay attention to the earth, to pray for the birds and the rivers and the grass, and to understand that everything is connected. It is a message he preaches wherever he can, a crusade of sorts that sends him often to the white man's world. But he comes back home whenever he is able, and slips away in the dugout canoe beneath the canopy of cypress growing by the creek. There, he thinks about many things, including the Seminole people in the past, who were slaughtered and desecrated in their graves.

According to some estimates, more than six hundred thousand Indian remains have been assembled for public display nationwide, an affront in the eyes of Native Americans that they have only recently been able to address. Billie has been a part of that attempt, and it was heartening to discover that he was not alone. From the tip of Florida all the way to Alaska, Indians have rallied around a recent act of Congress, the Native American Graves Protection and Repatriation Act (NAGPRA), which required, beginning in 1990, an inventory of human remains by every federally funded museum or university—and the return of those remains to the tribes.

In 1995, Billie met with the Seminoles of Oklahoma—including Ted Underwood, the former activist and member of AIM—to talk about the issue of repatriation. The Oklahomans had respect for their brothers in Florida. One official in the tribe, Alan Emarthle, had been visiting those reservations with his father, and every time, it felt like home. He and Underwood and their friend Tom Ahaisse were impressed by the legacy of economic progress amassed through the years by the Seminole leaders, and they were impressed also by the eloquent traditionalism of Bobby C. Billie. Since their activist days in the 1970s, Ahaisse

and Underwood had dreamed of a time when the Seminole people would finally come together. There had been some difficult issues through the years—chief among them a land-claim settlement offered in 1976 to compensate the tribe for lands that were taken in the 1830s. It was an important moment for the Seminole people, but it would take them another fourteen years to agree on how to divide up the money. How much for the Seminoles in Florida? The Miccosukees? And how much for Oklahoma?

And even when those questions were resolved, there were other divisions that were equally hard—divergent ideologies among the Seminole leaders and a range of different understandings of the future. But in the end, of course, they were all Seminoles—all heirs to the warriors of the 1830s who had fought so bravely to hold onto the land or to rebuild a nation in the hills of Oklahoma.

In Underwood's mind, the symbol that brought them together was a skull—the remains of a warrior who died at Fort Drane, an important battle in the Seminole War, in which the most debilitating enemy was malaria. Nobody knew how the warrior had died—or even for sure if that's what he was. But over the years, the cranial fragment, which was clearly an Indian's excavated at the fort, had made its way to Harvard University. The Seminoles decided it was time to bring it home.

Underwood thought the decision was historic.

For the first time since the wars of the nineteenth century, the Seminoles had gathered together as one—every part of the tribe, meeting near the Miccosukee Reservation. On December 9, 1997, they assembled in the spreading shade of an oak, as had long been their custom, and they talked about the reason why the issue was important. As Billie and Underwood understood it, the whites had set out to take away the land—to sweep the Indian people from the surface. But their roots and their bones were still underground, and now the whites were taking those, too, excavating the Indian remains to feed their voracious appetite for development. There were scholars and scientists who were part of it also, many of them good and well-intentioned people who saw value in a better understanding of the past, in searching through the mysteries concealed in the graves. But to Underwood, it was a matter of respect. If the Indian people were to dig through a place where the white men were buried—perhaps the national cemetery in Virginia—nobody would dare to defend that intrusion. Were the Native Americans really any different? Were their ancestors any less entitled to their peace?

Underwood is sure that the answer is no, and he is sure also that the question of respect for the Seminole dead is an issue that resonates with the people. It is essential, he thinks, to hold onto the past, for it is easy for the Indians to be blown off course in a world that many of them might not have chosen.

If they can only manage to remember that danger, they might find their way in the century just ahead. Certainly, the tools of leadership are there, and the heritage, too, if they can keep it alive. They are, after all, the unconquered people, who never found reason to surrender in the past. Perhaps they can profit from each other's wisdom—the adaptability of the tribal chairmen from Betty Mae Jumper to the men who followed, and the militant traditionalism of Bobby Billie.

Somewhere in the mix, there is the lingering hope that the Seminoles' finest days are still ahead.

CHAPTER NINE

The Pride of the Lumbees

SHE REMEMBERS THE FISHING TRIPS by the river, when the old man always seemed so serene. They would settle in on the bank, where the black waters swirled past the cypress trees and the great blue herons waded in the shallows, and sometimes they would talk. He would tell her of the prophecy his grandmother gave him, a spiritual gift handed down for generations, going back to the days before the white men came and mingled their blood with that of the Lumbees. Like most of his people, the old man was a Christian. He worshiped every week at a little Baptist church, where the people were touched and moved by the spirit. But Vernon Cooper believed—in fact, he was certain—that there was something in the soul of the Lumbee people, something more ancient than imported Christianity, at least among those who were willing to believe.

His grandmother had been the first to explain it. When he was eleven, she told him of the wisdom that had been handed down—the gift of healing that ran in the family, through generations reaching to the fifteenth century—

and she said that one day, he would possess it. As the years went by, Vernon knew it was true. There were herbs in the ground to cure any ailment, if the white man's pesticides didn't kill them, and there was also the power of the human touch. He could feel the fever sometimes in his fingers, and the jolt of pain almost like a shock, as he laid his hands on the people who came.

One of those people was Daystar Dial, a troubled young woman who was barely eighteen, newly married with a child, grieving over the recent death of her father. She had never met Vernon Cooper, but something in a dream had told her it was time, and as they began their fishing trips to the river, she found herself on a journey of discovery that led her, she says, to her Indian past. There was a time when she might have been tempted to deny it. Coming of age in the 1960s in the rich coastal farmlands of North Carolina, where the tobacco fields gave way to the swamps, she understood the sting of segregation and prejudice. But there was also a comfort she

DAYSTAR DIAL, TRADITIONAL LUMBEE HEALER,
PEMBROKE, NORTH CAROLINA, 1997

felt in that place. She was surrounded everywhere by extended family—cousins, grandparents, uncles, and aunts—whose identity was tied to each other and the land. They grew their tobacco in long, flat rows, and some of them worked at the meat-processing plant, turning turkey into cold cuts, and even those who moved away for better jobs—to Baltimore and other cities to the north—came home when they could. Later, she knew it was an Indian thing, this homing instinct that brought them back. She remembered the words of Vine Deloria, the great Sioux author, who argued that the core of Indian identity was an instinctive attachment to a people and a place.

In Daystar's case, the attachment was enriched by the spiritual powers of her friend Vernon Cooper, and later by the people she encountered in her job. She was assistant curator at the Native American Resource Center, a museum at the University of North Carolina at Pembroke, and she loved the art of the Lumbee people—the acrylic paintings of her cousin Karl Hunt and the pine-needle baskets of Loretta Oxendine, made in the traditional Lumbee style. But perhaps as striking as any of these were the hardwood carvings of Bernice Locklear.

The Lumbees have always worked with wood, functional items as much as anything else—bread pans carved from tupelo gum, much like those of other eastern tribes. Locklear's work was a little bit different. He had picked up the chisel maybe six years ear-lier and had begun to produce his impressionistic pieces—a mixture of styles, part Picasso, part Native American. His mother made quilts, and his father was always good with his hands, and Bernice set out to preserve that tradition with carvings that sprang from the struggles of his people. His walnut statue *A Cry for Hope* was done for the Lumbee children, he said, in an era when some of them were drifting into drugs or were confused by what it meant to be an Indian. Another of his pieces, *Canoe Water Spirit*, was a warning against the persistent abuses of the earth, and still others were intended as a tribute to God, creator of the land and the Lumbee people.

As far as Daystar Dial was concerned, there was an Indian spirit that lived in the work, a pride in the native identity of her people. She knew, however, that not everyone felt it. Bernice Locklear told the story of his teenage daughter, who declared one day that she and her family were not real Indians because, she said, "we don't wear feathers."

It's a point of view heard often among those outside of the Lumbee community—particularly from the Cherokees to the west and the office of Senator Jesse Helms. The Cherokees and Helms have led the fight against tribal recognition, an official acknowledgment from the United States government that the Lumbees, in the end, are like the Navajos and Sioux—Indians in the fullest sense of the word. The doubters point out that the Lumbees generally are a mixed-blood people lacking the outward symbols of identity. They speak no language other than English and wear the same kinds of clothes as their neighbors. Most of their religious ceremonies are Christian, and if many of the people clearly look like Indians, with jet-black hair and dark, olive skin, there are some whose hair is brown or even blond.

Like most other Lumbees, Daystar Dial disagrees with those who question her identity, mainly because she has no doubts. She has emerged near the close of the twentieth century as a Lumbee healer, heir to the wisdom of Vernon Cooper and respected by those familiar with her quest. She knows that her story is not unique, her journey of discovery that she shares with others of her own generation—with the Lumbee scholar Linda Oxendine and community organizer Donna Chavis, and lawyers Dale Deese and Arlinda Locklear, and artists Karl Hunt and Michael Wilkins. These are people in their thirties and forties, some a little older, who represent a bridge to the past. They have connected through the years with other native people—the Mohawks, Apaches, Lakotas, and Cheyennes, even the Hulchols in southern Mexico. But they've been inspired also by their Lumbee elders. In Daystar's case, it began with her grandmother Ester Dial, who taught her how to fish and tell time by the sun and revere the troubled history of her people.

It is a powerful story, the grandmother said, full of struggle and triumph, and it continues along those same paths today. Some of it is lost in the mists of antiquity, but much of it is clear—handed down not only in the history books but in the stories that Lumbees tell to each other.

Some people say the story first started to assume its shape in the autumn of 1587. According to the Lumbees' oral tradition, the remnants of several native tribes from the coast made their way over time to the fertile swamplands of what is now Robeson County, where the game was abundant, the dark river waters teemed with fish, and the corn crop flourished in the long summer season. According to the legend, there were others who had mingled with the Indian people—survivors from an early expedition of whites who had settled on the coast at Roanoke Island. They arrived too late for the planting of corn and were about to starve when the natives took them in.

Historians have debated the truth of that story, but this much is clear. In 1587, the English soldier and poet Walter Raleigh sent forth a group of about 120 people—including 9 boys and 17 women—to establish a permanent colony for the queen. They arrived in the summer and ran low on supplies, and as their situation became more desperate, their leader, John White, went to England for more. His return was delayed by the Spanish Armada, and when he finally made it back nearly three years later, he discovered that all of the colonists were missing. They had built a fort, which now stood empty and had the single word CROATOAN carved near the gate. White was encouraged by that enigmatic sign. Croatoan was a place where the Indians were friendly, and though he never located his people, he set sail for England assuming they were safe.

In the years after that, stories began to circulate along the coast of Indians who spoke in the white man's tongue and had gray eyes and lived in cabins much like the English. Then, sometime around 1730, Scottish settlers trickled into the area and were astonished to discover upon their arrival that many of the Indians who had settled in the swamps spoke in a peculiar dialect of English. They farmed like the British and lived in houses but retained their Indian ways also—holding their land, for example, in common. They abandoned that practice only when they had to—when the new arrivals began to carve up the land, claiming vast pieces of the earth for themselves. The Indians adapted to the white man's practice, filing individual claims of their own, but they remained in their minds a people set apart. Some of them fought in the newcomers' wars, and voted in elections when the day finally came. But as Indian people, it was never their intention to simply disappear, melting away into the white man's world—and the time soon arrived when they couldn't have even if they tried.

After almost a century of peace, attitudes changed in North Carolina. For people not white, the 1830s were a terrifying time. The tribes to the west—the Cherokees, Choctaws, Chickasaws, and Creeks—were ripped from the lands they had occupied for generations, and while the Indians in the swamps of Robeson County were unobtrusive enough to escape that fate, they could feel their status begin to slip away. When the slave Nat Turner launched his rebellion in 1831, killing sixty white Virginians before he was through, the wave of fear that swept through the South quickly hardened to a new kind of hate. Four years later, at a constitutional convention in North Carolina, the delegates agreed on a sweeping assumption. "This," they declared, "is a nation of white people."

For 135 years after that—some would say even longer—the Lumbees would feel the pain of that view. The Civil War was the worst. The Confederate States conscripted the Indians against their will to help build their forts. Many of the Lumbees retreated to the swamps, where they made common cause with runaway slaves and Union prisoners who had managed to escape. In the eruption of guerrilla warfare that followed, the Lumbees found a leader to admire—a handsome teenager with flashing eyes and a heart full of rage. According to the stories handed down in the tribe, Henry Berry Lowry had seen his father and his brother both killed—both forced to watch while their grave was dug by a Negro slave. Henry Berry vowed to exact his revenge, and

REEDY CHAVIS, GRANDDAUGHTER OF LUMBEE HERO HENRY BERRY LOWRY,
WITH HER GRANDDAUGHTER, SHANNON AHLFELDT,
ROBESON COUNTY, NORTH CAROLINA, 1997

for the next ten years, he and his band of a dozen young men—nine Lumbees, two blacks, and a white—staged their deadly raids from the swamps. To the whites who lived in Robeson County, Lowry was merely a bushwhacker and a bandit, killing from ambush and then retreating to his hideout deep in the bush. But to the Indians, he became a folk hero, a fighter in the war against the white man's oppression.

His only living granddaughter, Reedy Chavis, who was born shortly after the turn of the century, remembers the stories handed down by her mother. "I don't think much about it until somebody comes around and starts rooting it up," she says, "but my mother well remembered her daddy. She said it was no scandal, no disgrace. He was forced to do what he did. That was one way to get a fight out of her, if you said something you shouldn't about Henry Berry Lowry."

Throughout the Lumbee community, in fact, there's the same fierce pride in a legacy of resistance that grew even stronger in the twentieth century. Sanford Locklear says it was crucial. Born in 1933, he came of age in the era of segregation. He is a strong-willed man who worked as a farmer and later as the foreman of a dry-wall crew, and though he was proud of being an Indian, he understood the limitations of his status. There were places where he and his people couldn't go—local restaurants that refused to serve them, except perhaps at a window on the side.

"So we'd go to the window," he says with a shrug. "It was hurtful, but you had to do it."

But the Lumbees decided to draw the line when the Klan paid a visit to Robeson County. On January 13, 1958, crosses were burned at the homes of two Indians—retribution, apparently, for crossing the invisible lines of segregation—and a Klan leader by the name of Catfish Cole announced plans for a rally in the community of Maxton. Locklear and others decided to stop it. They talked about it first at a barbershop, and somebody suggested that they storm the meeting with guns and gasoline and a torch and burn every Klansman in the county to a crisp.

Locklear argued for a little more restraint. "I said, 'Just take our guns and tell 'em to leave,'" he remembers, which is what the Lumbees eventually decided to do.

They gathered at dusk on a Saturday night. It was bitterly cold as the Klansmen were making preparations in a field—setting up a speaker's stand, a mike, a single light bulb at the end of a cord, and a record player that was blaring Christian songs. As Locklear remembers it, he approached the person who seemed to be in charge, a skinny-looking man in khaki trousers with a look of fear and defiance in his eyes.

"I said, 'What are you-all here for?' and the guy says to me, 'We're having a meeting.' I said, 'You're not gon' have no meeting here tonight,' and then I slapped him, and my brother-in-law shot out the light."

GRANDSONS OF SANFORD LOCKLEAR, LUMBEE LEADER OF
1958 RAID AGAINST KU KLUX KLAN, ROBESON COUNTY, NORTH CAROLINA, 1997

With the blast from Neil Lowry's .22, the scene erupted into pure pandemonium. There were maybe three hundred Indians and only a handful of Klansmen, and as the Lumbees fired their weapons in the air—shotguns, rifles, whatever they had—the Kluxers made a howling dash for the trees. The Indians ripped the robes off those they could catch and turned over cars and seized Klan weapons, which they gave to police. Remarkably enough, nobody was killed, but in the minds of nearly everybody who was there, the message was clear. The Klan was not welcome in Robeson County, and the Indians were not afraid of anybody.

Locklear says he was much too angry to feel any fear. He was thinking of his wife and the baby she had begun to carry in her womb. He wanted something better for his child to inherit—a world more just than the one he had known—and he is pleased today that things have improved. He is careful, of course, not to take all the credit. The work of Martin Luther King, he says, profoundly altered the moral climate of the day, touching the hearts of his neighbors who were white and giving greater courage to those who were not. But Locklear believes that the Lumbees also have a right to feel proud. In addition to their hundred-year history of resistance—their refusal in the end to back away from a fight—they set about the task of building a community.

A major university was the cornerstone of it—a school that opened in 1887 as a place for the training of Lumbee teachers. It evolved through the years into the University of North Carolina at Pembroke, with a student body that included all races, but its Indian origins were still at its heart. More than a hundred years from its founding, a quarter of its students were Native Americans, who had at their disposal not only a traditional academic curriculum but a major in Native American studies. Under the leadership of Linda Oxendine, a Lumbee educator and writer, there were classes in Indian history and art, in archaeology and contemporary issues, and in the 1990s, hundreds of young Indians were studying their culture, searching for roots, for a deeper understanding of their own native past.

But in many ways, the role of the college has been more basic. Over the years, it has trained generations of Lumbee professionals— doctors, lawyers, and members of the clergy, politicians, teachers, and entrepreneurs—many of whom have remained in the county.

"We are problem solvers," declares Bruce Barton, a Lumbee teacher and newspaperman. "We have taken our frustrations and, as much as any Indian group in the country, we have parlayed those into a drive to succeed."

The tribal chairman, Dalton Brooks, agrees. He tells the story of the Lumbee Bank, founded in 1971, the first and oldest Indian bank in the country. It was a reflection, in a way, of an old tribal habit—Lumbees who had managed to save a little money loaning to those who might have a need. Dalton Brooks's own brother, Martin, was a struggling young doctor in Robeson County and was working one day to remodel his office when a Lumbee man, barefoot and ragged, came by on his bike with five thousand dollars.

"Pay me back when you can," the old man said. "I see you're gettin' started."

In the eyes of Dalton Brooks and others, it was, in effect, a banking structure based on trust, and when the Lumbees decided to make it official, they sold bank shares for five dollars each—a price that nearly anybody could afford. They raised a total of three hundred thousand dollars, most of it in cash, and according to a story circulated in the tribe, one of the directors took it home in a bag and kept it there until the bank finally opened. Nobody raised any questions about it. It was simply the Lumbees' way of doing business.

Connee Brayboy, a Lumbee editor, argues that in the midst of their adversity and triumph, her people have developed a strong sense of community, a tribalism running deep in their bones. "There are other cultures," she says, "other ways to survive. I think ours is the best."

But she also admits that even those who feel most proud can see there are difficult days still ahead, problems that linger in the Indian community—and a maddening refusal in the outside world to acknowledge that the Lumbees are Indians at all.

Michael Wilkins's anger is there in the wood, a piece of walnut polished to a shine. His carving took shape when he heard the news—the word out of Washington that the Lumbees again had been turned down in their quest for federal recognition as a tribe. It is a struggle that began in the 1880s and has continued off and on for more than a century. There was a flicker of hope in 1956, when Congress in fact did pass a bill affirming that the Lumbees were Native Americans. But in the last paragraph, the lawmakers stamped the tribe with an asterisk—declaring that, in contrast to most other Indians, the Lumbees were ineligible for federal programs.

Michael Wilkins, among many others, never worried very much about the money—the government dollars that went to other tribes. As an Indian artist who came of age in the 1970s, during a period of militancy that swept through native communities nationwide, he simply took offense at the government's presumption. He worried about the message handed down to the children, including his own, concerning the nature of their Indian identity. Were they Native Americans or were they not? He knew, of course, that it was silly to care, to get caught up in the government's hedgings, when most Lumbees knew exactly who they were. But the affront somehow seemed to be so stark, so thoroughly outrageous and unprovoked, that he was grateful for the fact that the tribe's best leaders refused to accept it.

The Lumbee Regional Development Association, a nonprofit corporation that began its life in the 1960s, started preparations to raise the issue of recognition once again. Working with genealogists, archaeologists, and a battery of lawyers, it prepared a petition of five hundred pages with that much more in supporting information and submitted the material to the BIA. One of the lawyers was Arlinda Locklear, a Lumbee graduate of Duke University who had worked on the recognition of other tribes, mostly in the East, and had won other cases for tribes in the West. She knew the Lumbees' case was compelling. They were clearly a people of Indian descent who had lived on the same piece of land since long before the coming of the European settlers. That much, essentially, was beyond all dispute. The Lumbees' disadvantage was simple. They were the largest Indian tribe in the East—forty thousand people in Robeson County and another ten thousand scattered all the way from Charlotte to Baltimore. Full recognition would entitle them inevitably to federal Indian programs and services at a time when the national budget was shrinking.

It was no real surprise when the Bureau of Indian Affairs turned them down. Officials there understood the realities, and in 1989, more than a hundred years after the struggle began, the BIA threw the issue to Congress. Congress immediately tried to throw it back. In 1992, the Republican Senate, deferring to the leadership of Jesse Helms, refused to recognize the Lumbees, and two years later, the legislation never even made it to the floor.

When word reached the people of Robeson County, Michael Wilkins was working on a carving. He had found a piece of black walnut wood, and he was chiseling out an Indian wrapped in a blanket, a look of pride and sadness in the eyes. Wilkins thought for a while about the news out of Congress, and as his feelings of rage began to take hold, he decided to make the blanket into a flag, turned upside down in a symbol of distress. On the backside of his piece, *The Shadow Dweller*, he carved out a delicate row of feathers recalling the verse from the Ninety-first Psalm: "Beneath His wings you will find refuge."

Wilkins often thought about things that way. Like most Lumbees, he was deeply Christian. He went to church on Sundays and listened to the preaching, and often there was gospel singing in the evening that spilled from the sanctuaries to the corners and the parking lots outside. But there was another expression of his faith also. For many years now, he had practiced the ancient Indian ceremonies—the smudge-pot rituals he had learned from other tribes. These things were part of his Indian identity, a passion going back to his teenage years—to the day, he says, when he first heard a drum. His scoutmaster, a Chippewa-Cree, had taken him to a Haliwa-Saponi powwow, and Michael was drawn to the rhythm and regalia, the chanting and the dances that called up emotions he didn't know he had. He became an activist in the years after that, marching on the White House in the 1970s and wishing he could be at Wounded Knee, where the Indians faced off against the FBI.

But there was plenty going on in Lumbee country. There were issues of political power and the environment, and toxic-waste dumps proposed for the area, and questions of police brutality and justice. For a while in the seventies, national leaders were streaming through the county—people like Dennis Banks, whose American Indian Movement was perhaps the most militant organization of its time, tapping the anger that existed in the country, the pride of Indian people nationwide.

Donna Chavis remembers those days. In the 1970s, she was a Lumbee who understood her own roots—a dark-haired woman still in her teens who was raised, she explains, at her grandfather's knee. The old man, Zimmy Chavis, was born shortly after the Civil War. He ran a country store in Robeson County and preached in the Indian churches on Sunday, sometimes walking from one to another— from the city of Fayetteville, just to the north, all the way to Georgia, where some Lumbees had gone in search of better jobs. But preaching was only one part of his gift. He was also a healer in the old-fashioned way, working with herbs and the power of his touch, and people came to him from all over the county. Donna herself had to turn to him once—actually more than that, she says, but one occasion stands out above the rest. She was in a

car wreck at the age of seventeen, and it left her with massive and terrifying headaches. But then one day, her grandfather took her head in his hands, and she could feel her pain disappear at his touch, never to return.

It was one of life's mysteries she never forgot, a reminder of the spiritualism of her people. Then as now, she regarded the world as the Creator's church, and the struggles of the Indian people to improve it were doomed to fail without that basic understanding at the core. It was hard sometimes to remember that fact. The Indian movement that took shape in the seventies was like many others—a blur of controversy and pain interspersed with occasional moments of triumph—and in Robeson County, the emotions only grew stronger with the years.

Donna Chavis was there for it all. With her husband, Mac Legerton, she started the Center for Community Action, a nonprofit agency that fought for social change—combating the creation of toxic-waste dumps and confronting the brutality of local law enforcement. In 1986, an unarmed Lumbee was shot and killed by a deputy sheriff, and a short time later, a black man died of asthma in the jail. In response to those events and others, a Lumbee attorney, Julian Pierce, decided to run for superior-court judge. His campaign galvanized the community, for Pierce was a popular and respected man, and most people thought he was going to win. Instead, he was murdered— gunned down in his home just before the election. The Lumbees voted for him anyway, and he outpolled his opponent, Joe Freeman Britt, a local prosecutor who was widely regarded by the Indians as oppressive.

"We won with a dead man," declared Connee Brayboy, editor of the *Carolina Indian Voice*, and in the years after that, the Lumbees continued to assert their power. By the 1990s, they held a plurality in Robeson County, with more voters than either the whites or the blacks, and they were slowly taking control of the government. The clerk of court was a Lumbee now, and so was the superintendent of schools, but no office was more symbolic than the sheriff's. In 1994, when an Indian, Glenn Maynor, successfully ran for that position, even the churches got into the act. They had seldom been involved in politics before, though they had long been critically important to the people as a source of spiritual comfort and nurture. The Burnt Swamp Baptist Association, an alliance of sixty-five Indian churches, was the oldest institution that the Lumbees had, and just before the election, its leadership invited Glenn Maynor to a meeting. It was quite a scene at Mount Elim Baptist—the sheriff's candidate surrounded by the preachers, who called him forward and anointed him with oil. Such was the urgency that all of them felt. They knew that Maynor, upon his election, would help heal the rift— the corrosive mistrust between the Indian community and the law-enforcement officials of the county.

They also knew that crime was a problem. Some of the Lumbees were drifting into drugs—a reflection of the times and also of the fact that Interstate 95, one of the great drug arteries in the United States, cut a path through the heart of Robeson County. A startling reflection of the new criminality came on the night of July 23, 1993, when the father of basketball star Michael Jordan was murdered on a Robeson County highway.

"The first thing I heard in the Indian community," remembers educator Linda Oxendine, "was, 'I hope it wasn't one of our people'."

But in fact, it was. Larry Demery, a Lumbee teenager, testified later that he and a friend, Daniel Andre Green, had talked all day about robbing somebody. Green had a .38 caliber pistol, and more and more in the past few months, the two of them were drawn to the idea of crime. Sometime after midnight, they found James Jordan sleeping in his car, a shiny, red Lexus that had to be worth more than forty thousand dollars. Jordan stirred as they approached the driver's side of the car, and according to Demery, Green shot him in the chest. The body was found a few days later by a Lumbee fisherman in South Carolina. It was a horrifying sight floating there in the creek. The arms were tangled in the branches of a tree, and the head was raised up out of the water, the face contorted as if the dead man were gasping for air.

Nearly three years later at the trial, when the killers were sentenced to life in prison, Larry Demery's mother testified for her son. She said that when he was ten, his father would threaten him sometimes with a gun, and

KERMIT CHAVIS, LUMBEE GOSPEL MUSICIAN,
ROBESON COUNTY, NORTH CAROLINA, 1997

Larry, in terror, would have to run away. For many Lumbees, it was a graphic reminder that even in the clannish world of the Indians, where the idea of family is a cornerstone of the culture, there are people among whom it is beginning to erode.

Donna Chavis isn't sure what to do about that, though she thinks it is important to keep it in perspective. For every Larry Demery, there are other young Indians who have gone off to college—to Harvard and Stanford, as well as the University of North Carolina at Pembroke. But she knows it is a time of uncertainty and crisis, and despite all the things her people have achieved—the political power and educational attainments—many of the young ones seem to be confused. The denial of federal recognition is part of it. For some of the Lumbees, especially the young, there is a disturbing ambiguity about who they are. Is their heritage something to be proud of, or merely a footnote to set them apart?

Chavis understands that the questions are out there for the Lumbees as much as for any other tribe. The answers, she thinks, are found in the past—in a history of struggle and building for the future, and in the spiritual legacy that has been handed down. The challenge at the end of the twentieth century is to find new ways to keep that legacy alive.

Karl Hunt wants to do what he can. He understands the path Larry Demery chose—and those of other Lumbees gone astray. He has walked those roads himself on occasion—though not in the early stages of his life. Like Donna Chavis, he had a grandfather who showed him the way—a Baptist preacher named Alex Jacobs, who understood the tenets of the Christian faith but believed in the power of the old knowledge, too. There is a reverence Karl feels for the Lumbee community, the bonds of memory that have been handed down and that work like something in the DNA, holding the Lumbee people together. He never thought about it much as a child, never analyzed his feelings of attachment or the simple sensation of being at home. But as soon as he left, he could feel its absence—the starkness of a world that was unfamiliar and sometimes condescending and racist. Partly as a salve for his sudden confusion, his private uncertainty about who he was—and partly as a simple act of hedonism—he began to drink and dabble in drugs, and the problem got worse until the day he sold cocaine to a narc.

Beginning in 1988, he spent seven years in a federal prison. In a way, he was grateful for that opportunity, for the bittersweet chance at salvation that it offered. At first, it was merely a salvation from drugs, a chance to go straight, but in the end, it was more. Behind the cold, gray walls of the Butner penitentiary, he found himself reconnected to his past. It was a change that began when he saw another inmate working on a painting. Fascinated, Karl

KARL HUNT, LUMBEE ARTIST,
ROBESON COUNTY, NORTH CAROLINA, 1997

pulled out a pencil and began to doodle, and he found himself drawing the figure of a chief. "I was just messing around," he says, "but I started drawing, and it just came out."

Soon, he was painting a little every day, and most of his work had an Indian theme. He found a book with pictures of the great native leaders, including Geronimo and Sitting Bull, and he began to wonder about their lives. Geronimo had been in prison also—in places that had to seem alien and cold—and as he stared at the pages and tried to imagine what it must have been like, Karl reflected on his own struggles, too. He had been so eager at first to get away, to join the navy and try to see the world, but he had lost a part of himself on the way. He knew the time had come to get it back, and he knew also that his painting held the key. It carried him back to his grandfather's time, to the sanity and perspective of his own native past, and as soon as his prison term was complete, he says, he knew what to do with his life.

He went back home. Almost immediately, he started working with the children, becoming one of many who were making that effort. He taught art classes at the North Carolina Indian Cultural Center, and he taught the old values on which he was raised. Identity, he says, is still at the heart of self-esteem, and he was pleased to discover that the young ones were curious—far more, he thought, than they had been in the past.

He knows the Lumbees' identity is subtle—invisible to those who are not looking for it. But Karl can see the signs all around. They are there in the face of Lonnie Revels, a Lumbee farmer staring out at his fields at the age of ninety-one and asking God for one more season, one more chance to feel the dirt in his hands. They are present in the work of the Lumbee artists and the spiritual journey of Daystar Dial, and they are clear in the films of Malinda Maynor, a Lumbee producer whose work is focused on the place of her birth.

Maynor had never lived in Robeson County. Instead, she was raised in the city of Durham, where her father, Waltz Maynor, was a professor of math and her mother taught English at North Carolina Central University. But Waltz and Louise wanted their daughter to be born at home, which was the word they used for Robeson County, and when that was accomplished, they held the tiny baby in their arms and gave her a name. Malinda Morningstar, they called her, a confirmation of her Indian heart. They raised her to know she could go anywhere—to Harvard University, where she got her undergraduate degree, and then to Stanford for her master's in film. But in the work that followed, she was drawn inevitably to Indian country, to the rich, flat fields of Robeson County, where the corn grows tall in the hot summer sun and her father owns land on the Lumbee River—a place for the family to come back home.

In her film *Real Indian*, she acknowledges that many people doubt her identity—even other

Indians she met in the West. But to Malinda, it is clear, and she is not alone in that. Daystar Dial, the Lumbee healer, is convinced that an attachment to a people and a place—tribal at its core—is getting stronger, not weaker, with the passage of time. She knows there are problems—the temptations of drugs and the rise in crime and the unfinished quest for federal recognition. But there is also a history on which they can draw and a core of new leaders to show them the way. She thinks they are living in an era of hope, when the century ahead seems to hold more promise than her Indian people have known in quite a while.

CHAPTER TEN
The Bayou Country

SOME PEOPLE CALLED THE OLD MAN A WITCH, and maybe he was. Nobody could deny that he had great power. He could touch a child who was sick with the fever, and people said the healing would happen overnight.

Rose Fisher remembers him well. His English name was Anderson Lewis, but in the Indian world, he was known as Falaya. As the twentieth century began to close in around him, he liked to spend long hours in the forest hunting with his blowgun and charming the bees in the wild honey trees. As a boy, he had lived in the woods by himself, banished by his tribe in eastern Louisiana when he came down with a case of tuberculosis—a disease the others were afraid they would catch. He managed to survive and came back tougher than when he had left, believing that the spirit people would provide. He could feel their presence in the trees and the bayous—a vitality the white men had never understood—and Falaya didn't want his children to forget. He was a man who believed in the Choctaw traditions, those that the ancestors had taken from Mississippi.

They were driven from their homes in the 1830s, after the Treaty of Dancing Rabbit Creek, and the Trail of Tears they took to Oklahoma led through the corner of northern Louisiana. They knew very little of their final destination, a mysterious land of wide-open spaces, but the bayou country in between was familiar. It was a hunting ground they shared with other tribes, and one night, a group of people slipped away. Five families left a camp on the Ouchita River and headed southwest toward Catahoula Lake. There they remained, setting up their community on a piece of land that was owned by a white man with an Indian wife.

Eventually, they became a tribe of their own, Choctaw people disconnected from any other band. "I thought we were the only Indians in the United States," remembers Clyde Jackson, a nephew of Falaya.

But their collective memories were nurtured and preserved, the traditions passed on as one generation slipped into the next. Jackson, who still speaks the Choctaw language, remembers the day when his uncle relented—gave in, finally, to his adolescent pleading—and taught him how to tan the hide of a deer. "Boy," said Falaya, "you need to be here Saturday." It took all day for a single hide, as they stretched it out and applied warm water and the yoke of an egg, and even today, the details of the recipe are a secret.

Rose Fisher, Falaya's granddaughter, says that's how it has to be. There are things the Indian people prefer not to talk about much, like the ancestors' habit of speaking with the animals. It's a gift that Rose herself has acquired, and sometimes in the thicket down by the creek, where the black-eyed Susans are scattered on the banks, she will take wild birds and hold them in her hands. There, in the solitude and the quiet, she will find herself thinking about the people who have died and how their spirit still seems to linger in the woods.

She and her teenage daughter, Anna Barber, a winner of the Miss Choctaw Indian Pageant who moves in and out of two different worlds, have written down the stories from Falaya and others—the creation myths and the bits and pieces of Choctaw history. They know that in the town of Jena, Louisiana, where the band now lives, times were hard a generation ago. Mary Jones, one of the elders in the 1990s, remembers how it was when she was a girl. Her mother worked in the white people's homes and her father in the fields, and sometimes even as a child, she would help. The cruelties, she says, were seldom overt—not many harsh words, no physical abuse—but there were the constant reminders of who was in charge. When it came time to eat, the Indians waited until the white people finished, then took what was left. "I always wondered," she says today, "why we had to wait."

There were no public schools for the Indian children, not until the end of World War II, when Mary as a teenager entered first grade. There is a picture of her class in the tribal office, Mary nearly twice as tall as the others, but she took it in stride, and in only two years, she made it all the way to sixth grade. There were things she knew that her classmates didn't, pieces of wisdom handed down in the tribe. Her father, for example, would always tell her that every time they took anything from the land—a rock, a flower, an animal killed to provide them a meal—it was important, out of simple respect for the earth, to give something back. Often, they would leave ceremonial tobacco sprinkled at the place where they took what they needed, but whatever it was, the lesson was clear. The earth was the cornerstone of creation, and it was the duty of the Indian people to remember.

There was a darker side to their story also—legends of witchcraft deep in the swamps, and passions sometimes giving way to murder. But all in all, the Jena Choctaws were proud of their community, proud of the history that held them together, and the band endured and grew stronger with the years.

In the 1980s, under the leadership of an

ANNA BARBER, JENA CHOCTAW, WINNER OF MISS CHOCTAW
INDIAN PAGEANT 1997, JENA, LOUISIANA, 1997

MARY JONES, JENA CHOCTAW ELDER,
JENA, LOUISIANA, 1997

aggressive new chief, Jerry Jackson, they filed a petition for federal recognition. They knew from the experience of other eastern tribes that it would not be an easy thing to accomplish. But Jackson was certain they could meet the criteria. They had governed themselves in an unbroken line since they left Mississippi, and on several occasions since the turn of the century, they had been identified as Indians by the government. Still, it took them nearly a decade, a time of politicking and meticulous documentation of their history, before they were recognized in 1995—a tribe of 186 people who owned a total of three acres in common.

Nothing much changed in the early years of recognition. There was a little money for health-care services, but the new designation came at a time when the federal government was cutting back its budget. Jackson saw no end to the trend, and he assumed his people would have to make it on their own. As a student of history, he understood the past—the Trail of Tears, and the racial prejudice of the twentieth century, and the tenant relationship with the whites. He saw a painting one time that captured that spirit. It was the work of a Frenchman, Alfred Boisseau, hanging in the New Orleans Museum of Art—a haunting image of an Indian family trudging along the shores of a Louisiana bayou. There was no identification of the tribe, but in Jackson's mind, the people in the painting—burdened but together in the moss-draped land they had

chosen for their home—could well have been his Jena ancestors. He sought permission to make the painting an emblem of the tribe, the centerpiece of the Choctaw seal, for he thought it was important to honor the Indians' survival.

But Jackson is not a man to live in the past. If history is a part of what holds them together, he also believes that the moment has arrived for the Jena Choctaws to build something new. If they manage their current opportunities correctly, they can buy more land and build better houses and establish a scholarship fund for their children. They can open a museum and create jobs and attack the old problems of alcohol and drugs. And as far as Jerry Jackson is concerned, the key to all of those initiatives is clear: The Jena Choctaws need a casino.

There are other examples in the Louisiana swamps. The Coushattas and Chitimachas are bringing in millions of dollars every year—some say every week—to use for a variety of tribal programs, and while nobody assumes the opportunity will last, the tribes have vowed to get it while they can.

For the Jena Choctaws, the first challenge is to find an appropriate site, a place where a tribal casino could flourish, and early in 1998, Jerry Jackson was working hard at the task. He knows there are doubters in the ranks of his tribe, people who worry about a change in values and the loss of identity that can come with sudden wealth. For Jackson, however, the opportunities are simply too great to ignore, and if he ever harbors any doubts of his own, all he has to do is look to the south, where his neighbors, the Coushattas, are entering a period of prosperity and promise unlike anything the tribe has ever known.

You can see the difference on a weekend night—the neon flashing in the Louisiana fog while the parking lot, as always, is jammed full of cars. They say that in 1995, when the Coushattas' casino first opened its doors, there were days when the traffic was stacked for twenty miles. Three years later, the two-lane roads are still overloaded leading to the hamlet of Kinder, Louisiana, but most people agree that the benefits are greater than the inconvenience. Certainly, the Coushattas feel that way. With casino money, they have built new housing and a recreation center that is state of the art, complete with a sauna and a racquetball court, and a new health center that opened its doors in 1998. Their casino employs more than two thousand people—whites and blacks, as well as Native Americans—and by 1997, it was pumping $40 million into the local economy.

It's an unaccustomed role for a struggling community of seven hundred people, a tribe that came to Louisiana in the 1790s. Before that time, the Coushattas were part of the Creek Confederacy, living on the waterways of Alabama. By the eighteenth century, they were caught in a swirl of diplomacy and war as the European settlers pressed in from every side. There were the French in Mobile, the Spaniards in Florida, and the English out of Georgia and South Carolina. The Coushattas understood that hard times were ahead. With their neighbors, the Alabamas, they began moving west, many of them settling in the Big Thicket area of eastern Texas.

As luck would have it, they were on the winning side of Texas's war for independence, and Sam Houston, a hero in the fight who had been raised by the Cherokees of Tennessee, saw to their reward. He set aside a reservation of twelve hundred acres, which was expanded substantially in the twentieth century and by the 1990s was home to more than five hundred people. Their culture and language are still intact, and the same is true for their Louisiana cousins, a contingent of Coushattas who had broken away and were officially recognized in 1971. But on both reservations, there are people who worry. The language is slipping in the television age, when Indians, like other people in the country, are becoming more passive in their search for entertainment. There aren't many storytellers anymore—the keepers of the legends and the history of the tribe.

"With television," says Burton Langley, a traditional Coushatta flute maker and artist, "there's nothing left to imagine."

Myrna Wilson agrees, and she says the problem becomes even worse when people marry

BURTON LANGLEY, COUSHATTA FLUTE MAKER AND ARTIST,
ELTON, LOUISIANA, 1997

outside the tribe and simply stop practicing the traditions at home. That hasn't happened in the Wilson household. Myrna and her husband, Wilfred Wilson, an offshore oil worker, still speak the language in their moments alone and when friends come to visit from the Alabama-Coushatta Reservation in Texas. They still do most of their cooking outdoors in the old-fashioned way, and Myrna still works with the pine-straw baskets, intricate creations that she sells to the tourists or sometimes uses herself in the home. She says they are perfect for storing her food. The pine-straw scent keeps the insects away.

"We're so used to the old ways," she says, and it worries her to think that someday they'll die. But there are others who insist that it may not happen, that the Coushattas' casino, ironically enough, may be the salvation—their gaudy institution of neon and greed, where white people come and play the machines and leave so much of their money behind that the Indians can use it any way they choose. Burley Sylestine, the public-relations director for the tribe, says a part of the money has gone for the children, for lessons in Coushatta traditions and crafts.

The same is true for the neighbors to the east, the Chitimacha Indians, whose reservation lies on Bayou Teche, where the Acadian prairie gives way to the swamps and the sugarcane fields stretch in a green and endless expanse. Unlike the Coushattas and the Jena Choctaws, the Chitimachas are natives of the

Louisiana low country. Until the coming of the French in the seventeenth century, they lived in a string of fifteen villages starting near the shores of the Mississippi River and stretching west and north to the country that was occupied by the Houmas. But the wars went badly in the eighteenth century, and the Chitimacha Nation was nearly destroyed, reduced to a remnant on Bayou Teche, where the people tried to keep to themselves in the swamps.

The low point came in the twentieth century, when their last bit of land was about to be auctioned away for taxes—a system that the Indians had never understood. Fortunately enough, they had a well-placed friend, a Louisiana heiress named Sarah McIlhenny, whose family made its fortune, starting in 1868, by blending red peppers from its own plantation with rock salt quarried on a Louisiana island. The result was a sauce now known as Tabasco, tangy enough to make the McIlhennys rich, and Sarah spent some of her money through the years buying river-cane baskets from her Chitimacha neighbors. She admired their artistry, the intricate weaves and the handmade dyes, and on the day that their land was about to be lost, she simply bought it and gave it back to them—a new reservation, protected this time by the federal government.

In the 1930s, the Chitimachas opened a reservation school—their first opportunity at a formal education. Their building in the early years was a castoff, a white frame structure that was battered and condemned, but the tribal leaders quickly made the repairs, and within a generation, there were college graduates among its alumni. Today, the old school building is gone. In its place is the pride of the Chitimacha people—a brick schoolhouse built in 1979, where a staff of twenty well-trained teachers serves a student population of eighty. Casino money makes the ratio possible, for education is now a Chitimacha priority. Every year, the tribe puts $350,000 in a scholarship fund, sending their brightest young people to college wherever their talents can get them accepted. In return, the students must come back home, at least for a time, and offer the fruits of their learning to the tribe.

One of the graduates is a Chitimacha teacher by the name of Kim Walden, who has developed a cultural program for the school. Among other things, she is trying to resurrect the Chitimacha language, which began to dwindle in the 1930s and apparently disappeared from the face of the earth with the death of the last Chitimacha speaker, a tribal elder named Benjamin Paul. But there are recordings of Paul in the last years of his life, and using those resources and others, Walden and the members of the cultural department have put together a new dictionary, as well as language tapes and CDs, for use in the school. The goal is to teach every Chitimacha child at least 150 words every year—or more than 1,000 by the time they are twelve, which is enough for conversational Chitimacha.

Nick Stouff is one of Kim Walden's supporters. He is an old man now, a wisdom keeper who was raised in Texas and never spent much time on the reservation until he came there to stay after World War II. His mother was white, his father Chitimacha, and Stouff, who looked more white than Indian, could have chosen either world. But he found himself drawn to the Indian ways—to people like his grandmother Delphine Stouff, who was regarded by the tribe as a woman of medicine. Her specialty was snakebites, and her legend in the bayous was so well established that one day, some doctors came in to observe her. They tried to be polite but lost interest quickly when she got to the prayers, the Indian words necessary for the healing. Nick, however, continued to believe. There was, he thought, something fundamental in the workings of the world that many white people, including the members of his own family, had never allowed themselves to understand.

So he threw himself into the world of the Indians, traveling the state with his uncle Emile, a Chitimacha chief who was trying to unite the Louisiana tribes. It was frustrating work in the 1950s. The Houmas, the Coushattas, the Tunica-Biloxis—all of them were scattered through the bayou country, isolated and alone, fighting those battles that they couldn't avoid and otherwise doing what they could to survive.

Times have changed in the past forty years.

The Indians are stronger now than they were. The federally recognized tribes, including Stouff's own, have attained a measure of economic power, which has given them resources for building their future and preserving their traditional links to the past. There are young people now—like Stouff's gifted neighbor, Melissa Darden—who are making the traditional Chitimacha baskets, their work as fine and true to the craft as any the ancestors left behind.

Toby Darden, administrator for the tribe, says the times quite clearly are better than they were, and the Chitimachas are trying to make good decisions. Among other things, they are searching for investments more permanent than casino money, which they believe could disappear at any moment. With that in mind, the Chitimachas are working on real-estate developments, including a planned community in the bayou country, as well as other enterprises that are still taking shape. "Diversification," says Darden, "is the key."

The Coushattas are proceeding along that path, and the Jena Choctaws are hoping they can follow. But some of the other Louisiana Indians—those who are not yet federally recognized—know that the road ahead of them is hard. The dreams of casinos can seem far-fetched to those whose legal status is different, and who are embarked on a difficult struggle—unsuccessful so far—to have their Indian identity reaffirmed.

On the eastern shore of the Sabine River, just a few miles from the Texas border, there is a faded brick building in the town of Zwolle, sandwiched away between an empty motel and the Tabernacle of Love. Out front is a sign with hand-painted letters proclaiming that the building is now the headquarters of the Choctaw-Apache community of Indians.

Inside, the tribal chairman, Tommy Bolton, is hard at work with his staff of three, tracing the complicated history of his people. Their name, they've discovered, is a little misleading. There *were* some Choctaw people in the area. There were Choctaws scattered over much of Louisiana, from the town of Clifton on the eastern border all the way to the Sabine. There were also Apaches imported as slaves—Lipan people from the plains of central Texas—but Tommy Bolton's native ancestry began to assume its distinctive shape sometime early in the eighteenth century. That was the era when the Spaniards arrived, pushing east out of Mexico through Texas to set up a mission in 1716.

Their targets for conversion, as they challenged the growing empire of the French, were the Adaes Indians, who were indigenous to the flatlands of western Louisiana. But many of those who came in the eighteenth century were, in fact, Indian people also—Tlaxcaltecan and Coahuiltecan soldiers from northern Mexico and Texas. They were mixed-blood subjects of the Spanish empire who had accepted the culture of Hernando Cortez and

MELISSA DARDEN, CHITIMACHA BASKETMAKER,
CHITIMACHA RESERVATION, CHARENTON, LOUISIANA, 1997

TOBY DARDEN, CHITIMACHA TRIBAL ADMINISTRATOR,
CHITIMACHA RESERVATION, CHARENTON, LOUISIANA, 1997

brought it with them to the Louisiana frontier. The community that resulted was unlike any other—a mixture of Adaes, Apache, and Mexican, with a little bit of Choctaw thrown in as well. The people embraced the Roman Catholic religion and a variety of Spanish not heard in other places. It was a trade language, really, the syntax altered by the Indian roots, the vocabulary sprinkled with Indian expressions.

In the 1990s, there were still a handful of people who spoke it. Amy Parrie and Glenda Etheridge both heard it often as they were growing up, and even when they came to work for the tribe—documenting the history of the Choctaw-Apaches and the traces of the Indian culture that remain—they would spend time periodically with a handful of elders who never spoke English unless they had to. Elvie Parrie was one of those people—a woman of medicine, many people said, who could dig up roots and gather wild herbs and cure everything from pneumonia to warts. She was partial to her grandson, Garland Parrie, the husband of Amy, and spoke to him often in the Indian tongue.

"It's blood," says Amy. "My husband can speak it." And she says their daughter has taken an interest and given them hope that the culture will survive.

It consists of more than the old trade language. Glenda Etheridge says there are customs that are nearly unnoticed—a frugality, for example, in which nothing goes to waste.

At hog-killing time, people eat the brains, the liver, the feet, and when it's time to put away the peaches or the pears, even the peelings are boiled to make jelly. Throughout the centuries, the people were proud of their ability to survive, to use whatever resources were at hand. The stands of cane that grew by the river were a source of blowguns, arrows, and rafts, and the men were hunters, and every family had a garden. Even today, there are people who seldom go to a store, preferring instead to grow what they need. They make quilts and shawls and baskets from the cane, and the knowledge has been handed down through the years.

But now, it's time to do something more. Under the leadership of Tommy Bolton, the tribe has applied for federal recognition, which may be a problem, given the record-keeping flaws of the nineteenth century. When the census takers came, says Stephanie Pierrotti, a tribal historian, there were times when the Indians hid in the woods. Now, however, they have clearly reemerged, and whatever the BIA may decide, Bolton and the others are laying claim to their roots. There are cultural programs at the tribal office—classes in dance and the making of shawls—and Choctaw-Apaches like Amy Parrie are pushing for the day when their Spanish trade language will be taught in the schools.

"I think the culture will survive," she says. "The children are interested. A lot of it depends on what we can teach them."

But there is also the matter of the outside world, the very strong possibility that the government will deny their Indian identity, and that even other native leaders in the area—those whose tribes are federally recognized—will continue to scoff at the tribes that are not.

It's a disturbing pattern to Grey Hawk Perkins, a traditionalist in southern Louisiana who traces his roots to the Oklahoma Choctaws but more directly to his mother's people, the Houmas, whose petition for federal recognition has been denied. Perkins is old enough to remember when there was never any doubt about the Houmas' identity—when, for example, the Indian people in the vast river deltas south of New Orleans were not permitted to go to public schools. There were facilities for whites and African-Americans, but the first Houma graduates from the public high schools did not appear until the 1960s. Nobody argued back then, he says, that the Houma people were not real Indians.

But the Houmas are a large and loosely organized group who, according to Perkins, could easily emerge as an unwanted force—a competitor with other Indian tribes for federal money, or an impediment to powerful economic interests that want to drill for oil or develop the wetlands unimpeded by the presence of the Indian people. Whatever the reasons, the Houmas are stalled in their tenacious pursuit of federal recognition, and like the Choctaw-Apaches, they are sometimes belittled by native leaders in the state. One chief noted that the Houmas speak French instead of a native language like his own, and that their blood has clearly been mixed with their neighbors'. "The BIA just laughs," he said.

When he heard the story, Grey Hawk Perkins shrugged and shook his head. He knows that the competition is out there, the destructive backbiting among Native Americans, but he tries to stay clear of political debates. His goal, he says, is to bring people together in a collective understanding of their culture. He has built a museum on the Mississippi River, in the town of Kenner just west of New Orleans, and he spends his days with his wife, Annette, a Chippewa-Huron who grew up in the industrial cities of the North and has come to take pride in her Indian roots. Together, they are building authentic reminders—palmetto houses like the kind that disappeared in the sixties, and dugout canoes like those that carried the people through the swamps. Their museum is mostly an outdoor display, a waterfront tract of an acre or two, where rabbits and waterfowl wander through the grounds, falling victim occasionally to the red-tailed hawk, and the great blue heron soars in from the marsh, resting for a while in the afternoon shade.

There are Indian artists who visit also, representatives of more than two dozen tribes who conduct workshops and demonstrate their crafts, and for Grey Hawk especially, the museum is a place of contemplation and study. He has spent many hours poring over the various

GREY HAWK PERKINS, HOUMA TRADITIONALIST,
KENNER, LOUISIANA, 1997

histories of his tribe, the accounts of the people's early contact with the French, when they met an explorer named Henri de Tonti, who paddled down the Mississippi River from Canada and confronted the Indians in 1699. The Houmas were a little awe-struck at first. De Tonti was a strong and flamboyant man, a fashionable dresser with flowing black hair and a strange metal hook replacing his hand, which had been mutilated by a grenade.

As the French set out to establish their empire, the Indians made concessions, adopting the European language as their own and moving south to the swamplands just off the gulf. But in the twentieth century, they have changed as reluctantly as any tribe in the country, maintaining a traditional way of life that is tied to the land and the black-water rivers that flow through the swamps. They hunt for the alligators and the fish, and there are still people like Antoine Parfait, a trapper who putters through the marsh in his skiff, searching for the signs of the muskrat and otter. Even though his age is creeping up on him—he is now pushing eighty—he dreads the day when he will finally have to stop.

"This," he says, "is just what I do."

He lives in the Houma town of Dulac, sharing a house with his middle-aged son, who has gained a measure of national renown as a native woodcarver. Roy Parfait is one of many artists who work in the bayous, preserving the ancient skills of the people. Not far away, his friend and mentor, Lawrence Billiot, still makes occasional dugout canoes, carved from the handsome wood of the cypress, and Marie Dean—"Miss Marie," as everybody calls her—still makes her fans and palmetto baskets. These items were once the staples of life, functional pieces used for transportation or storage or battling the heat in the Louisiana summer. But in more recent times, as the tourists have trickled in from afar, Parfait and others have discovered a market for their Indian art, and the crafts are slowly beginning to evolve. Roy Parfait, for example, does animal carvings that are vaguely abstract—panthers, turtles, fish, and raccoons fashioned out of cypress or tupelo gum, whatever he can find. His work is different from that of Ivy Billiot, a friend whose carvings of alligators and crabs are so lifelike you expect them to move. But in either case, there's a deep sense of place—a feeling for the water and the Houma way of life—reflected in the intricate shapes of the wood.

"I've done a lot of traveling," says Roy Parfait. "I've been to Switzerland. I've seen the Inside Passage to Alaska. But I've never seen a prettier place than Dulac."

It's not just the sea gulls skimming on the waves or the Spanish moss streaming from the live oak trees. For Roy Parfait, there's a sense of identity that's tied to his place, a feeling of familiarity and trust measured in part by the unlocked doors. He knows it is changing. There are racial problems in the town of Houma just up the road, and there's a new fear of crime that many people say is destined to spread. There are also changes in the local economy. The fishermen say there are too many laws and not enough shrimp, and some of them say they are about to give it up.

There are others, however, like Rodney Parfait, a young cousin of Roy's who can't imagine another way of life. He fishes for the crabs and trolls for the shrimp and hunts rabbits and alligators in the swamp. He knows there are better-paying jobs on the coast, including work on the oil rigs out in the gulf, but as far back as anybody can remember, his family has made its living on the boats.

Ricky Higgins, who is part Houma and part Chitimacha, understands the power of that kind of tradition. "It gets in your blood," he says with a shrug, and against all the odds, he finds himself year after year chasing crawfish deep in the basin—wading in the shallows and feeling like his life is a part of something old.

"I'm like a dinosaur," he explains.

Whatever the analogy, there is something that endures in the Louisiana bayous. From the Houmas near the gulf to the Jena Choctaws farther to the north, there are Indian people tied together by the past—and despite their divisions and the differences that exist in their current circumstances, their identity is simply too strong to disappear.

RAY BUCKLEY, LAKOTA, NASHVILLE, TENNESSEE, 1997

CHAPTER ELEVEN
City People

RED NIGGER.

Ray Buckley stared in disbelief at the ugly words that were painted on his door. He hadn't lived in Nashville very long, and already it struck him as a little bit strange—very different, certainly, from the rugged grasslands of South Dakota, where he was raised in the traditional world of the Sioux. His ancestry has many roots, which became intertwined in his parents' generation. On his mother's side, the people were Scottish, and he says he loves that part of his family—the European forebears who came to America to build new lives—but in his heart of hearts, he is Native American. His paternal grandfather, White Antelope, survived the Battle of Wounded Knee, plucked from the slaughter by a sympathetic soldier who hid the terrified baby in his coat. For Buckley, the lesson of the story was clear. The world sometimes is a brutal place, full of cruelty and pain, but there is a goodness that coexists through it all, for those who can muster the strength to understand it.

That was always his article of faith, tested many times in the course of his life, most of which he spent in the West. It was the land of the mountains and the wide-open spaces, and whenever he left it, he yearned for the people who understood how he felt. They were Indians, mostly, and they were nearly invisible in the cities of the East—in places like Boston, where he went to study in the 1980s. But every now and then, they appeared.

One day in 1984, he was reading through a book of poems at McDonald's and left it behind as he walked out the door. When he went back to get it, he found a young woman leafing through the pages. Her name was Sally O'Callahan, and she was a classical dancer who was part Irish and part Nez Perce—a background not very different from his own. They began to talk, and he was struck by her beauty and the ease of companionship and conversation. Within a year, they were married and living in Colorado, which was a part of the country that both of them loved. Six years later, a baby was born, a little boy named Jason, and for a while, at least, each day blended sweetly into the next. But then, unbelievably, Buckley's world came apart. Jason was barely six months old on a day he and Sally were riding in the car. They were on a steep mountain road outside of Denver when a truck lost control and crossed the line, and mother and son both died in the crash.

He stayed for a while in Estes Park, but the place was too small and too full of reminders. His family and Sally's were not far away, and there was never anyplace to go to recover, to deal with the grief that was tearing at his heart. Eventually, he made a trip to Africa, a teaching mission with a group of musicians, many of whom had ties to Tennessee. They urged him to try that part of the country, and he took a job with the Methodist Church, settling in slowly in a place that was odd and unfamiliar, where the sky was smaller and the sunsets were blotted away by the trees. Still, he did his best to adjust, and after about a year, his grandmother and sister came east to see him. They dressed one day in their traditional regalia and set out for a powwow sponsored by the Indians of middle Tennessee. When they came back home at the end of the day, they found the words spray-painted on the door: RED NIGGER.

It was a slur that Buckley had never encountered, and he wondered at the level of hate it contained. His grandmother must have wondered also. She pulled a rocking chair out on the stoop and sat for hours, waiting in silence for the racists to return. They never did. As he watched her there in her vigil of defiance, Buckley was struck by her dignity and courage, this ninety-five-year-old Tlingit-Cheyenne whose Indian name was Moon of the Silver Fox. He knew in the moment of the old woman's stand that he had no choice. Whatever his discomfort or the familiar yearning for his home in the West, he would not be driven away by the hate.

The next morning, his doorbell rang. It was his next-door neighbor, Sandy Vandercook, a white Tennessean who was horrified by the message on the door. She wanted him to know that there were good people, too, people who wanted him to feel at home, his culture and his dignity respected by his neighbors. "I'm sorry," she said, and it was a sentiment repeated again and again for the next several days, as the story quickly spread and people came calling to see if there was anything they could do. Buckley was touched by the outpouring of support, and he wrote a letter of thanks to the daily newspaper, *The Tennessean*, telling the story of the slur and the response of the decent people in the city.

Even then, however, there was something fundamental that was missing in his life. It was one thing to know that the bigots in Nashville were outnumbered and there were people who respected his Indian identity, but it was another thing to find other people who shared it. The loneliness was sometimes hard to define. He could talk to his neighbors easily enough—the NASCAR fans, the black man who recently moved in from Texas—but there were places where the conversation couldn't go. He couldn't really talk about his grandfather's portrait that was hanging on the living-room wall of his apartment, except perhaps to say he had done it as his personal tribute to a man he revered. But the spiritual identity represented in the face and the great bald eagle that hovered in the background were images that were simply too hard to explain. How could he tell his neighbors from the South about the sun-dance ceremony back home, when his gentle grandfather took the talon of an eagle and carved an incision into Ray Buckley's chest? How could it sound anything but barbaric—even to people who worshiped in the blood, who believed in the sacrifice of Jesus Christ?

What he needed, he knew, were some Indian friends—and slowly, over time, they began to appear. A few were people he met in his work—JoAnn Eslinger, a Cherokee from North Carolina, and Ginny Underwood, a Kiowa-Comanche who had moved to Nashville with her husband, John, a Seminole from central Oklahoma. All of them seemed to be searching for answers, wrestling with decisions that were basic to their lives. John, for example, was a young traditionalist who had been asked by one of the Seminole elders to become his apprentice—to study the ancient ways of the tribe and to serve his people as a

spiritual leader. But John and Ginny had made other plans. They believed, as Ginny was fond of saying, that Native Americans had to "be at the table." They had to be educated and resourceful, able to cope in an era when the continuing threats to their people often took bewildering and sophisticated forms. Ginny was a journalist, and John was getting his degree as a coach, hoping one day to work with the children and help them learn to live in two worlds.

"It's always a duality," he told one reporter. "You live almost two separate lives."

That seemed especially true in the cities, where they could go for a month without seeing other Indians, and where the urban landscape of concrete and steel offered its chilly reminders every day that they were living among strangers. But for Buckley and the others, the feelings of isolation were relieved whenever they got together for a cookout. They could laugh and tell stories like any group of friends, or they could talk about the deeper issues of identity that confronted every Indian person in the city. Granted, there were some with more pressing problems—like the homeless Navajo who stumbled through the streets and the Apache in desperate pursuit of the wine. But the search for common ground was universal.

Certainly, Jennifer Welch understood it. She was another of Nashville's Indian professionals, a woman who came to the city with her songwriter husband. She fit in well with his circle of friends—a generous and talented community of musicians that included people like Emmylou Harris and country-rock songwriter Marshall Chapman—and she had her own career also. She was an educator who was determined to make a dent in the dismal statistics—the dropout rates and all the rest—that crippled the lives of so many children. But she awoke to a nagging sensation every morning that something irreplaceable was missing in her life, and after a while, she knew what it was. In Nashville, she simply didn't know any Indians. She was an Osage raised in Oklahoma and accustomed to the traditional dances every summer and the feelings of fellowship and understanding, which were so much a part of her everyday life that it was easy sometimes to take them for granted. But not in the city.

So Welch set out to build a community. She established a new nonprofit organization—the Tennessee Indian Education Association—and in 1998 agreed to host a national convention that brought several thousand educators to the state to talk about the needs of Indian children. On the 160th anniversary of the Trail of Tears, she liked to think of the meeting as historic—an opportunity for native people to return to a part of the country that had been swept clean. But whatever the symbolism of the moment, it was also a chance for her to connect—to meet other Indians and to affirm her own identity in the process.

It's a story that's repeated in city after city, in many cases on a much larger scale, as Native Americans search out their peers, sometimes crossing old borders in the process. In Boston, for example, they come by the hundreds to a rambling brick building south of downtown that has served as a haven for twenty-five years. To the casual observer, the North American Indian Center doesn't look like much. The brick exterior has faded over time, and the cavernous hallways could stand a little paint. The institution itself has survived its share of troubles through the years, including a bankruptcy in 1989. But there are traces of beauty at the center also, especially the Micmac murals that are painted on the walls, a gift from the most populous tribe in the city.

Joanne Dunn is the acting director, a second-generation immigrant from Canada whose mother came to Boston as a girl of seventeen, looking to find some way to survive. She spoke no English when she first arrived, and even today, she prefers the native tongue of her people, a Micmac band on Cape Breton Island. They were a close-knit community that eked out a living from the land and the sea, but there were times when the poverty got to be too much, and a family here or there would break away. They never lost touch with the people at home, returning when they could, and a connection developed over half a century between the Micmac reservations and Boston. The network was formalized in the seventies, as Indians began to gravitate toward the North American Indian Center, a place that provided training and jobs and, more than that, a space to be together.

Joanne Dunn's mother, Nannette Francis, remembers how in the first few years of living in the city, her Micmac language began to slip away. She could still understand it, and even speak it when she had to, but she noticed over time that she was thinking more and more in English. In a way, she didn't mind. It was a sign of her adjustment to a new way of life. But she longed sometimes for the Micmac phrases, the rhythms that echoed softly in her mind, and it was like a piece of herself was being lost. And then something happened. As she started spending more time at the center, often in the company of other Micmacs, she found herself speaking the language once again, feeling more like herself— even thinking and dreaming in the Indian words she had known as a child.

Joanne, meanwhile, made her way through school, eventually getting her degree from Radcliffe and becoming a symbol of the new generation. But there is, she believes, a common thread between people like herself and those who came to the city in the past. Many of them have simply refused to be absorbed, to disappear into the jumbled mass of ethnicity and work that some people call the melting pot of America. While making their concessions to economic progress, they have held on stubbornly to a sense of who they are.

"And we couldn't have done it," says Dunn, "without this place. People have found their role models here, and all of us have learned a lot from each other."

Perhaps the greatest strength, she says, is that the Indian community in Boston is multitribal. In addition to the Micmacs, there are Wampanoags and Nipmucs from Massachusetts, the Iroquois from New York State, and Penobscots and Passamaquoddies from Maine. In all, there are more than thirty different tribes, ranging from Cherokees to Nez Perce Indians, and all of them have found a home at the center.

Janis Falcone is an Onondaga who believes that Indian people in the city, a minority so small they are in danger of drowning, must concentrate on things that bind them together—"similar feelings, a similar philosophy," she says, which are too often taken for granted back home and therefore, on occasion, get lost. It's strange that it should be that way. As late as the fifties, the federal government was working to move Indian people to the city on the theory that assimilation was the answer. Instead, they simply turned to each other. Even those who adjusted and made their mark were at least as likely as their brothers back home to wear their Indian identity as a badge, to reflect on its meaning and give it a prominent place in their lives.

For Falcone, at least, that reality came into focus more sharply that it had in the past on a recent visit to her own reservation, the one where her father served as a chief. In the Iroquois tradition, her tribal identity came from her mother, a Turtle Clan member of the Onondagas. But her father, Roy Poodry, was a Seneca chief, a respected leader at the Tonawanda Reservation who was known for his spirit of moderation and tolerance. He died in the spring of 1997, a troubled time for the Indian people. At the moment of his passing, Senecas on other reservations in the state were facing off against the New York police, part of an ongoing battle over taxes—and everywhere, it seemed that the Iroquois people were deeply divided, in desperate need of some common understandings. How could they live with their history and tradition and still find a way to do business in the world? It was a question that threatened to tear them apart, but with the death of Poodry, they put it aside, calling a cease-fire for twelve days of grieving, carefully structured as they had done it in the past—a time of solemn ceremonies and feasts.

"In his death," concluded Falcone, "he brought people together."

But it simply couldn't last. The tensions among the Iroquois were too strong—the divisions too deep—in battles with the state and battles over ideology and power that had led the reservations to the brink of civil war. And so, when her grieving was over, she packed up her suitcase and headed back to Boston—torn, as always, by her feelings of attachment to her people and her place and the spirit the Native Americans had managed to build in the city.

The irony sometimes was difficult to bear—this ability of the Indian people in Boston, coming together from so many places, to recapture a spirit of unity and peace that often eluded the Iroquois at home. It didn't happen everywhere, she knew. But somehow at the North American Indian Center, it seemed to be too important not to try.

In Baltimore, many miles to the south, there's an Indian mural in the row-house district just north of the harbor—a beacon of sorts for a center that resembles its counterpart in Boston. There are more than six thousand Indians living in the area. Most are Lumbees with ties to the farmlands of Robeson County, North Carolina, which they refer to as home, even though many of them have never lived there. Their gathering place on the southeast side is the personal legacy of Herbert Locklear, a dark-skinned man with curly, gray hair who came to the city in 1958. He is a sharecroppers' son, the lone sibling out of ten who made the daring move to the North, an ambitious young teacher in search of a job. He wound up instead as a social worker with a de facto specialty in the needs of his people, and he could see immediately in the 1950s that they needed institutions. They had nothing in Baltimore to hold them together.

That began to change in the 1960s with the founding of a church, South Broadway Baptist, which served as a rallying point through the years, and then in 1968, the people began the Baltimore Indian Center. The programs in the early years were modest—study groups, mostly, where Indian families learned about their culture, trying to build a bedrock of identity. In North Carolina, they could take it for granted—their sense of connection to the land and each other—but in a city like Baltimore, it was different. In the area around Broadway and Lombard Streets, they felt outnumbered, surrounded by people very different from themselves, at least on the surface. These were the ethnic neighborhoods of the city, full of Ukrainians and Poles and Italian-Americans, many of them caught in the same new awakening, the same intermingling of alienation and pride that was becoming commonplace among the Indians. In the 1970s, they began to come together in a loose coalition called the Southeast Community Organization (SECO), and Herbert Locklear was one of the leaders. He shared the fundamental premise of the group—that it was possible for the ethnic groups to work together while also remaining true to who they were. He discovered, in fact, that his own identity grew stronger through the years as he battled for a place in the life of the city, doing his part to make things better.

"The ability to move comfortably in the larger world strengthened my sense of being Indian," he says. "I am different. I am also equal. That's the way I'd like to see people live."

To some extent, that's the way it has happened. There are second and third generations of Lumbees who have lived in Baltimore all their lives, getting their degrees, holding good jobs, and sometimes moving away to the suburbs. Milton Hunt, for example, became director of the Baltimore Indian Center in the nineties. He grew up nearby on the fringes of the harbor, where Polish women scrubbed the sidewalks with Comet and the smell of salt water drifted in on the breeze. It was a landscape as different from North Carolina as any the Indian people could imagine, but for many in Milton Hunt's generation, there was peace on the other side of their adjustment. Not all of them found it. There were those who longed every day for Carolina and cursed their jobs and the streets full of cars. But whatever their feelings or their level of success, there was always the Indian center to sustain them. It provided job training and day care for their children, a museum to remind them of their history and culture, and, in a site nearby, a place for their elderly people to gather.

And so the Lumbees remained close-knit, and a few of them tried to reach out to other tribes, for they were not quite alone in the Baltimore area. There were Meherrins and Haliwa-Saponis from the South and Oneidas and Tuscaroras from the North, and there were the Piscataways from the Maryland coast, the modern survivors of a once-proud confederacy shattered by the power of the European invasion. Keith Colston did his best

KEITH COLSTON, LUMBEE-TUSCARORA CULTURAL DIRECTOR,
BALTIMORE INDIAN CENTER, BALTIMORE, MARYLAND, 1997

to serve every group. As cultural director at the center, he thought the people had no room for division, for the native population was simply too small. It was true, of course, that every tribe was different, but it was also true, as they learned in the city, that the differences were smaller than the things that they shared—their feelings for the land and their place in the world.

That, at least, was the way Keith saw it. He came from North Carolina himself, but he didn't refer to himself as a Lumbee. He was instead a Lumbee-Tuscarora, a young man in his twenties embracing not only his modern identity but his ancestry, too. It was clear early in the 1700s, as the remnant groups of native survivors drifted into Robeson County, seeking shelter in the swamps, that the Tuscaroras were a significant part of that mix. He thought there were lessons embedded in the story—the Indians turning to each other for survival, crossing old boundaries that had kept them apart. If not for that spirit, they might not have made it, and even in the shadow of the twenty-first century, he still saw the need. So he held his classes wherever he could, in Baltimore and the Piscataway communities out in the country, doing his best to bring people together. But he also knew that the Lumbees were clannish, and that Baltimore was different in that way from Boston. There was less interaction among the different tribes.

Within each group, however, there were bonds, particularly among people who came to the city. There were personal jealousies that cropped up occasionally, and individuals who didn't get along, but there was also a sense of being in it together. Herbert Locklear always said that if there was a Lumbee in trouble anywhere in the world, it was a matter of concern for them all. So they held to each other through the years and the miles, and whenever they could, they went back home—a pilgrimage made several times every year to the black-water swamplands of North Carolina, where the Indian people had found a place to survive.

In the 1990s, Gary Revels, the minister at a Lumbee church in Charlotte, would lead his people once a year to the river, loading up a convoy of buses or vans for the two-hour drive to Robeson County and a late afternoon of baptizing and hymns. The fervor of the moment, he said, was twofold—part Pentecostal, a ceremony of faith, and part homecoming, a private celebration of identity and place.

The impulse appeared to be widespread, a ritual for the Lumbees and many other tribes. In Hollywood, Florida, the Seminole community was clustered in the shadow of the tribal headquarters, where the reservation had been engulfed by the city. Many of the Seminoles had done very well, making their mark as entrepreneurs. But there was a longing also that many of them felt—bittersweet memories of a simpler time, when they lived in the camps hidden deep in the swamps. For some of them, those memories were nourished at least once

BAPTISM IN LUMBER RIVER LED BY CHARLOTTE MINISTER
GARY REVELS, TUSCARORA, ROBESON COUNTY, NORTH CAROLINA, 1997

a week when they gathered to worship at the Chickee Church—a familiar place where the ceiling was made out of palmetto thatch and the hymns were delivered in the Seminole tongue. For the Indian people, it felt like home—a cultural journey they were able to make without ever leaving the place where they lived.

For others, of course, it took more work. In the city of Buffalo, for example, Joyce Pembleton was a Cayuga educator who made her seasonal journeys every year to the long-house ceremonies of her tribe. She took her grandchildren with her when she could—Joel Pembleton and Sarah Nichols, who were eager for the chance to mingle with the elders as the people gave thanks in the season of the harvest. Joyce understood from her years in the classroom that it was important for the children to know who they were. When she came to Buffalo as a teacher back in 1975, there was a single Indian graduate that year— a total of one. But after twenty years of work, the dropout problem had all but disappeared, and Pembleton was sure that she understood the reason. Teachers were able to bolster the students' self-esteem, and the heart of the effort was a magnet school in an old brick building just a few miles from the Canadian border. Not all of the students who went there were Indian, but all of them were interested in the history and values of Native Americans, and for the Indian students, it was a source of great pride. They studied the contributions of the Iroquois people, the dominant confederacy in New York State, learning about the government and the values that held their communities together.

Many of the teachers who came to the school were astonished by the spirit. There were hardly any discipline problems at all. True to the things they were taught in the classroom, the children treated their elders with respect, and all the teachers had to do was return it.

There were exceptions, of course, to the overall pattern, children for whom the lessons didn't take. But most of them got it. There was no going back to a time in the past when the Indian people were firmly in control. Their numbers were small. But Pembleton and the others could see great hope in the students who graduated from the schools and began to make their way in the world. Most were proud without being bitter, which was always the goal.

"Back when we started," says Pembleton today, "there were parents who didn't want their kids to be identified as Native American. To my knowledge, nobody feels that way anymore."

In Nashville, Ray Buckley says that's how it should be. He rejects the notion he has heard many times that Native Americans have to live in two worlds. There is only one, and the circle of life, as the old people say, includes everybody. It may be true that there are things that native people see clearly, and that their

SARAH NICHOLS AND JOEL PEMBLETON, GRANDCHILDREN
OF CAYUGA EDUCATOR JOYCE PEMBLETON, OUTSIDE
SIX NATIONS RESERVE, ONTARIO, CANADA, 1997

vision is sometimes sharpened in the city. "In family ties, in reverence for the land, in the sense of history and a sense of hospitality, in food and music and storytelling," he says, the Indians have something important to offer— not only to themselves but to their neighbors all around. But there is a need also to cling to each other, and not to lose themselves in the noise or to assimilate at the expense of their native identity and spirit.

That can happen in the city, but the opposite experience seems to be more common. For the Indian people who have made it their home, the urban landscape is a place for remembering, for holding to the values and the sense of tradition that have made the native people who they are.

CECIL GARVIN, HO-CHUNK, MANAGER OF
BUFFALO RESTORATION PROJECT, MUSCODA, WISCONSIN, 1997

CHAPTER TWELVE

Signs of the Times

FORTY MILES EAST of the Mississippi River, on a sloping meadow in southern Wisconsin, the big bull stood at the edge of the herd. He was wary and defiant as he approached the strangers who had entered his domain—snorting, pawing, then pausing to stare with eyes too small for his great, shaggy head. Cecil Garvin smiled. "That's Kunu," he said. "He's the leader of the group. In the Ho-Chunk language, his name is First Son." In the summer of 1997, Kunu's empire was not very large—only fifteen animals, mostly cows and a few young bulls that spent their days on an isolated range safe from the prying eyes of the public.

But to many of the people in the Ho-Chunk Nation, particularly the elders, the return of the buffalo is important. They once roamed freely in the Wisconsin hills, and because of that fact, the Ho-Chunks today are part of a movement, a growing crusade in Indian country that includes more than forty tribes nationwide. They have set out consciously to restore an old link—the tie between the Na-

tive American people and the buffalo herds that were once a cornerstone of their existence.

The effort was led in the 1990s by a South Dakota–based group, the Intertribal Bison Cooperative, and not surprisingly, the Great Plains people were the first to get involved. The buffalo, historically, were their key to survival, their primary source of shelter and food, and in the time of decimation and defeat, the prophets of the nineteenth century proclaimed that the buffalo herds would be the next sign. When they were restored, coming once again to live on the plains undaunted by the winds and the deep winter snows, the spirit of the people would rise up as well.

The tribes in the East understood such talk, though the buffalo for them had never been as central. There were also the deer and the fields of corn and the wild blueberries growing free in the thickets. But the buffalo were there. They roamed from the prairies of southern Alabama all the way to New England and west to Wisconsin and the Great Lakes region. The Cherokees and the Creeks had a buffalo dance, and the Ho-Chunk Nation had its Buffalo Clan.

Cecil Garvin knows the story very well. As the project manager for the buffalo herd, he sees it as an enterprise of the spirit. He knows that the bison were driven from Wisconsin at about the same time that his own people were. There was a series of treaties beginning in 1829 in which the Ho-Chunks—or Winnebagos, as they were called at the time—were forced to give up most of their land. They moved to Iowa and then to Minnesota, where they prospered for a while, but a Sioux rebellion in 1862 led to still another cry for removal. The Ho-Chunks, who had taken no part in the war by the Sioux, were driven from their homes and sent to live in South Dakota, where a third of them died in the terrible winter of 1863. The following summer, they slipped away in canoes and headed south to Nebraska, where the Omaha Indians took them in, and where a contingent of Winnebagos lives to this day.

But there were the renegades who kept coming home. Individually or in small bands, they drifted back across the Mississippi River to the place the Creator intended them to be. Cecil Garvin's great-grandfather remembered those times. His name was John Swallow, and he lived to the age of 106—an old man full of Indian stories and songs. When he died in 1965, he left his family with a strong sense of history and a respect for the culture and the Ho-Chunk traditions. His great-grandson still speaks the language, and his spiritual identity is rooted in the time when the Indians' survival was tied to the land.

"Our people," says Garvin, "were able to survive because of the natural environment around them. They had access to game or crops. Ask the old people about the Depression, and they hardly know what you are talking about. This money machine we are part of now is quite new to the tribe. The window for economic development is here right now, and it needs to be developed with a long-range plan. But the four-legged creatures would still exist if the market collapsed. With the return of the buffalo, if we have enough land, the herd can sustain itself and the people."

In addition to the matter of physical survival, Garvin sees the buffalo as a symbol—part of a larger reclamation of the past. The Ho-Chunks are working hard at that task. In 1994, they took back the ancient name of the people, rejecting *Winnebago*, and the tribal elders, like those among the Cherokees to the south, are teaching the children in the day-care centers, trying to make certain the language will survive. There is a tribal department of historic preservation that protects the burial mounds in the state—some of them going back twelve hundred years—and the nation is trying to buy back the land, to restore a part of what was lost in the treaties. The buffalo herd is a part of all that—a tangible reminder of identity and place and the capacity of the Indian people to survive.

The Ho-Chunks are not alone in that view. Their Oneida neighbors near the shores of Green Bay and the Menominee people to the north are also working to restore the buffalo, and by the early winter of 1997–98, the Oneidas were well along in the process.

The driving force behind their success is Pat Cornelius, director of the Oneida Nation Farms. She is a cheerful woman in love with her work, and nothing gives her greater pleasure than the bison. From the very beginning, she was fascinated by the Intertribal Bison Cooperative, how the members would gather from all over the country and begin each meeting with a sacred ceremony. There were Indian prayers and the burning of sage and a staff that was placed in the center of the room with an eagle feather for every tribe in the group.

She was deeply impressed with the spirit of the effort, and later she talked about it with her sister, Loretta Matoxen, who serves as the Oneidas' tribal historian. Matoxen had done some research on the subject, and she confirmed what Cornelius had already guessed— that for many of the Indian tribes in the East, the buffalo were a part of their story. They had lived for centuries in what is now New York State, where the Oneidas were members of the Iroquois Confederacy, and there were herds in Wisconsin in the 1800s, when many of the Oneidas were uprooted from New York and packed onto barges in the Erie Canal. Looking for a place they could live in peace,

they boarded steamboats at the end of the line and made the journey across the Great Lakes until they came at last to the shores of Green Bay, where the Menominee Indians had agreed they could live.

Those were the early days of removal, when the new federal policy was first taking hold. Within a few years, if the government got its way, there would be no Indians anymore in the East.

In Wisconsin, the Oneidas did their best to adjust. They adopted the English language of their neighbors, and at least on the surface, many of the old ways began to disappear. But then something happened in the 1970s. Oneidas from Canada who had also been driven from their ancestral lands began to visit their Wisconsin cousins, and they carried a gentle word of reproach. In Wisconsin, they said, the Oneida language was almost gone, along with the ancient ceremonies of the tribe. These things were their birthright, the center of their definition as a people, and it was simply unthinkable to allow them to die.

Carol Cornelius was one of those who listened. She was a young Oneida with a Ph.D., and she began making regular trips to Canada—a twelve-hour drive if she did it by car, and perhaps even longer when she traveled with her friends in an old school bus. With the help of the Canadians, she began to relearn the Oneida language, and to practice once again the long-house religion, and to understand the values on which she was raised. Those had never died—the respect she felt for the elders in the tribe, the connection to her people, a deep sense of place, the gratitude for the good things around her. These were at the heart of her Indian identity, and now she understood the source.

She came back home and went to work for the tribe, plunging into the task of cultural preservation. She says she is pleased by the Oneidas' progress. There are language programs in the tribal schools, and there is another project involving the elders. Eleven of them fluent in Oneida are teaching a group of adult trainees, all of whom will teach other groups, and the tribe is hoping for a geometric progression. But of all the work being done in the nineties, all the efforts to reconnect with the past, nothing is more exciting to Carol Cornelius than the Oneida Nation Farms.

The Oneidas historically were agricultural people, as were all of their Iroquois neighbors. There are accounts from a war in the seventeenth century when an army of the French attacked the Indians and laid waste to a million bushels of corn. A hundred years later, George Washington exacted the same kind of toll, conducting a scorched-earth war against the Iroquois in punishment for their support of the British. His army burned more than three dozen villages and destroyed their food, which consisted of orchards full of succulent apples and hundreds of acres of corn. As Cornelius read through the bitter accounts, she

was struck by a sense of tragedy and loss, but she was also proud of her ancestors' knowledge. They clearly understood how to make things grow.

One of their methods was to plant corn, beans, and squash in the same small hill. The corn took nitrogen out of the soil, the beans put it back, and the leaves of the squash helped choke back the weeds. Carol tried the technique in her garden and was astonished to discover how well it worked. But the most impressive thing was the farm—the vast operation run by the tribe. In 1989, when Pat Cornelius took it over, it consisted of thirty-five head of cattle and 350 acres of land. Nine years later, it was one of the largest operations in the state—more than 4,000 acres in corn and apple orchards and cattle, a throwback to the days when the Oneidas and all of the Iroquois tribes ran the most prosperous farms in North America.

For the Oneidas in 1997, the buffalo were the final piece of that revival. There were doubters at first, people who wondered if a herd was really worth it, but then came a miracle in Indian country, and it happened a few miles south of the farms. A Wisconsin rancher by the name of Dave Heider—a white man, as it happened—had started a buffalo herd of his own. One day, he awoke to a startling discovery. A white calf was born to one of his cows. The odds against it were huge— 10 million to one, some people said—but for the Indian people, the tiny new calf was more than a matter of genetic curiosity. There was a legend that began among the Lakotas about a white buffalo woman who came to the people and gave them the wisdom for living in the world. "You will walk like a living prayer," she said.

Because of that myth, white buffalo are seen by many tribes as a sign, and Indian people from all over the country began to make their way to Dave Heider's farm. There were others who came for less noble reasons—curiosity seekers and a few who were hostile—and the Oneidas stood guard, making sure the buffalo calf was protected.

"We patrolled the pastures twenty-four hours a day," remembers Nori Damrow, an elder in the tribe.

If there was ever any doubt, the birth of the calf so close to their home sealed the Oneidas' commitment to the bison, and Pat Cornelius put together a herd. The first animals arrived on an October day. There was a chill in the air and a drizzling rain, and the arrival ceremony was modest—maybe thirty Oneidas who gathered for a prayer and the burning of sage as the animals were brought on a truck from South Dakota. There were thirteen buffalo at the start, turned loose on a sixty-acre preserve, and as autumn gave way to the Wisconsin winter, they continued to thrive.

The same was true for other herds in the East—the Onondagas' back in New York State, where the tribal leaders had written their purchase agreement on a hide, and a Poarch Creek herd in south Alabama, where the tribal chairman, Eddie Tullis, wanted the Indian people to remember.

He also wanted to bring in the tourists. For Tullis and many native leaders in the East, there is a practical edge to their notions of revival. Without new jobs and an economic base, it is silly to think of rebuilding their communities. The people have to live, and for many of the tribes—the Choctaws, Coushattas, Pequots, and Creeks—perhaps the most encouraging sign of the times is a fundamental change in their standard of living. But there are others. For the tribes split apart by the forces of history, including the Trail of Tears in the 1830s, there are bold new attempts to bring them together.

Among the Creeks, for example, there are young traditionalists who make their regular trips to Oklahoma, where the culture is stronger than it is in Alabama. It's the place where the majority of Creeks now live and where a medicine man, Sam Proctor, has adopted the Alabama Band as his own. Sam is an elder, a carpenter by trade, who still speaks the language and knows all the Indian dances and the prayers—the theology of humility and purification that are at the heart of most of the Creek ceremonies.

Every summer for the Green Corn Dance, they gather at the Tallahassee ceremonial grounds in the scrubby hill country near Okemah, Oklahoma. The Alabama people

SAM PROCTOR, OKLAHOMA CREEK MEDICINE MAN,
AIKEN, SOUTH CAROLINA, 1998

make the difficult trip every year, which even today is a drive of fourteen hours or more. But the pilgrimage also goes the other way. For more than twenty years, Sam had made his regular journeys to the East, and he is proud of the fact that a movement that began with a handful of people has now grown larger. There is a committed core among the Poarch Creek Band that is eager to keep the old ways alive, and Sam understood from the start that it would happen. The Alabama Creeks, he says, are like the land, a fertile piece of ground that has not been cultivated in a while. But he knows they are Indian people in their hearts. On one of his trips, he met an old woman named Clara Rolin who was dressed like the elders he had known as a boy—in a long, straight dress hanging nearly to the ground, with soft shoes and an apron and a scarf looped carefully around her hair.

"When I saw that," he says with a smile, "I knew that they were my people, my blood."

Not all of the Oklahoma people agree. Some tribal officials are privately contemptuous of the Poarch Creek Band and other Creek descendants still living in the East. "They had the opportunity to come here," says one. "They turned their backs on their own people."

But many of the tribes have rejected that view. The Seminoles, for example, have worked to overcome the history and division, banding together with their brothers in Florida to recover the remains of the ancestral people, those whose bones were extracted from the earth and put on public display in museums. It was a desecration that took them back into time, to the days when the Seminole people were one and found their home in the swamps. And so today, many of the Seminoles have turned their eyes once again to the East. In 1998, the tribe was bidding on a tract of land—some two thousand acres of Florida real estate near a well-traveled exit off of Interstate 10. Their motivation, in part, was economic. They envisioned a massive entertainment complex, a source of revenue for a people whose unemployment ran near 70 percent. But for Oklahoma Seminoles like Alan Emarthle, the project stirred something deep in the bones. "This was the motherland," he said. "This was our home."

Other tribes feel the same kind of pull, and there are people who are working to heal old wounds. Recently, the Narragansetts and their Mohegan cousins held a ceremony of reconciliation. They were often at odds in colonial times, both because of their own competition and because of the diplomacy imposed by the whites. But both tribes survived, and they were living in the twentieth century as neighbors. The Mohegans had struggled for federal recognition, their identity preserved through the work of elders like Gladys Tantaquidgeon, who opened a museum in 1931—an institution that became a focal point for the tribe. There were younger Mohegans who worked at it, too, including Melissa Fawcett, a tribal historian whose award-winning book, *The*

Lasting of the Mohegans, helped to document the story of her people.

After receiving federal recognition in 1994, the Mohegans reached out to the neighboring tribes, including the Narragansetts. On a late summer's day, the traditionalists gathered at the historic sites where the tribes had battled each other in the past, and together, quite literally, they vowed to break the old arrows of war. The message was simple, says Lloyd Wilcox, a medicine man for the Narragansett tribe. They were proclaiming to each other and the rest of the world that it's a whole new era for Native Americans, a time to put their divisions in the past. They know there are signs of better days ahead. But there are problems also, as chilling and familiar as any the Indian people have ever faced, and their spirit of reconciliation and peace is sure to be tested in the days just ahead.

Some people say it's already begun.

In the hot, murky lowlands of North Carolina, there's a breakaway faction in Robeson County, where the remnant survivors in the eighteenth century drifted into the swamps and built a new community from the wreckage. They were the victims of wars and European epidemics, and by the middle decades of the twentieth century, most of them thought of themselves as Lumbees. But there were others who rejected that particular designation— who claimed instead a lineage going back to the Tuscaroras, a coastal people who fought a war against the whites, then fled for their lives. Many of them went north and took their place in the Iroquois Confederacy, but others found a hiding place in the swamps.

Robert Locklear says his own ancestors were a part of that group. Lockiear is a painter whose work hangs on the walls of the Tuscaroras' office in North Carolina. The paintings have a Native American theme— sunrise on a woodland river in the South, an Indian standing ankle deep in the snow. Locklear is proud of his native ancestry, and he and others have set out to reestablish the link between themselves and the Tuscaroras now living in the North. It's a reversal of history, in Locklear's view, and he has made the pilgrimage to New York State to affirm that the Tuscaroras are one.

The exchanges, in fact, have gone both ways. There have been delegations coming south from New York, attending powwows, meeting with the leaders in North Carolina, including Locklear and the chief, Cecil Hunt. In many ways, they had to be impressed. Locklear has studied the Tuscarora language, and he knows the history of the people by heart—the bloody warfare of the eighteenth century and the long and bitter migrations that followed—and he and other Tuscaroras from the South have defended the rights of native people nationwide.

But there are skeptics in the ranks of the Tuscarora people. Rick Hill, for example, is a

Tuscarora scholar from New York State who lives on the federally recognized reservation and teaches at the University of Buffalo. He says the Tuscarora Nation "will never recognize" the people in the South who have laid their claim to a Tuscarora ancestry. Among other things, it's difficult to prove—difficult to show that of all the survivors who eventually came together in Robeson County, the Tuscaroras somehow were the dominant strain. But in addition to the basic historical debate, the issue has been contaminated by money—the possibility that a land-claim settlement would have to be divided in a whole different way if the band in North Carolina were affirmed.

That's the way it is in Indian country. There are divisions that are tied to ideology and power—a scramble for resources and a debate over how to respond to the pressures that the outside world still seems to generate.

"It never stops," says Eli Rickard, the eloquent son of a Tuscarora chief.

The proof came recently in the United States Congress. In 1995, under the prodding of Republican senator Slade Gorton (known as "the Indian Fighter" to the tribes), the lawmakers slashed appropriations to Native Americans, cutting more than $200 million in social programs. In 1996, Rhode Island senator John Chaffee introduced an amendment to deny the Narragansett tribe the right to build a reservation casino. There was no discussion or debate on the issue. Chaffee quietly attached his rider to a federal budget package that Congress had to pass to keep the government from being shut down. The Indians cried foul. If the Narragansetts could be singled out, they asked, what fate might await the rest of the tribes?

The answer came in 1997, when the floodgates opened. There were proposals to tax the revenues from tribal casinos, to cut federal funding to tribes like the Choctaws that had managed to develop successful enterprises, and to prohibit the expansion of Indian reservations unless the tribes in question negotiated a tax agreement with their states. To the outside world, the issues were complicated and obscure. To the Indian people, however, they were basic—a backlash hidden in the cloak of reason, which was a pattern they had seen many times in the past. At the turn of the century, the government decided to divide up the Indian land, "allotting" to the individual members of the tribes the reservation tracts that were held in common. The goal, in the words of the national reformers, was to turn the native people into farmers and to find them a place in the American mainstream. But the primary result was to take away the land through scams and taxes that the Indians couldn't pay, and by the time it was over, their holdings had dwindled by 100 million acres.

The avalanche of 1997 was like that. On the surface, it sounded reasonable enough to suggest that an Indian tribe with successful enterprises would need less money from the

ELI RICKARD, TUSCARORA, TUSCARORA RESERVATION, NEW YORK, 1997

BIA. If the Mississippi Choctaws were able to build new schools or send students to college with casino money, or if the Coushattas could expand their system of health care, why should the BIA foot the bill? The Indians' answer was rooted in their definition of a tribe. It is not, they say, a community of individuals defined by their race. It is a legal entity much like a state—a government raising money for the needs of its people. In nearly every case, the tax base is small, and so the Indians have turned to other enterprises, most of which are struggling and even the most prosperous of which are still new. Almost every tribe has problems, epidemics ranging from alcohol abuse to suicide to diabetes, and if the federal government turns its back now in a final violation of its treaty obligations, Native Americans understand what will happen. Their fragile progress will soon be reversed, and the problems that have festered for the last hundred years will begin getting worse.

The Indians also see a double standard. Nobody is suggesting that states with lotteries ought to have their federal programs cut, or that the lottery money coming into the states ought to be taxed by the United States government. But to the Republican Indian fighters in the Congress, the reservation casinos are a whole different matter. And why? Native leaders say there's a longstanding pattern—a history of capricious changes in the rules every time the tribes begin to make a little progress.

To combat that problem, they have banded together, forming alliances all over the country. In the East, one of the most important of these is USET, the United South and Eastern Tribes, a sophisticated coalition that began in 1968. From an original membership of only four—the Cherokees, Choctaws, Seminoles, and Miccosukees—the organization has grown to twenty-three tribes. Their slogan from the start was "Strength in Unity," and in 1997, the USET tribes were part of a national movement that defeated the most damaging legislation in Congress—at least for the moment. But they know that the unity at the heart of that achievement is often a difficult thing to accomplish. Every tribe has its factions, and the battles over ideology and power have sometimes skated to the edge of civil war.

In the 1990s, despite the presence of extraordinary leaders, the Iroquois Confederacy seemed on the verge of coming apart. And even in the South, where the Catawba Indians of South Carolina gained national renown for their successful pursuit of a land-claim settlement, the tribal factions have occasionally come to blows.

Everybody knows that the Indians can't afford it—that the threats from the outside world are too serious to allow them the luxury of internal division. USET does what it can to keep the peace. But some critics say that even that alliance helps to perpetuate a fundamental division, perhaps the most basic among Native Americans. The USET tribes are federally recognized, and the organization has kept its distance from those that have not yet achieved that status. There are reasons, of course, for USET's stance. There are impostors today, people with only the faintest trace of native blood who find it romantic to say they are Indian. But there are also groups with a historic claim—the Paugussetts in western Connecticut, the Ramapoughs in northern New Jersey, the Western Abenakis of Vermont. Some are expecting their recognition any day, while others have had their petitions turned down. But in nearly every case, they have worked as hard to preserve their identity as many of the federally recognized tribes.

The Miami Nation of Indiana, for example, was federally recognized until 1897, when the BIA decided that the real Miamis were those in the West. Fifty years earlier, more than six hundred Indians had been shipped away to Kansas and then to the territory of Oklahoma, where they put down roots and managed to survive. Those who escaped the deportation soon lost their land—the familiar story of speculators and taxes—but they have continued to struggle for the last hundred years to restore their federal recognition as a tribe. Throughout that time, they have held their annual reunions every summer, recognizing the importance of those cultural occasions, and in 1992, they bought thirty-eight acres on the Mississinewa River, where they built a long house—a place for the ceremonies of the tribe.

A few miles to the north, the Potawatomis, too, have maintained their sense of identity and tradition. There are Potawatomi communities that are scattered through five different states, three of them east of the Mississippi River. In Wisconsin, the tribe has been recognized since the 1930s, but the bands along the border between Indiana and Michigan only recently attained that status. Even so, they have managed to hold onto their traditions and culture, with a core of elders still speaking the language and a younger generation now trying to learn it. They have joined a coalition of Potawatomi bands that meets once a year and works to reestablish their ties to each other and to preserve the ceremonies of the tribe. Federal recognition, they say, has helped, making programs available that were not there before. But in the seventy years that recognition was denied, the members of the tribe still knew who they were—still believed in their own identity as a people, regardless of whether the government understood it.

From the Shinnecocks on Long Island Sound to the Waccamaw-Siouan in North Carolina to the Nanticokes in southern Delaware, there are tribes with similar stories they can tell. There are pretenders also, and Joseph Bruchac, an Abenaki writer, understands the need to be careful. There have to be standards in the recognition process.

But whatever the federal government may decide, Bruchac knows the story of his people. He was raised in a family where they didn't talk about it. His grandfather Jesse Bowman was a dark-skinned man, part Abenaki, part French Canadian, who referred to himself most often as a mongrel. "Mongrels are tough," he told his grandson, and Joseph often wondered about that toughness and the subtler qualities his grandfather possessed. There was a kindness about him and an inclination to trust, and there were days when he would climb to the tip of his roof and stare off at the mountains rolling away in Vermont. It was there that the Abenakis had lived, in communities scattered from the Adirondacks through the hills of New England and on into Quebec. They called themselves "the People of the Dawn," and for centuries, they flourished in the mountainous land that lay between the Iroquois and the sea. But their chiefs were murdered in the nineteenth century, and the story is told of the day in Vermont during the patriotic fervor of World War I when a village of Abenakis disappeared. The people were living in the old way then, their wigwams clustered on the fringe of the city. They hunted and trapped and traveled by canoe—a band of "gypsies," in the eyes of their neighbors. And so one night, the white people came. At the point of a gun, they herded the Abenakis into trucks, and according to the story that the old people tell, many of the Indians were never seen again.

It is a story that Bruchac heard many times, and he thinks it explains, at least in part, his grandfather's reluctance to acknowledge his Indian identity to the world. But there were others who kept the traditions alive, the language and the stories that made the Abenakis a tribe, and beginning sometime in the 1960s, Bruchac was part of a great reawakening. He was a graduate student at Syracuse University, a young poet who was drawn to the native storytellers. He began to spend more time with the elders, especially at the Onondaga Reservation, which was just down the road from the Syracuse campus. They embraced his fascination with his roots and said it was time for native people to share—to speak the language and listen to the drums and learn whatever they could from each other.

Bruchac began to travel after that. He was soon spending time at Odanak, an Abenaki reservation outside of Montreal, and later with the Anishinabes and Mohawks and even the Mayas in southern Mexico. He could see that the native people had problems. Every reservation had its alcohol and drugs and reports of abuse and teen suicide, and in many places, there was also the fear. "They are going to come and get us," said an Abenaki woman in the 1970s. She was responding to the militant expressions of pride, the proclamations of identity that were spreading from Canada to the United States. The Abenakis were a part of that movement, and the Bruchac family was right at the heart.

As the years went by, Joseph's young sons, Jim and Jesse, began to follow in their father's footsteps. Jesse is a linguist, and in the 1990s, he was working with an elder at the Odanak

Reserve, Cecile Wawanolett, to learn the dialect and teach it to others. Jim spends his time outdoors teaching the traditional skills like tracking—an area where the native people are the masters. Joseph is proud of both of his sons. They help give him hope for the Indians' future. But there are other signs also, other people whose lives are reminders of the strength that brought the Indian people this far. There is Oren Lyons, the wisdom keeper at the Onondaga Reservation, who still believes in the Great Law of Peace, and Tom Porter, a Mohawk who led his people to the fertile river valley where the long house stood in the ancestors' day and where, even now, they can speak the language and offer up the prayers and plant their Indian corn in the spring.

All over the East, there are people who simply refuse to let it go—that kernel of identity that each generation hands down to the next. Jolene Rickard, a Tuscarora scholar, works every season with her father, Eli, to put in the seed and celebrate the miracle of life it contains. The Seminoles and Creeks keep the Corn Dance alive—a symbol of the harvest— and in the north woods of Maine, Maliseet basket maker Fred Tomah still does his work in the old-fashioned way.

Far to the south, in the Louisiana bayous, Janie Luster does the same. For as long as anybody can remember, the Houmas have made baskets out of palmetto fronds. They always use whatever is at hand, and Janie's mother,

Mary Verret, who lives next door, still makes her dolls out of Spanish moss. "Somebody asked if they were voodoo dolls," she remembers with a smile. "I said, 'Actually, no, they are toys.'"

Today, she can sell those toys to the tourists, and the power of the market has helped to keep an old art form alive. But Janie and Mary would do it anyway. They can remember the days when they were mostly undisturbed—an Indian community hidden deep in the swamps, the alligator country of Bayou DeLarge. Janie's father grew up in a palmetto hut, but nobody lives in those dwellings anymore—and of course, that is good. The Indian people have a right to their comforts. Still, there are things they are trying to preserve—intangible qualities in addition to the crafts, like the tendency of families to stay close together. Janie and her mother believe they can do it. Even in the younger generation, there's a pride, a respect for the values passed along over time.

Jane Mt. Pleasant sees it every day. As director of the American Indian Program at Cornell, she works with students from more than two dozen tribes, many of them in the East. For the most part, they are conscientious people grappling with the issues of Native Americans, from questions of sovereignty to environmental justice. And there are personal issues that they struggle with, too. What does it really mean to be an Indian?

"There's an incredible excitement," explains

MARY VERRET, HOUMA DOLLMAKER, THERIOT, LOUISIANA, 1997

Mt. Pleasant. "These young people are saying, 'We are going to recover the roots and then move on. What it looks like in the next fifty years will be different. But that will not make it any less native.'"

They know, of course, that it will not be easy. Nothing about their history ever is. "The red road is hard," says Owen Smoker, Jr., a Cherokee traditionalist from North Carolina.

But the good news is that whatever their confusions, missteps, and mistakes, it is the road that the Indian people have chosen. Not all of them, certainly, but enough to establish what Joseph Bruchac describes as a "lifeline"— a chain of understanding that extends from the past to the generations that are not yet born.

Notes and Acknowledgments

We have tried to say in the pages of this book that the history of the Indians is not something that ended in the nineteenth century, but is a dynamic story that continues to evolve. Or perhaps more precisely, there are many stories that are now intertwined. If we have done justice to any of them here, it is because of the Native Americans who helped us, who told us their stories in a spirit of trust. There were also the scholars and a handful of journalists who traveled this road—or at least a part of it—long before we did. We want to acknowledge our debt of understanding. The final product, of course, is ours, especially the errors or misunderstandings. The credit for the truth belongs to the following.

PROLOGUE

LaVerne McGhee Pohronezny spent many hours with us in Alabama, telling her story and introducing us to members of the Poarch Creek Band. William Bailey also was gener-

ous with his time, and Barry Dana from Maine gave us the story of how he learned the Penobscot language. For the historical overview, we relied on *Bury My Heart at Wounded Knee* by Dee Brown, *Custer Died for Your Sins* by Vine Deloria, Jr., *Rivers of History* by Harvey Jackson, and *Alabama: The History of a Deep South State* by Rogers, Ward, Atkins, and Flynt. Our thanks also go to Ray Littleturtle and his father, Ray Spottedturtle, of the Lumbee Tribe and Tom Porter of the Mohawks for the wisdom and overview they provided.

CHAPTER ONE

The story of the Catawba renaissance was the inspiration and the starting point for this book. Our special thanks go to Wenonah Haire, director of cultural programs for the tribe, for urging us to expand our account to include all of the Indian nations in the East and for helping us to see the connections. Thanks also go to Gilbert Blue, the chief of

EMMA TAYLOR, CHEROKEE BASKET MAKER,
BIRDTOWN, NORTH CAROLINA, 1997

the Catawbas, for his friendship and support and to Keith Brown for the extra time that he gave us at the start. Anna Brown Branham and Monty Branham were patient and open and also generous with their time, as were most of those we interviewed. We spoke at length with Faye Greiner, John George, Warren Sanders, Cheryl Sanders, Brian Blue, Carson Blue, Wanda Warren, and master potters Earl Robbins, Evelyn George, and Georgia Harris. (The interview with Georgia Harris occurred several years before this project began.) We also talked to Fred Sanders, the former assistant chief of the tribe, who is now a critic of the land-claim settlement, and with others who oppose the current tribal leadership but in some cases did not want their names to be used. It is clear that there are significant divisions among the Catawbas—problems for the Indian people to address. But like most people who have covered this story, we are deeply impressed with their progress. In that connection, we benefited from the writings of Anna Griffin and Dan Huntley in the *Charlotte Observer* and from the knowledge and wisdom of Thomas Blumer, a historian at the Library of Congress.

CHAPTER TWO

Our introduction to the Cherokees came through tribal council member Jim Bowman, who not only told us his own story and introduced us to officials in the tribe but also took us to the Cherokee communities deep in the mountains. We are grateful to him for the time that he spent and for the insights he offered into the life of the tribe. We also spent time with the Cherokees' progressive chief, Joyce Dugan, with the director of cultural affairs, Lynne Harlan, and with tribal council member Delores Davis. In the community of Snowbird, where many of the Cherokee full bloods live, we were greeted with warmth by Lula Rattler, Mose and Mark Wachacha, Ed Chekelelee, Marlene Garland, Owen Smoker, Jr., and many other residents. We visited the community center, the public library, and the day-care center, where elders in the tribe are teaching the Cherokee language to the toddlers. The tribal museum in the town of Cherokee is a rich storehouse of history and information, as are many of the tribal elders. Through Jan Brooks and Doris Colter, we met Amanda Crowe, a Cherokee woodcarver who spent many hours in conversation with us. Robert Bushyhead is a linguist who talked to us in the company of his daughter, Jean Bushyhead Blanton. Emma Taylor is a basket maker who has passed that tradition on to other members of her family, including her daughter, Katrina Maney. We are grateful to all of these artists for their time.

The story of the Cherokees' removal to Oklahoma is told with grace in John Ehle's book *Trail of Tears* and in the informative *Trail of Tears across Missouri* by Joan Gilbert. Jim Bowman is also a historian by personal inclination, and he took us to the grave of Trail of Tears survivor Junaluska. Bo Taylor, who works in the schools, organized a demonstration game of Cherokee stickball, and tribal police officer Jeff McCoy talked about the problems that some of the young people are facing, despite the best efforts of the Cherokee schools. "It's about like everywhere else," he says. But Chief Dugan believes that with better education and a deepening sense of identity and pride, the future of the Cherokee people is bright.

CHAPTER THREE

In the Poarch Creek community in southern Alabama, tribal chairman Eddie Tullis not only spent time talking to us but gave his personal stamp of approval to our visit. His assistant, Amy Bryan, helped us organize a wide range of interviews that included tribal leaders and elders, as well as critics of the current leadership. LaVerne McGhee Pohronezny, a former council member, went out of her way to be helpful, as did tribal historian Gale Thrower. Thanks also go to Houston McGhee, Hattie Morris, Veronica McGhee, Joe McGhee, Jr., Mabel Jackson, Edgar and Ruthie Mae Rackard, Buford Rolin, William Bailey, Billy Smith, Carolyn Rackard, and others.

The story of Calvin McGhee and his efforts to restore the identity of the Creeks is beautifully told in the documentary film *The Chief: Calvin McGhee and the Forgotten Creeks*, produced for the University of Alabama Center for Public Television. We benefited also from the writings of Dr. J. Anthony Paredes, the scholar of record on the Poarch Creek Band and editor of the book *Indians of the Southeastern United States in the Late Twentieth Century*. But there was no substitute for the oral history offered to us by the Creek people themselves.

Chief Phillip Martin of the Mississippi Choctaws spent several hours with us on our visit, despite a hectic daily schedule that resembles a corporate CEO's. Chief Martin urged others to cooperate as well, and they did. Our thanks go to Melford Farve, Lester Dalme, Morris Carpenter, Terry Ben, Kenneth Carleton, Jay Dorris, Pat Kwachka, Deborah Boykin, Roseanna Nickey, Maggie Chitto, Nelda Lewis, Trina Cheatham, Creda Stewart, Kennith York, and others. Thanks go to John Egerton for sharing his essay "Philadelphia Story" and to tribal historian Bob Ferguson for the excellent work he has done through the years. We also read the essay "Choctaw Self-Determination in the 1980s" by John H. Peterson, Jr., which appears in the Paredes book mentioned just above.

Special thanks go to Rose Bryan for introducing us to the Choctaw basket makers, including Lula Mae Lewis, Mallie Smith, and Esbee Gibson, and to stickball player Vince Smith, a young man who is part of an ongoing Choctaw tradition. (The tribe is host every year to the World Series of Stickball.) And finally, our thanks go to Melvin Tingle for introducing us to his fascinating Okla Museum, which includes, among other things, a remarkable collection of Choctaw baskets.

CHAPTER FOUR

We visited the Mowa Choctaws twice, the second time on the day of their powwow. Chief Wilford Taylor talked to us at length, showing us around the tribal grounds and sharing a part of the documentation in the Mowas' current quest for federal recognition. Thanks also go to Craig Taylor for the background information he provided. The historical account of the Choctaws' presence in Mobile County is taken from the book *Mobile: The Life and Times of a Great Southern City* by Melton McLaurin and Michael Thomason. In the archives of the Historic Mobile Preservation Society, we found pictures by documentary photographer William E. Wilson showing Choctaw women in Mobile County around the turn of the century, further supporting Chief Taylor's contention that his people have long been a presence in the area. The story of Geronimo's captivity in Alabama is based on the book *Once They Moved Like the Wind* by David Roberts. At the Mowa powwow, we spoke with Heather Wilkinson, a Mowa Choctaw student who showed us her traditional Choctaw dress, handmade in Philadelphia, Mississippi. We talked also to Tracy Weaver, who emphasized the importance of Indian identity to her children. "It keeps them out of the streets," she said. But some people say the Mowas' heritage is simply too mixed to be considered Choctaw, and federal recognition so far has been denied.

The story of the Burt Lake Band of Ottawa-Chippewas was told in the *Detroit News* on July 20, 1997, in an excellent article by Laura A. Potts. We spoke also to Gary Shawa, the executive director of the Burt Lake Band, to update the story and reconfirm the specifics. The encyclopedia *Native America in the Twentieth Century*, perhaps the best reference book on the subject, provided additional background material on the Chippewas, who are also known as Ojibwas and Anishinabes.

Our introduction to the Haliwa-Saponis came through Greg Richardson, executive director of the North Carolina Commission of Indian Affairs; Barry Richardson, executive director of the Haliwa-Saponi Tribe; and Archie Lynch, a Haliwa artist and leader in the Indian community of Charlotte. We spent several fascinating hours with the Haliwas' charismatic chief, W. R. Richardson, and with Earl Evans, one of the bright young leaders in the tribe. Thanks also go to A. Kay Ensing, Pat Richardson, Allie Richardson, Sharon Harris, Johnny Hedgepeth, and James Lynch.

In researching the Chicoras of South Carolina, we spoke with Gary Deese, their federal acknowledgment officer, and benefited from the work of Gene Joseph Crediford, author of *Those Who Remain: Native Americans in South Carolina*. But most important, we spent a day with Gene Martin, the remarkable and strong-willed leader of the group.

In visiting the Pamumkeys, we spoke with

Warren Cook, a longtime leader in the tribe, and his father, Tecumseh Deerfoot Cook, a former chief. We also visited the tribal museum, which is excellent, and the burial mound, which is said to contain the remains of Chief Powhatan. We benefited also from the writings of Helen Rountree, whose essay "Indian Virginians on the Move" appears in the book *Indians of the Southeastern United States in the Late Twentieth Century*.

We visited the Tunica-Biloxi Tribe in the summer of 1997, as it was hosting a meeting of the United South and Eastern Tribes (USET). Despite the demands of that occasion, we were able to talk to tribal chairman Earl Barbry, historic preservation director Bill Day, tribal leader John Barbry, linguist Donna Pierite, basket maker Lula Cryer, and Juanita Ducote, the guide at the Tunicas' fascinating museum. Other historical background came from *On the Tunica Trail*, a publication of the Louisiana Archaeological Survey and Antiquities Commission featuring essays by Jeffrey P. Brain and Bill Day, and from the September–October 1995 issue of the magazine *acadiana profile*, which features articles by Jefferson Hennessy and Trent Angers.

CHAPTER FIVE

We were welcomed to Maine by Butch Phillips, a Penobscot traditionalist, and John Banks, the tribe's director of natural resources. Banks sent us a copy of the film *Penobscot: The*

People and Their River, produced for the nation by Gunnar Hansen and David Westphal, and he invited us to visit the Penobscot community during the annual running of the Katahdin 100. At that event, we met other members of the tribe, including the artist Stan Neptune and his sister Neana, the tribal elder Sam Sapiel, and Barry Dana, the organizer of the Katahdin ceremony. In addition, we talked with Steve Francis, a Penobscot now living in Boston; Bill Phillips, a Micmac from the north woods of Maine; and Dave Almenas, a Penobscot who said he would like to develop a connection to the Odenak Reservation in Canada, where the Abenaki people still speak a language very much like the Penobscots'. We spent time also with Joan Dana Tomah, a Passamaquoddy, and her younger friend Joanne Predham. Predham was raised as an African-American, but she knows she is also part Choctaw and is now in search of her Indian roots. The Penobscots and Passamaquoddies have embraced her, respecting the obvious sincerity of her search, which is typical of the hospitality of those tribes.

That is a part of the story in Maine, but the rest of it is harsher and more political. Our chronology of the land-claim settlement and the jurisdictional battles between the Indians and the state comes from a number of different sources. Paul Brodeur wrote a thorough and highly readable account of the land-claim issue for *New Yorker* magazine, and it was later expanded into a book. After reading Brodeur,

SYMBOL OF PRIDE, CATAWBA INDIAN NATION, SOUTH CAROLINA, 1996

we talked at length with many of the important people in the story, including the Indians' attorney, Tom Tureen; the Passamaquoddies' governor, John Stevens; Butch Phillips, who served as one of the Penobscots' negotiators; and another Passamaquoddy governor, Clive Dore.

In helping us to update the story, John Banks invited us to an otherwise private negotiating session between a representative of the governor of Maine and a delegation from the tribes. Evan Richert represented the state, facing off with Fred Moore, Dwayne Sockabasin, Eric Altvater, and attorney Greg Sample of the Passamaquoddies and a Penobscot contingent headed by Banks and Mark Chavaree. We are grateful to all of these participants for allowing us to be there for the hours of difficult negotiation, as well as the conversations that followed. We are grateful also to Wayne Newell, a Passamaquoddy educator, who offered additional perspective on the issues. The good news is that as this book goes to press in the summer of 1998, there are signs of progress in the Maine legislature on the issues of fishing rights, land use, and sovereignty—a foreshadowing, perhaps, that justice will prevail.

The final dimension of the story in Maine has been a renewal of Indian culture and art. Stan and Neana Neptune and Stan's multitalented son, Joe Dana, talked to us at length about those developments, and Theresa Hoffman, head of the basket makers' alliance in Maine, not only spent time talking to us herself but introduced us to many of her fellow artists. We spent hours with Molly Neptune Parker and members of her family and with Mary Gabriel, an award-winning Passamaquoddy basket maker, and we were introduced to the work of Fred Tomah, a Maliseet. We also traveled to northern Maine, where the Micmacs Donald and Mary Sanipass and their son, David, took us through every stage of making a basket—from cutting the trees to splitting the ash to weaving the utilitarian baskets that they often sell to the farmers in the area. They also told us their personal stories, sometimes in painful and intricate detail. We are grateful, of course, for their candor, as well as their hospitality and kindness.

One footnote: In the spring of 1998, Theresa Hoffman was part of a workshop for Maliseet children at which a little girl named Nicole was studying the technique of several of the artists. "Now I remember," she said with a smile. Theresa asked what she meant, and Nicole replied that when she was only six, she had seen her grandfather Aubrey Tomah, one of the legendary Maliseet weavers, working at his craft. It was a reminder to Hoffman that the basket-making art is there in the blood, but it's a fragile gift that could easily be lost unless each generation does its part.

CHAPTER SIX

Understanding the painful and complicated story of the Iroquois would have been impossible without the extraordinary assistance of Rick Hill, Jolene Rickard, Dwayne Sylvester, and Oren Lyons.

Hill, a Tuscarora, is a professor at the University of Buffalo who spent several hours in conversation with us and pulled together a thick file folder of background articles, including (as we had requested) many that he had written himself. Some of the most informative came from the *Syracuse Herald American*, the *Niagara Gazette*, and the *Toronto Star*, as well as the Native American publications *Akwesasne Notes* and *Native Americas*. The latter devoted most of an issue in the summer of 1996 to the complicated questions of taxation and sovereignty.

Jolene Rickard, also a professor at the University of Buffalo, shared some of her articles, including a particularly helpful piece in *Akwesasne Notes*, and invited us home for dinner with her family. We were privileged to spend an evening listening to the stories of Eli Rickard, the son of a former Tuscarora chief, and to get a firsthand feeling for how the oral tradition has been preserved.

After some initial skepticism, Dwayne Sylvester, a Seneca who was caught in the middle of the violent demonstrations of 1997, spent several hours talking to us and helped open doors on the emotionally charged Seneca reservations—especially his own Cattaraugus Res-

ervation, where the president, Michael Schindler, talked to us at length, as did a Seneca poet and elder, Edna Gordon. We were fortunate in Schindler's case that a *New York Times* reporter, William Glaberson, had visited the reservation shortly before us and had done a thorough and evenhanded job on the taxation issues affecting the Iroquois and other New York tribes, including the Poospatucks on Long Island. Glaberson's work, it was clear, helped reinforce Michael Schindler's natural inclination toward openness, and we were the beneficiaries of that.

Oren Lyons, the Turtle Clan chief of the Onondagas who is profiled eloquently in *Wisdomkeepers* by Steve Wall and Harvey Arden, spent several hours with us patiently explaining the background of the struggles of the Iroquois. He introduced us to the documentary called *The Dark Side of Sovereignty*, a hard-hitting look at Indian criminality that aired on Canadian television. Rachel Zolf, who worked on the film, was kind enough to provide us with a copy. Lyons also introduced us to Doug George, a Mohawk journalist, and Doug's wife, Joanne Shenandoah, a beautiful and talented Oneida musician who spent many hours with us as well. Doug and Joanne are critics of the Oneidas' controversial leader, Ray Halbritter, and talked to us about their misgivings. Except for a brief introduction at a USET conference, we were unable to speak with Halbritter himself, who was unavailable during our two-week stay in New York. His quotes in the chapter are taken from an exhibit at the Oneidas' cultural center—a remarkable place that even some of his critics admit is a tribute to Halbritter's vision. We benefited also from a long interview with one of his supporters, Keller George, and from the thoughts of Jane Mt. Pleasant, director of the American Indian Program at Cornell, who shared her insights on a variety of subjects.

Many other people were generous with their time as well: Tom Porter, the Mohawk traditionalist who led a small contingent of his people back to the valley where his ancestors lived; Francis Hill, a Mohawk educator in Buffalo; Joyce Pembleton, a Cayuga who took us to the long house ceremony at the Six Nations Reserve in Canada; Randy Johnson, a Mohawk sculptor; Louise Hill, principal of a Cayuga immersion school at Six Nations; Jonathan Wagers, a young Mohawk; Peter Jemison, a Seneca artist; and Ed Smoke, who gave us an excellent tour of Akwesasne and introduced us to his mother and father, Ed and Selena, who remembered the terrible days of the fighting.

For additional historical perspective, we relied on the excellent displays at the Oneidas' museum and on Laurence M. Hauptman's *The Iroquois Struggle to Survive* and E. Lawrence Lee's *Indian Wars in North Carolina*, which provided an account of the Tuscarora War in the early eighteenth century. We are grateful, finally, to our friend Rosa Winfree, a Lumbee educator in Charlotte who introduced us to the story

of Charles and Tammy Bluewolf, and to Tammy herself, who told us more about the story of Charles, her Anishinabe husband who died but helped her find the meaning for her life. "I had an awesome husband," she said, and everybody who knew him seems to agree.

CHAPTER SEVEN

Sam Sapiel, the Penobscot elder, introduced us to the Mashpee Wampanoag community on Cape Cod. He had moved there to be with Shirley Mills, a Wampanoag activist who had once been married to the chief, Earl Mills, Sr. Sam, Shirley, and Earl were all exceptionally generous with their time and opened as many doors as they could. We talked with Peter Hendricks and Earl Mills, Jr., two younger Wampanoags who have defended the hunting and fishing rights of their people, and to Russell Peters, a leader in the tribe who helped to launch its land-claim case. The story of that case is told in the books *Restitution* by Paul Brodeur and *The Mashpee Indians: Tribe on Trial* by Jack Campisi. Our account of testimony at the trial is taken from Campisi. The callous quote from one developer—"The Mashpees can go along or not. It won't make any difference"—is taken from Brodeur. Additional insights into the case and its continuing implications came from our own interviews with Russell Peters, Earl Mills, Sr., and Mashpee tribal leader Jim Peters.

Our initial contact with the Gay Head

BARRY RICHARDSON, HALIWA-SAPONI,
HALIFAX COUNTY, NORTH CAROLINA, 1997

Wampanoag community came through Alfred Vanderhoop, a fisherman and member of the tribal council. Through Vanderhoop, we met Berta Welch, the cultural director, and her husband, Vernon, whose hospitality and insights were unexceeded anywhere in our travels. Through Berta, we met Beverly Wright, the tribal chairman, and several members of the cultural committee, including Gladys Widdiss and Donald Widdiss.

Those most helpful among the Narragansetts were Randy Noka, Matthew Thomas, and Hiawatha Brown—who are part of a young generation of leaders who have helped to guide the restoration of the tribe—as well as the medicine man, Lloyd Wilcox, who shared his perspective on the long years of struggle.

The Pequots' story was taken primarily from the book *The Pequots in Southern New England*, edited by Laurence M. Hauptman and James D. Wherry and containing essays by some of the finest writers and scholars in the field: Alvin Josephy, Jr., Jack Campisi, Neal Salisbury, and others. Staff members for the tribe provided us with information on its current enterprises, and Betty Fayerweather, an Eastern Pequot, described the efforts of her own family to preserve a sense of Pequot identity. Thanks also go to Russell Patrick, an Ojibwa now living among the Pequots.

The account of the Day of Mourning demonstrations and police brutality in Plymouth in 1997 was taken in part from the *Boston Globe* and from the eyewitness experience of Sam Sapiel and Shirley Mills. One non-Indian witness who thought the police had gone too far did not want her name to be used. Others did speak for the record in the *Globe*. The text of the speech by the Wampanoag Frank James at the first protest is found in the book *Chronicles of American Indian Protest*.

The brief history of AIM that appears in this chapter is based in part on the summary in *Native America in the Twentieth Century: An Encyclopedia*.

CHAPTER EIGHT

For an overview of the Seminoles and Miccosukees, we relied on a commemorative issue of the *Seminole Tribune* published on the occasion of the fortieth anniversary of the Seminole Tribe of Florida and its new constitution, approved in 1957. The special issue contained informative essays by a number of writers, including Patricia R. Wickman, a historian who works for the tribe, and Peter B. Gallagher. Wickman's book *Osceola's Legacy* offers a very good account of the Seminole Wars. A briefer account is contained in Wyatt Blassingame's *Seminoles of Florida*. (Blassingame is also the author of a well-crafted children's book, *Osceola: Seminole War Chief*.) In addition, we benefited from an essay by Harry A. Kersey, Jr., "Seminoles and Miccosukees: A Century in Retrospective," which appears in the book *Indians of the Southeastern United States in the Late Twentieth Century*.

To add some flesh to our basic understanding, we were fortunate to be able to talk to Betty Mae Jumper, a former chairman of the Seminoles who now works in the tribal communications office. We benefited as well from an interview with Jumper by Margo Harakas, made available in pamphlet form by the tribe, and from an interview by Dan McDonald that appeared in 1997 in a commemorative issue of the *Seminole Tribune*. We spoke also to Buffalo Tiger, former chairman of the Miccosukee Tribe, who led the effort for separate recognition for that group of traditionalists living along the Tamiami Trail. Buffalo Tiger's airboat company took us on a tour of the southern Everglades, including a hammock where the Indians once made camp.

Through Shannon Larsen, a Florida environmentalist, we met Bobby C. Billie, a medicine man for a group of highly traditional Seminoles who have tried to hold onto the ancestral ways. Bobby spent half a day with us, talking about his view of the land and the Creator's laws for preserving the earth. He also led us on a canoe trip along a swampy little creek where the light slanted in through the limbs of the cypress trees, and he talked about the oral history of the tribe—the accounts of the Seminole Wars passed down through the generations, and his own recollections of the terrifying night in the 1950s when a band of drunken hunters attacked the traditional camp of his family.

We visited all of the Seminole reservations, including Big Cypress, where the tribe has opened a new museum, and Brighton, where we met Lottie Huff, a maker of dolls, and a couple of teachers, Loreen Gopher and Jenny Shore, who are working hard to keep the Seminole language alive. We are grateful to all of them for their time, and to David Blackard at the Ah-Tha-Thi-Ki Museum, which is located on the spot where the dynamic Seminole chairman James Billie once had his camp.

And finally, we spoke to several Seminoles in Oklahoma, including Ted Underwood, Tom Ahaisse, and Alan Emarthle, who are part of a coalition seeking to find a peaceful resting place for the remains of Indians that have been unearthed—and sometimes put on display in museums. Among their allies are the Oklahoma Creeks, who are working to prevent the further desecration of an ancient burial site in Georgia and to achieve the return of ancestral remains. Their historic preservation officer, Joyce Bear, sums up the issue this way: "Our ancestors have been on the shelves too long."

Underwood hopes the Seminoles can rally around the issue of repatriation to find new unity for facing the future. But the divisions run deep. Progressives sometimes view traditionalists as hopelessly out of step with the times, and traditionalists are fearful of the lifestyle changes and potential corruption that can accompany high-dollar tribal enterprises.

POTTER BRIAN BLUE, DIGGING THE CLAY,
CATAWBA NATION, SOUTH CAROLINA, 1996

CHAPTER NINE

Our understanding of the Lumbees comes primarily from many hours of interviews in Robeson County, North Carolina. We did make use of Adolph Dial's *The Lumbee*, as well as a short but comprehensive history, *Pembroke State University*, written by David K. Eliades and Linda Ellen Oxendine, and the chapter in *Wisdomkeepers* on the respected Lumbee healer Vernon Cooper. We also watched Malinda Maynor's film *Real Indian* and spent several hours at the Native American Resource Center, a superb museum under the direction of Dr. Stanley Knick. Among other things, the center contains the work of Lumbee artists and fascinating exhibits on Lumbee history, including the Indians' 1958 raid on the Ku Klux Klan. The account of the tragic murder of James Jordan was taken primarily from the *Charlotte Observer*.

We relied, of course, on all of these resources, but there was no substitute for long conversations with the Lumbees themselves, including Rosa Winfree, Daystar Dial, Wanda Carter, Malinda Maynor, Waltz Maynor, Connee Brayboy, Linda Oxendine, Dalton Brooks, Michael Cummings, Bruce Barton, Ray Littleturtle, Ray Spottedturtle, Ben Jacobs, Herman Oxendine, Loretta Oxendine, Michael Wilkins, Bernice Locklear, Karl Hunt, Donna Chavis, Hays Allen Locklear, Reedy Chavis, Arlinda Locklear, Mary Chitwood, Kermit Chavis, James Hardin, Sanford Locklear, and others. Thanks also go to Mac Legerton, a non-Indian activist in Robeson County who has a deep commitment to the well-being of the area, as well as a wealth of historical perspective.

CHAPTER TEN

The book *The Historic Indian Tribes of Louisiana* by Fred B. Kniffen, Hiram F. Gregory, and George Stokes offered a good introduction to the Indian people of this area. So did the personal knowledge of Louisiana folklorist Mike Luster. But again, there was no substitute for the perspective of the native people themselves. Thanks go especially to Roy Parfait, a man of irrepressible good cheer who gave us a couple of days of his time and introduced us to the wonderful community of Dulac. Roy is a woodcarver, a Houma Indian who learned his craft not only from other members of his tribe but from the great Cherokee artist Going Back Chiltosky. We are also grateful to Chief Jerry Jackson of the Jena Choctaws, who made himself available for several hours on a Saturday, and to Mary Jones and Cheryl Smith, who did the same. Among the Jena Choctaws, our special thanks also go to Rose Fisher, Anna Barber, Clyde Jackson, Ricky Jackson, and Chris Allen. Among the Choctaw-Apaches, we enjoyed our time with Amy Parrie and Glenda Etheridge and the tribal historian and folklorist Stephanie Pierrotti, who is working on the issue of federal recognition.

Among the tribes already recognized, including the Coushattas and their cousins in Texas, the Alabama-Coushattas, we spoke to Burley Sylestine, Burton Langley, Myrna Wilson, Wilfred Wilson, Randy Robinson, Barbara Langley, and the non-Indian director of social services, Joan Fullilove, as well as other employees of the tribe. Both the Coushattas and Alabama-Coushattas also supplied us with extensive written information on the tribes. Our introduction to the Chitimachas came initially through Lois Rider, a non-Indian social worker who has become a good friend. She introduced us to the tribal administrator, Toby Darden, who gave us a tour of the Chitimacha Reservation and helped set up interviews with other members of the tribe: Kim Walden, Nick Stouff, Melissa Darden, Ricky Higgins, and several people we met more briefly.

Our Houma interviews included Roy Parfait, Antoine Parfait (who still makes his living as a trapper), Marie Dean, Janie Luster, Mary Verret, Kirby Verret, Rodney Parfait, Ivy Billiot, and Grey Hawk Perkins. Our thanks go again to all of these people for their hospitality and time and also the knowledge they were willing to share.

CHAPTER ELEVEN

The idea for a chapter on the urban experience began to take shape when we read John Egerton's powerful account in *The Tennessean* on Ray Buckley's life in the city of Nashville—the racial slur he endured and his search for an Indian community of his own. Egerton introduced us to Buckley, who patiently answered all of our questions and suggested other friends that we might want to talk to, including John and Ginny Underwood. We also talked to Jennifer Welch, a Native American educator in Nashville, and then moved on to other cities in the East.

In Boston, we spent several hours at the North American Indian Center, which has become the focal point of the native community in that city. We are grateful especially to Joanne Dunn, Janis Falcone, and Shirley Mills for the time that they gave us. In Baltimore, we visited an Indian center that was similar in many ways to the one in Boston, especially in the thrust of some of its programs. The founder of the center, Herbert Locklear, and the current director, Milton Hunt, gave us a good overview, as did another member of the staff, Keith Colston. The difference between Baltimore and Boston is that the center in Boston is more multitribal. Joanne Dunn is Micmac. Janis Falcone is Onondaga. Shirley Mills is Wampanoag (with a little bit of Navajo thrown in as well). Nearly all of the leaders in Baltimore are Lumbees. But one of the overriding similarities—a refrain in every urban community we encountered—was the connection the city people maintain to their homelands. Gary Revels, a Tuscarora minister in Charlotte, leads the members of his mostly

Lumbee congregation on frequent trips back to Robeson County. The same pattern is present in Buffalo, where people like educators Joyce Pembleton, a Cayuga, and Francis Hill, a Mohawk, go home often to their multitribal reservation in Canada. "It's important," says Joyce, "to maintain the ties."

CHAPTER TWELVE

On our visit to Wisconsin, we talked at length to Cecil Garvin, the manager of the buffalo herd for the Ho-Chunk Nation, and also to his brother, Larry Garvin, and Roxanne Owens, who are working to protect the historic sites of the tribe. For historical background on the Ho-Chunks, we relied on several essays pulled together for us from the tribal archives by Larry Garvin and Owens, including "Winnebago" by Nancy Oestreich Lurie, "The Winnebago" by David Wooley, and "History of the Territory of Wisconsin," compiled by Moses M. Strong. Among the Oneidas, we spent several hours with Pat Cornelius, director of the Oneida Nation Farms, who introduced us to Nori Damrow, a tribal elder, and Carol Cornelius, a scholar and teacher who gave us our introduction to the history and culture of the nation. We also talked with historian Loretta Matoxen and several of the Oneida young people, including Deacon Powless and Ruben Ortiz, Jr. We talked to representatives of the Intertribal Bison Cooperative and read several issues of the organization's newsletter, *Buffalo Tracks*, provided to us by Pat Cornelius. We visited the buffalo herd at the Poarch Creek Reservation, and at Onondaga, Oren Lyons told us the story of the purchase agreement that was signed on a hide.

In documenting the continuing contact between the Indian nations of Oklahoma and their counterparts in the East, we met in Oklahoma with Seminoles Ted Underwood, Alan Emarthle, and Tom Ahaisse. The Creek medicine man Sam Proctor was generous with his time, as was Joyce Bear, the historic preservation officer. We also spoke to repatriation officer George Coser and several other members of the tribe.

The story of the healing ceremony between the Narragansetts and the Mohegans was told by Narragansett medicine man Lloyd Wilcox. The Mohegans' story was taken primarily from the writings of Melissa Fawcett, the tribal historian whose book *The Lasting of the Mohegans* has been important in calling attention to her people.

In North Carolina, the Tuscarora leader Robert Locklear described his efforts to reestablish connections with the Tuscaroras in New York State. Two Tuscarora scholars, Rick Hill and Jolene Rickard at the University of Buffalo, offered us a very different point of view. The staff at USET guided us to a number of published accounts of the troubling legislation that has recently been introduced in the Congress. Joseph Bruchac, the great

BOBBY C. BILLIE, SEMINOLE MEDICINE MAN, EVERGLADES CAMP, 1998

Abenaki writer, shared his thoughts on the story of his people and shared his book *Bowman's Store*, a moving account of his own growing up. Jane Mt. Pleasant, director of the American Indian Program at Cornell, was patient and helpful during our visit to the campus.

The stories of the Potawatomis and the Miami Nation of Indiana were based primarily on essays in *Native America in the Twentieth Century*. It should be noted that the Miamis are not alone in their part of the country in trying to stay close to the ancestral land. In northern Ohio, a band of Shawnees led by Chief Hawk Pope has moved back to the homeland of the legendary Tecumseh, who tried to unite the eastern tribes in a stand against the massive encroachments of the whites. Chief Pope's United Remnant Band of the Shawnee Nation has worked to hold onto important traditions—including the Green Corn Ceremony—based in part on his boyhood memories of the way they were practiced by the Shawnee elders.

One final note on terminology: We have used the terms *Indians, Native Americans,* and *native people* interchangeably, taking our cue from the people we interviewed. *Indians,* by far, was the most common term, but the others were used quite often also. We found little concern for political correctness among Native Americans, but a great deal of concern about basic respect.

Our effort to document the Indians' story was encouraged by James Martin, the executive director of USET, and by a number of friends and fellow photographers, writers, and artists, including Vine Deloria, Jr., Amy Rogers, Jay Lamar, Joseph Bruchac, Deborah Luster, John Egerton, Patti Meredith, Christie Taylor, Judy Hermitte, Rebecca Turner, Carl Bergman, Tim Buchman, Jan Brooks, Paula Fraher, Marilyn Barrier, Cordelia Williams, Bruce Lineker, and others. Thanks also go to NationsBank for a grant that covered a part of our travel, and to the Light Factory for putting together an exhibition of photographs, and to Melinda Farbman for her help with research. And finally, our special thanks go to Mike DeMeritt and Nancy Gaillard, without whose support this book quite literally would have been impossible.

Appendix

Tribes in the South and East and the states where the largest communities reside:

SOUTHEAST

Alabama-Coushatta (Texas)
Catawba (South Carolina)
Cherokee (North Carolina)
Chickahominy (Virginia)
Chicora-Siouan (South Carolina)
Chitimacha (Louisiana)
Choctaw (Mississippi, Louisiana, Alabama)
Choctaw-Apache (Louisiana)
Coharie (North Carolina)
Coushatta (Louisiana)
Creek (Alabama)
Edisto (South Carolina)
Haliwa-Saponi (North Carolina)
Houma (Louisiana)
Lumbee (North Carolina)
Mattaponi (Virginia)
Meherrin (North Carolina)
Miccosukee (Florida)
Monacan (Virginia)
Nansemond (Virginia)
Pamunkey (Virginia)
Peedee (South Carolina)
Person County Indians (North Carolina)
Rappahannock (Virginia)
Santee (South Carolina)
Seminole (Florida)
Tunica-Biloxi (Louisiana)
Waccamaw-Siouan (North Carolina)

NORTHEAST

Abenaki (Vermont)
Cayuga (New York)
Maliseet (Maine)
Micmac (Maine)
Mohawk (New York)
Mohegan (Connecticut)
Nanticoke (Delaware)
Narragansett (Rhode Island)
Nipmuck (Massachusetts)
Oneida (New York)
Onondaga (New York)
Passamaquoddy (Maine)
Paugussett (Connecticut)
Penobscot (Maine)
Pequot (Connecticut)
Piscataway (Maryland)
Poospatuck (New York)
Ramapough (New Jersey)
Schaghticoke (Connecticut)
Seneca (New York)
Shinnecock (New York)
Tuscarora (New York)
Wampanoag, Gay Head (Massachusetts)
Wampanoag, Mashpee (Massachusetts)

GREAT LAKES, UPPER MIDWEST

Brothertown (Wisconsin)
Chippewa, Ojibwa (Michigan, Wisconsin, Minnesota)
Ho-Chunk, Winnebago (Wisconsin)
Menominee (Wisconsin)
Miami (Indiana)

Oneida (Wisconsin)
Ottawa (Michigan)
Potawatomi (Michigan, Wisconsin, Indiana)
Shawnee (Ohio)
Stockbridge-Munsee (Wisconsin)

Note: This list of tribes in the South and East was compiled from popular reference sources on Native Americans, including *Native America in the Twentieth Century: An Encyclopedia; The Native American Almanac: A Portrait of Native America Today; Indian America: A Travelers Companion; Indians of the Southeastern United States in the Late Twentieth Century*, edited by J. Anthony Paredes; *The Historic Indian Tribes of Louisiana* by Fred B. Kniffen, Hiram F. Gregory, and George A. Stokes; *The Pequots in Southern New England*, edited by Laurence M. Hauptman and James D. Wherry; and *Those Who Remain: Native Americans in South Carolina* by Gene Joseph Crediford. The North Carolina Commission of Indian Affairs and the United South and Eastern Tribes (USET) also helped in compiling the list. All tribes listed here are located east of the Mississippi River (except for the tribes of Louisiana) or are members of USET.

Index